WHY WE WALKED AWAY

Twelve Former Catholic Priests Tell Their Stories

Libri Agni

Indianapolis   *Evansville*   *Chicago*

Libri Agni

WHY WE WALKED AWAY
Twelve Former Catholic Priests Tell Their Stories
Copyright © 2014
by Libri Agni
Evansville, Indiana
All rights reserved.

Published in the United States by Libri Agni

ISBN-ISBN-10:193766886X
ISBN-13: 978-1-937668-86-0

Printed in the United States of America

Graphic artist Whitney Arvin

Excerpt from "Searing criticism emerges in laments" by Dan Morris-Young, from the National Catholic Reporter, July 5-18, 2013 issue is reprinted with permission.

WHY WE WALKED AWAY
Twelve Former Catholic Priests Tell Their Stories
General Editors: Bill Field & Ed Griffin
Literary Editor: Kerry Griffin Bergeron

Dedication

To
Pope Francis

Pope Francis has made it clear he wants the Church to be the home of all. He has reached out to the homeless, to those outside the Church seeking the truth. His example of spirituality is one we all hope we could emulate.

Pope Francis does not mince words. He has shown over and over again the trappings of a former age must be left behind so as to speak to the modern world.

We twelve priests, who have left the active ministry, recount our stories in this volume. We have not given up ministering. We hope the struggles this book describes can serve as a point of reference for lay people who seek to understand how priests today could best function in a world ever more in need of evangelization. We are hopeful this book could also help bishops and the pope himself evaluate the possibilities a married priesthood would help the Catholic Church evangelize as it should in our ever more secularized world.

In this spirit, we respectfully dedicate this volume to Pope Francis who, like his namesake, wants to adapt the Church to a changed world.

Advance Praise for *Why We Walked Away*

I had the pleasure of reading *Why We Walked Away* and was very impressed by its content. I believe it can make a substantial contribution to a variety of fields like ecclesiology, spirituality, faith development, and sociology.

The book provides a broad description of the church of fifty years ago, especially in relation to the lives of priests.

First of all, we get a description of the Catholic Church before Vatican II. The church then was stable and predictable. Parents encouraged their sons to become priests, which often meant that they entered a minor seminary; later they moved to a major seminary without having much of a life experience.

The church and its seminaries were strongly structured, like IBM or the armed forced; disagreement was unknown as one was not supposed to think by oneself. That was fine in the Eisenhower era, but not under Kennedy and the Vietnam war. In the 1960s the world changed; the church did not; the human cost of this lack of adaptation is described in this book.

Then as today people in uniform were not expected to have emotions, neither in the military not in the priesthood; they were only expected to perform. They performed well, but the cassock often hid loneliness, which in turn led to nagging questions. What is the purpose of celibacy? Is it my personal vocation to be celibate? What will I do if I fall in love? Many priests were spiritually and socially "homeless" in their rectories.

Appointments in the pre-Vatican II church (and often today) came through the bulletin, the news, or a formal letter. There was little personal contact between the bishop and his priests. Both were called "father," but it was a stereotypical name. There was little recognition of one's personal gifts and wishes. Priests were mainly cogs in the diocesan administrative machine.

How long shall one continue to pretend? To live a double life is not gratifying. In order to move out of it one had to confront the bishop. The confrontations were seldom friendly; those who left because of their inner burden often felt rejected.

For many priests, Vatican II offered a new vision for the church and new ideals of social justice. These ideals were often both "a way out of darkness" and an invitation to first seek the Kingdom of God. Many priests blossomed in their new vocation.

Much can be learned from this book in terms of applied ecclesiology, as the examples given above suggest. One can also find practical points of spirituality about the religious vocation, its nurture and growth, and the issue of celibacy. When children enter religious life to unconsciously please their parents, how can authentic vocations be recognized? Not just through obedience to religious superiors, as this book makes it plain. Vocations should not be protected by monastic seminary isolation, at the end of which celibacy was accepted quasi automatically, like teenagers entering marriage based on romance and fiction.

Pierre Hegy
Sociology Department
Adelphi University
Garden City, New York

Table of Contents

Introduction

In its July 5th, 2013 issue the National Catholic Reporter covered the recent conference of the Association of U.S. Catholic Priests in an article *"Searing criticism emerges in laments" by Dan Morris-Young*. The focus of the report was the opening session on the evening of June 24th. The session was titled "Laments." A sampling of the priests' laments follows:

People feeling a strong sense of being devalued.

We lament the pervasive, arrogant abuse of power on all levels.

We lament that power is exercised without accountability.

We lament the fallout from the sexual abuse crisis, the double standard that exists in the treatment of priests as compared to bishops—we lament that we are not a forgiving church.

We lament that Jesus came to our door and we turned Him away.

We lament that too many bishops are too much CEO's and not enough pastors. Anger (frustration) at our failure as a church to live what we believe and teach! We teach the dignity of each human person but treat the gays, divorced, etc., with disdain. Disconnect between Theology of Church and Reality of Church. Frustration and anger at the new translation of the Roman Missal.

We lament that the Roman Missal makes prayer impossible and causes me to stumble and fall.

1

We lament the gulf that exists between clergy and laity, and the abuse by episcopacy. Pain and anger of women in the Church who feel discriminated and excluded by leaders. Devaluing of theology within official Church culture today. Lack of support of new and young pastors—being "left hung out to dry. "Disappointed on local, regional and universal levels for not facing evasive problems of ministering in the Church. Grave disparity between priests and bishops over Eucharistic theology. Not being able to have wider sharing of lay ecclesial leadership in the Church. Authority that leads by criticizing others. Hurt of people due to inflexible, dominant pastors. Domineering approach to pastoral situations creates a church of anger, frustration and pain where there should be grace and growth.

(This article appeared in the National Catholic Reporter, July 5-18, 2013 issue. It is reprinted here with permission).

In the chapters that follow, twelve Catholic priests from the last half of the twentieth century detail the events in their priesthood which led them to abandon their childhood dreams of a sacramental ministry to the people of God. Tragically, their reasons for leaving were a near mirror image of those identified by the priests attending the conference of last June 24th. The only difference is that the priests of the twentieth century believed leaving was their only option; the possibility of change within the Church's hierarchical structure was not a consideration. Present day priests are hopeful of being heard.

Why We Walked Away was conceived as a priestly ministry to the present and future Church and its priesthood. The authors of the book feel that the veil of secrecy which sustains the callous treatment of priests and people, must be pierced, and the windows of Vatican autocracy opened wide.

The theological thesis behind this book is that the source of Christian life and power comes with the sacrament of Baptism; the primary role of bishops, through the sacrament of Holy Orders, is one of service to both the baptized, as well as to those who do not believe in Baptism. The model for leaders within the Church is Jesus on His knees, washing the feet of his Apostles.

* * * * *

Like Rip Van Winkle the twelve men in this book woke up during the sixties and seventies. They hadn't been asleep, but the church they belonged to had slept for centuries. Then Pope John XXIII called the Vatican II Council and asked the church to open its windows and let in some fresh air.

Turmoil surrounded the church in America in those years, the civil-rights movement, the war in Vietnam, and poverty in America. New leaders arose – Martin Luther King, John Kennedy and Robert Kennedy. New religious leaders defined what it meant to be a modern Catholic – Hans Kung, Teilhard de Chardin, and the liberation theologians.

Most of these twelve entered the seminary in high school. Here they found a quasi-military organization with a strong hierarchy. Because John Ardizzone's father and mother had not married in the church, his bishop considered him a 'bastard' and refused to let him join the seminary there.

The director of the seminary held Phillip Field back from the first steps of ordination because, "you ask too many questions in class" and "the faculty doesn't think you like them."

The seminary director gave Jim Koerber a test. "He showed me a yellow wooden pencil lying on the desk. He said, "If I told you that the pencil was green, and asked you to say that it was green, would you do it?" He was fully aware of the requirements of blind obedience, and truthfully replied, "Yes, I would." Then what little integrity I had would not be denied, and I added, "But I would know it was yellow." The director came alive immediately. "I knew it," he exclaimed. "You have no vocation to be a Redemptorist" (an order of priests).

These twelve survived the unnatural loneliness of seminary life and the unnatural restrictions against normal romantic feelings. They were ordained and began to work in parishes.

One day the sister-principal of the parochial school asked young Father Raymaker, "Why didn't you tell us you were being reassigned?"

He asked her what she was talking about. She told him she had read that news of his reassignment in the local Catholic newspaper.

When these twelve caused trouble, bishops moved them from parish to parish like pawns on a chessboard.

Loneliness hit them. "I found living alone very difficult," said Bill Field. "There can be little doubt that many priests suffer from the same loneliness that gradually seeps into the soul like a silent winter, placing so many limits on opportunities for personal growth, even as their outward life appears as normal as any other. Most priests are, in reality, 'homeless,' even though they have a warm place to stay and a roof over their heads. People may fill their lives all day long, but at night the priests' companions are the walls and a television or computer screen. This all too often leads to social and interpersonal abnormalities and debilitating addictions."

These priests started to leave. "The chancery officials (bishop's staff) asked me why I was leaving," writes Jim Koerber, "and I told them I was unable to believe one thing and preach something else."

Gerry Charbonneau says, "My transition to the lay Christian lifestyle became a spectacular gift from God. I took on a personal mantra in my faith life: "Where God has been, God will continue to be."

These twelve tried to implement the changes of Vatican II. They were opposed at every turn. Yet, as John Raymaker says, "The conservatives now run the Church; they intend to keep it that way. Still, the Vatican cannot highjack the Kingdom or its values. Nor can the *official* Church completely undo what Vatican II wrought. The bishops and the Vatican cannot silence such publications as the *National Catholic Reporter* or *Commonweal* which reflect the views of a *loyal opposition*; this opposition wants to prioritize the Kingdom and its justice as well as the rights of all the faithful."

Note that three brothers wrote their stories. The Field brothers, Bill, Clark and Phillip from Owensboro, Kentucky were raised in a very fervent Catholic home, encouraged by their mother to become priests. They were ordained and given parish assignments typical for priests of the 1960's and 1970's. This book relates what happened to them.

Much of what is expressed in these stories goes back to the early 1960's. When Pope John XXIII and John F. Kennedy were in office, these two "Johns" inspired and encouraged our writers' faith and activity. In a prophetic way, the church and the world were to be renewed–or so the writers hoped.

The Second Vatican Council prescribed many changes in the Church. The next pope, Paul VI, did his best to accommodate both the conservatives and the progressives, but succeeding popes, John Paul II and Benedict XVI, tried to suppress the changes in subtle and not so subtle ways.

In this atmosphere the young men in this book lived their priesthood.

OUT OF DARKNESS

William Overstreet Field

For many years, the famous radio commentator, Paul Harvey, had a noonday segment called "The Rest of the Story." He would begin each program by recalling some historical event or facts about a well-known public figure but without disclosing the identity. He would then relate some surprising background information few people would ever associate with either the event or the person. Finally, as his listening audience waited in rapt anticipation, Mister Harvey would reveal "The Rest of the Story."

On his way home for lunch each day, my father always listened to Paul Harvey, and would entertain us with some fascinating information from the master story-teller. Many years later as I ate lunch in my law office in Frankfort, Kentucky, I too was captivated by the same program.

Now, how does this relate to the subject matter of this book? Let me connect the dots. When I was a child, growing up on a farm in the Diocese of Owensboro, Kentucky, the term used for a man who had left the priesthood was "fallen." It happened only rarely, and was always without any public announcement by the Diocese. Everyone was mystified, and spoke of the matter as though someone had died in disgrace. Of course there was always speculation: had he "run off" with a woman; had the bishop sent him away because of an alcohol problem; had he openly defied the bishop; or did he lose his faith altogether?

The reason I agreed to contribute to this book is because the people of God have a baptismal right not to be left in the dark about whatever transpires in the diocese that affects their faith experience. But also, when a priest leaves there is always a "Rest of the Story" that needs to be told, either in charity toward the priest, or for the benefit of future clergy, or both.

For these reasons, and on behalf of the many friends and parishioners of the churches I have served, I want the rest of my story to be told and understood. In telling my story I have decided to begin with my first full day as a parish priest. The date was June 9, 1959. Fresh out of nine years in the seminary, my dream was now coming true.

It was about 7:00 in the evening, and the sun was still high in the summer sky as I drove into the rectory driveway at St. Francis de Sales Church in downtown Paducah, Kentucky. As I was attempting to find a place to park, a short, balding priest in a long black cassock, hurried out to point me toward a church parking lot. No "Hello," or "Welcome," just a crisp directive. After maneuvering my car into a proper space, I began a very awkward entrance up some steps and through the back door of the rectory.

From the time I came into view until I was safely in my room at the top of the stairs, there was the incessant, shrill barking by "Nippy," the housekeeper's toy terrier, letting me know in no uncertain terms that I was an unwelcome intruder. The housekeeper, who was the pastor's sister, seconded the motion with not so much as a nod.

Once my belongings were unpacked, I asked about the pastor, and was told he should be returning shortly from his annual retreat. Some two hours later I inquired again, and was told he was downstairs watching television. When I approached him, he only glanced in my direction and offered a limp handshake. That was it; nothing more until the next day.

At breakfast the next morning the pastor, a dour, graying man, speaking in a low, modulated voice, informed me that I would be taking care of the mission parish in Calvert City at Kentucky Lake, which would entail a fifty mile round trip twice a day, transporting high school children back and forth to Paducah. I would also be teaching religion classes from grades one through twelve at St. Mary's Academy. In addition, I would have the early Mass at St. Francis each Sunday, and the later Mass at St. Pius X at Calvert City. And, by the way, I was the newly appointed Catholic chaplain to the maximum security prison at Eddyville, Kentucky, including death row, where an execution was scheduled for late summer. In addition, I was to be a full-time Assistant at this large inner-city parish in Paducah.

In retrospect, I see this, my first day on the job, as the actual beginning of my long journey out of the priesthood because it turned out to be a preview or snapshot of so many things to come: the cool detachment of the pastor as he laid out his expectations (and those of the Bishop) almost as though I had been assigned as his servant; his lack of enthusiasm toward any aspect of my ministry; his obliviousness to the fact that I had no training or preparation for ministering to death row inmates–especially those about to be electrocuted; and the absence of any offer of help or guidance from him or the Bishop.

At the time, in the afterglow of ordination, this was all interpreted as part of God's call to the priesthood. In spite of feeling overwhelmed by inadequacy, I was somehow confident that God's grace would see me through.

Throughout my six years at St. Francis de Sales, this same professional and personal, but cordial, aloofness prevailed: three priests, each marching to his own drummer; no shared ministries, and few mutual interests other than sports, finances, or politics.

Priests assigned, other than myself, would come and go. One priest vanished without warning just before my first Christmas. Another older Assistant would disappear for days at a time, then return in the middle of the night, eat a jar of peanut butter, and sleep for forty-eight hours. Still another very pleasant former Trappist monk was literally ushered out of the diocese under embarrassing circumstances, with no explanation to anyone. However, as he was hurriedly packing his bags, he told me he had been accused of homosexuality.

Except for my ministry to death row where the condemned men were given to cursing the guards, each other, and God himself, I loved my work with a wide variety of convert classes, and enjoyed my contact with the students at St Mary's Academy. Also, I had formed a new couples group dedicated not only to learning more about the Gospel, but committed to living it out. The group was a branch of the Christian Family Movement (CFM) which I had learned about in my seminary studies. We were able to engage a broad segment of the community in building and furnishing a new home for a large family in destitute circumstances. Few things in my years of ministry have been more rewarding than witnessing this family move into their new home.

Then in the spring of 1962, a beautiful young woman came to the rectory seeking to learn about the teachings of the Catholic Church. As I opened the door, my first impression was of the famous movie actress, Elizabeth Taylor, only with dark brown eyes. Since I handled close to 100% of all such inquiries, I was more than happy to set her up on a typical twice-a-week one-on-one schedule. From that night in early May until her baptism in July, we had many long discussions about the Catholic faith and its authoritative position on many theological issues. I had never known anyone more absorbed in these discussions, nor more serious about their impending baptism.

Over a period of time we developed a warm and trusting friendship. I discovered she had lived a short time in California where she became involved in the Catholic Youth Organization (CYO). When I asked if she would be willing to help organize a group for our high school students, she readily accepted the invitation, and ultimately became the first president.

This mutual interest and involvement increased our time together, and resulted in many planning sessions in the rectory front office, which often ended up in personal revelations about our families and our dreams for the future.

From the time I was seventeen I had lived in an all-male environment. I had lots of friends among my schoolmates, and enjoyed our years together, but had never experienced an intimate sharing of feelings with an adult woman who was now unlocking something within me that I never knew existed. Never before had I felt safe enough to lay my innermost self out there without the slightest fear of rejection or disapproval. I realized that the highlights of every week were our times together in the same office where we first met. While we were comfortable with silence, we never ran out of things to talk and laugh about. Often times her humorous one-liners would provide much appreciated comic relief. In groups or social gathering we could communicate volumes with our eyes.

In time, we both became aware of how deeply we felt about one another, but by mutual but unspoken agreement, we understood that our love must remain platonic. Not only did my vow stand in the way but, for me, I couldn't risk taking a chance on anything that might change the nature of our cherished friendship. I suspect her thinking was along these lines also.

She eventually accepted a proposal of marriage, and moved away, leaving me with a broken heart. But I was a richer, more whole and wholesome human being because of her. I now knew what I wanted and desperately needed in my life, which I would discover in my lovely wife years later.

For those who voluntarily choose celibacy, and who have a deep relationship with Jesus Christ, which sublimates the need for an intimate human relationship, a life of celibacy can be highly rewarding. I know that to be true from the lives of several priest friends of mine. However, enforced celibacy will always inhibit growth, both human and spiritual. After all, no less an authority than the Book of Genesis tells us that, "It is not good for man to be alone."

The defense for mandatory celibacy had always been that Jesus was never married, and that a priest with a wife and family would have less time to carry out his primary duty of saving souls, but no mention was ever made about the first priests, the twelve Apostles, most of whom are believed to have been married. Nor was an explanation given as to how priests were doing more good works than Protestant ministers in the same community. We were simply asked to believe that celibacy made priests holier and more pleasing to God.

My experience as a priest, who worked closely with a variety of other Christian ministers, belied these improbable and fatuous conclusions. There can be little doubt that many priests suffer from the same loneliness that gradually seeps into the soul like a silent winter, placing so many limits on opportunities for personal growth, even as their outward life appears as normal as any other. Most priests are, in reality, "homeless," even though they have a warm place to stay and a roof over their heads. People may fill their lives all day long, but at night the priests' companions are the walls and a television or computer screen. This all too often leads to social and interpersonal abnormalities and debilitating addictions.

In many ways, the genuinely human and transforming relationship I had with one I loved, gave me a new perspective on the life to which I was called. I became more proactive in the face of diocesan policies which lacked human compassion and at times, all rationality. One example of which involved the annual diocesan collection designated for the "poor, the hungry, and the homeless." After ten years in the diocese, I had not seen nor heard of one dime of that collection being used for its stated purpose. So, following a small but devastating tornado, rather than sending the funds from this collection to the Chancery Office, I informed the Chancellor that they had been used to help the victims of the storm. Predictably, I was called on the carpet to explain why I had not complied with diocesan rules. With no regard for the needs of the victims, the Bishop's concern was that I, a thirty-five year old pastor, had made a decision without first getting his permission.

Clearly, my inner spirit, the core of my being, was taking a beating. It was more and more difficult for me to interpret cold, unrelenting, mandates to be the will of God.

At a specified time each year the Bishop would juggle priests from one parish to another. You never knew when your number would be drawn, or why. A note would come in the mail, without consultation as to the merits of such a change either for the priest or the efforts and dedication of many men and women, a parish program would be underway, only to be abruptly terminated because of the disinterest of the newly assigned priest. Such occasions as this only highlighted just how inconsequential and insignificant the faithful of the Church were to the primary "shepherd of the flock."

This is how it played out for me with my first transfer. At the breakfast table on a Saturday morning in mid-April of 1965, the pastor, in a loud and cheery voice, announced that my vacation would begin the following morning, and that he would be taking all the Masses, and would explain my departure to all the people. At the end of my vacation, he continued, I would report to my new assignment at the other end of the diocese.

Thus, after six years at St. Francis de Sales, there would be no good-byes, no opportunity to sign-off on any programs or scheduled meetings. At the age of thirty-one my only option was to obey. Except for a different pastor, nothing had changed since my first day on the job.

As the years passed, I began to realize how infantilizing this hierarchical system was: assistant priests were subjected to the biases and whims of the pastor, and the pastors experienced the same expectations from the bishop. (I know a pastor who, because he disagreed with his bishop over the location of a new building, was demoted to assistant for the rest of his career.) The tragic consequences of such a lifestyle are that many God-given gifts and talents are likely to go undiscovered. Much potential for creative growth remains dormant, and many personal landscapes and far horizons can never be explored. The obvious question remains: can the God who created such potential be pleased with a system that stifles its development?

On May 1, 1966, the seventh anniversary of my ordination, I decided to share my observations and disillusionment with the Bishop in the form of a letter. Since I had the habit of filing all of my correspondence with the Bishop, I can quote from it here. As I looked at so many priests throughout the diocese, I expressed my deep concern that "the priesthood may have made them better builders and administrators...but it has not made them better men....Rather than having formed them as men, they have been fossilized into clerics."

When the Bishop's only response to my letter was a promise of prayer, I phoned my spiritual director while at St Mary's Seminary in Baltimore to make an appointment to fly up to see him in Washington, DC. As I set by the window during the flight, I remember looking down at how tiny the homes, even the cities looked, and wondered how my problems could be so enormous.

Father O'Shea took me out to dinner at a restaurant popular among members of Congress, and listened attentively as I told him how out of place I felt in the priesthood, and what I feared it was doing to me as a person; that it seemed so unnatural to live in such isolation from the normal human context. I explained how I was frequently walking the floor well into the night, obsessed with the conviction that, at some future date—maybe a hundred years—people would be looking back at the lifestyle of Catholic priests—AT MY LIFE—and chuckling in disbelief. I could not bear the thought of having my life and its very purpose, dismissed as a medieval misreading of Scripture.

I was also tired of having the conversation abruptly changed when I would happen to join a group of men parishioners. I was tired of living in a bubble simply because I wore a Roman collar.

I'm not sure whether my old confessor and friend was even aware of what he was eating, but what I needed more than ever before in my life, was a priest with compassion. His response was like a warm comforting breeze that almost literally lifted me up. Clearly, he had heard my soul talking. He felt my anguish, and in the kindest, most fatherly way, he said, "Bill, I cannot encourage you to leave, but be assured I will support you in whatever decision you make."

When I took the plane back the next morning, I was flying in more ways than one. Within myself, I was assured that should I leave the priesthood, it would not be a sin of betrayal against Almighty God.

What lingered now more than anything else were thoughts of my parents, and their disappointment—even humiliation—at my abandoning the priesthood they had always held in such high esteem.

These thoughts and questions as to how I would support myself outside the priesthood, would remain major deterrents to any final decision to leave. But my spirits were soaring when I arrived back at my new parish of St. Mary of the Woods in Whitesville, Kentucky. I was enjoying my new life as Athletic Director, and coach of the Junior High boys' basketball team. I was good friends with the pastor, who was a bit older than my father, and the housekeeper made the best pot roast I had ever eaten. In many ways, these were the best two years of my priesthood.

Then in August of 1967, I was assigned as pastor of the two western-most parishes in the diocese. This assignment included the original church, which I will refer to as the "home" parish, and the mission parish of St. Edwards located eighteen miles away in Fulton, Kentucky. The Bishop called me to his office to give me fair warning that the people of the home parish were the most racially prejudiced of the entire diocese. But, having grown up in Kentucky, I thought I understood what the Bishop was talking about; but I hadn't a clue as to the degree of hatred to which he was referring.

Just a couple of examples here might give a glimpse of the depth of this bitterness. Shortly before I arrived, there was a temporary African American resident of the town who received Holy Communion on his first Sunday morning, after which he was given a stern reprimand by parish members, and told, if he wanted to receive Communion, he could never do so until all the white members had returned home. (This was told me by a disapproving member of the parish when I arrived.) Within the first few weeks of my arrival, one of the pillars of the church informed me through clinched teeth, that "there ain't no good nigger, but a dead nigger." And when I prayed for Dr. Martin Luther King, Jr. the Sunday after his assassination, there was a resounding "No!" shouted back.

Although I preached the "Good News" of Jesus' commandments of love each Sunday, I realized my true ministry was to the larger community, and to the mission parish in nearby Fulton, who were open and responsive to God's Word.

Within a few months I was elected to the local board of the Office of Economic Opportunity (O.E.O.), a Federal program which provided various kinds of economic assistance to families living below the poverty level throughout several counties in Western Kentucky. I was also active in four ministerial alliances in the area. These were the kinds of ministries to which I felt called as a priest.

Members of the home parish thought differently, and as a result, what problems I may have had with the Bishop, had only just begun.

It was with deep resentment the people of that parish reacted to my involvement in the O.E.O., since I was not only working shoulder to shoulder with black community leaders, but with ministers of other denominations, whom they held in utter contempt. This came to light in a conversation with a wealthy member of the parish who informed me with remarkable clarity: "Father, you wouldn't be so bad, if you didn't spend so much time with the niggers and the Protestant ministers."

It was not long before their animosities toward me were boiling over. Because of the high mileage on my car, I decided to buy a new one in the fall of 1967. It only took days for the slander to circulate that the purchase was made with church funds.

In the spring of 1968, the Head Start Program learned that our school was closing, and inquired to see if they might use our classrooms for their pre-school children. After getting the approval of the Parish Council, I gave the go-ahead. However, within twenty-four hours, the Parish Council had reversed its decision since they had been unaware that close to ninety percent of Head Start children were black. The nearly seismic reverberations reached me on Sunday morning at the mission parish of St. Edwards in Fulton.

It so happened that I had an appointment with the Bishop on Sunday afternoon, regarding the new church we were building in Fulton. When I told him what was going on in the home parish, and that he could expect to hear from some very angry people, he appeared genuinely surprised, and said they had a very similar arrangement with Head Start in Owensboro, and that it was a good thing. As I was leaving, he assured me he would stand behind my decision.

The next morning a small caravan of people the Bishop had called the most racially prejudiced in the diocese, arrived at his door. They came with both demands and threats. Within forty-eight hours, I received a letter from the Bishop, advising me that the meeting with this "loyal group of people lasted two hours and twenty minutes," and that "you are trying to push them harder than they are able to go." He went on to say we were not to use the school for Head Start unless no other facility was available, and then only with a contract "allowing some compensation for the use of the building facilities."

Rarely in my life have I been devastated as I was with the Bishop's about-face. In a lengthy reply, I challenged his attribution of "loyalty." I reminded him these were the same people who had denounced Pope John XXIII and shouted out in anger at the very mention of Martin Luther King at Mass. These were the same people who were bold enough to say, "If we don't want to live like Christians, that's nobody's business but our own." Without responding to this letter, containing these and other highly incriminating allegations as to the sincerity of their Christian faith, the Bishop stood by his decision.

Sometime later I learned what I already suspected: these "loyal" people had threatened to withhold their financial support if the Bishop did not accede to their demands.

The final indignation that sealed my fate in Western Kentucky as well as in the Diocese of Owensboro, was committed in the early fall of 1968. I was instrumental in putting together a biracial panel which we called "Operation Communication." The purpose was to invite responsible members from both the black and white communities for an open discussion of how their relationships might be improved. The mayors of five small cities representing the states of both Kentucky and Tennessee, all of whom were white, agreed to be on the panel, along with five businessmen who were leaders in the black community. An Episcopal priest friend of mine completed the panel. I served as moderator. The location for the public dialogue was City Hall in Fulton, Kentucky. The media was well represented, including

TV Channel 6 from Paducah, Kentucky, the largest city in the area.

To a person, the panel recognized the gravity of the occasion, and related to one another with respect and candor. Problems which had never before been addressed and shared in a public forum were brought into the open as mutual concerns of the greater community. And, by all accounts, real progress was made that night toward bringing both communities together.

The only exception came from the members of the parish the Bishop had called loyal. Each effort I made to reach out to the black community was interpreted as a declaration of war against them. For them this was the last straw. They informed the Bishop they would withhold their financial support so long as I remained their pastor. In addition, they demanded he come down and listen to their complaints, to which he complied. He also insisted I be present for the meeting between him and the parish.

At the meeting in the fall of 1968, approximately thirty parish members were present. The Bishop, a large, stolid, man with rimless glasses, sat quietly as they took turns denouncing me for various reasons, none of which was the real basis for their antagonism, which of course the Bishop must have realized. While he had been unwilling to say anything in my support, he infuriated everyone else by not siding with them in condemning me.

The die had been cast. In the absence of strong Church leadership, the differences were too profound for either a meeting of the minds or for reconciliation to be reached.

Several weeks later, in a letter dated the day after Christmas, the Bishop informed me I was being appointed pastor of two small parishes effective, "at noon at the 9th of January." And further, I was to sign a resignation letter from the present parishes "in order to have the parishes vacant for the appointment of the new pastor."

By return mail, I told the Bishop my conscience would not allow me to sign the letter of resignation or accept his new appointment. This prompted a phone call from the Bishop. His voice was filled with indignation, as he asked if I did not believe in obedience. I assured him I had a long record of obedience, but that could not be the highest value in the case at hand. I reminded him that everything leading up to the proposed transfer was public; that everyone over a three county area knew what was behind the move, and that he was capitulating to a group long recognized for their bitter hatred for a whole race of people. I told him I could not be a party to such a public scandal in the Church.

In spite of many letters and petitions to the Bishop, along with editorials by two local papers objecting to the Bishop's decision, and requesting him to visit the people of St. Edwards, the Bishop remained adamant. Therefore, on January 9, 1969, I drove away from St. Edward parish and many people, both in and outside the parish, I had grown to love, as well as a new church which was about to be dedicated. At the time, I had no plans for the future except to return to my home and live with my parents.

In a letter written earlier that day to all the priests of the diocese, I wanted them to know the basic facts and background in my decision. I concluded with the following: "We are told we are ordained *propter homines*, [for the people]. I believe this! I believe that my first obligation is to the people who are entrusted to me—the People of God. Conscience demands, therefore, that I do everything within my power to see to it that the inherent rights of the laity, so clearly enunciated in the Documents [of Vatican II] of the Church (Paragraphs #30 and #37) are respected.... I am writing this to you because I see no good purpose in remaining silent. For until such anachronistic and unchristian policies are exposed to the light of public scrutiny, there will be no end to them." In response to my letter, out of the sixty-five priests in the diocese, I received one post card of support and one phone call.

*   *   *   *   *

Postscript:

As the National Catholic Reporter was covering the story, they contacted the Diocesan Chancery Office in Owensboro, Kentucky for its position on what had happened. In the February 12, 1969 issue of the NCR, the official response given by the Chancery Office spokesman was that I had so "inflamed the people of Fulton" that the Bishop was reluctant to meet with them, and further, that many of the names on the petitions to see the Bishop were "babes in arms." Once again, truth was at the service of convenience and pragmatics.

Had the laws of the Church been based on the Good News of the Gospel rather than the rule of life in medieval monasteries, and had the Bishop's Chancery Office reflected a modicum of the compassion and the humanity of Christ, I would happily have retired as the priest I was called to be. However, my decision to leave the Catholic priesthood in no way interrupted my ministry to others.

While earning a master's degree in Guidance and Counseling at Xavier University in Cincinnati, Ohio, I worked part-time as a re-socialization therapist at Longview State Mental Hospital. In the fall of 1972, I ran the McGovern Campaign for President in Upper State New York, as my wife, Barbara, was lining up job interviews for me in neighboring Vermont. Her efforts led to a position with the State of Vermont Division of Vocational Rehabilitation as a psychiatric counselor for eight highly rewarding years.

Following the completion of Law School at the University of Kentucky I devoted nearly ten years protecting the wild life, waterways, farmlands, and forests of my dearly loved native State of Kentucky, as an environmental attorney with the Kentucky Cabinet of Natural Resources.

And finally, after returning to the ministry as an Episcopal priest, I served parishes in Louisiana, Maryland, and Delaware, from which I am now retired along with my cherished wife and invaluable helpmate of thirty-nine years, for whom I would not take all the riches of the Vatican.

This, in brief, is the rest of my story.

Becoming A Man

Ed Griffin

I was just three years a priest in 1965, when I marched in Selma with Dr. Martin Luther King. It was the high point of my life as a Christian. Finally I had done something significant for my faith. When I returned to my suburban Cleveland parish, I discovered that people had gone to the pastor and the bishop and demanded my transfer. "Either you get rid of that nigger-lover young priest, or we'll never give you another dime," they told the pastor.

Instead of standing up to the racists, the bishop and the pastor complied with their wishes. I was hurt and shocked. The church to which I had given my life, did not stand behind its own proclamations. Money ruled.

I was transferred to Cleveland's slum area and transferred again when I got too popular with the people and my fellow priests.

Two years after I marched in Selma, I was stationed with an alcoholic pastor, Father Lynch. The bishop had placed him here in the central city as his last chance to sober up. He was failing the test.

*   *   *   *   *

As the fall went on, I grew angrier and angrier with what I saw in the community. One day I mustered my courage and decided to tell the bishop about the failure of the Catholic Church in the central city. I had always been told that the bishop spoke for God. At ordination I had promised him absolute obedience. This was a big step for me.

The bishop lived in a rich suburb, near the central city, but separated from it by a major freeway. I got in my VW minibus and drove along East 105th Street toward Lake Erie. This street was one of the worst in the city. Deteriorating stores, sleazy bars and houses of prostitution lined the street. Riots and near riots often started at the big intersections. Garbage, abandoned cars, and half-burnt buildings littered the street. The sun was just coming up on this fall day so not much was stirring on the street at this hour.

East 105th Street went under the freeway near the lake and the scene changed as rapidly as a movie montage might switch from a barrio to a luxury subdivision. Expensive homes, mansions really, lined the street. Gardeners manicured the lawns to perfection, trimmed the shrubs, and picked up litter. As usual, a police car sat on the Bratenahl side of the underpass, I assumed to keep black people out. When they saw the Roman collar, they waved me on. I drove on and noticed that they had even changed the name of East 105th Street to Bratenahl Road. In the minds of most Clevelanders, East 105th Street was a slum. It wouldn't do for the owner of a mansion to have his return address listed as East 105th Street.

I turned on to Lake Shore Boulevard and drove to the Bishop's mansion. It was right on the lake. I parked and absorbed this large, well-kept home. One old man and a few nuns lived here in luxury, while just across the freeway, thousands of men, women and children lived in poverty. What had happened to the message of Jesus – "Sell what you have and come follow me"?

I rang the bell and a nun came to the door. "I want to see the bishop," I said.

She looked at me like I had asked her for a handout. "This is emergency?" she asked.

"Yes."

She had an accent, but I couldn't identify it. She let me into an atrium. "You wait," she said and hurried into the mansion.

There was one straight-back carved wooden chair in the atrium, what I thought of as a bishop's chair, appropriately enough. An ornate large mirror gave me a picture of myself, a young priest with cigarette ashes and a bit of breakfast on his black coat, a receding hairline and an earnest face.

On a small end table, I saw an old fashioned statue of the Virgin Mary. My mother had a statue like that, and it put me in mind that this is where she wanted me to end up–a bishop. No thank you. I wanted no part of this luxury.

Next to the statue was a box of matches encased in a knitted sleeve. I laughed out loud. Who in their right mind would spend time knitting such a thing? I couldn't help myself–I pocketed it–it would make a great souvenir.

Finally the bishop came down. He was a man in his sixties, a stern look about him. He sat down in the carved chair and left me standing. I caught a whiff of aftershave lotion.

"What seems to be the problem, Father? I allow priests to visit me in my home if they have an emergency problem of faith or morals. Is this an emergency?"

"Ah... Yes."

"Is it a moral question?"

"Yes, indeed."

He sighed and leaned back in the chair. "What is it?" he asked.

I blinked, took a deep breath and started. "Bishop, the church is failing the inner city. People are dying, children aren't getting proper care and what is our church doing? Nothing."

The bishop's resigned look turned to one of anger. His face reddened. "That's not true young man. Our Catholic Interracial Council tries to help the inner city."

"By making statements? Much more is needed, Bishop. Action."

He stared at me and I boldly stared back. But what I saw was not an evil person but a tired old man. For a moment I felt sorry for him.

"This is not really a matter of morals, Father Griffin. We set this opportunity up for priests to come and talk about moral issues, you know, like sexual things or stealing from the church."

"Helping the poor is not a moral issue? You build new churches far out in the suburbs and our parish has a beat up old school and no extra money to make a difference in the neighborhood. We Catholics–you, Bishop–we don't take a strong stand on racism or on poverty. We let the Presbyterians and the Anglicans take the lead. What's the matter with us?"

"You're wrong, young man. We subsidize inner city parishes, including the one you're in. And just last month I had a letter read in all the churches condemning racism. So don't tell me we're not doing anything."

I paused. What would my hero, the prophet Isaiah do in the Bible? Surely, he would not mince words. He would tell it like it was.

I gestured in a circle, pointing to the walls around me. "This mansion, Bishop, why don't you sell it? Give the money to the poor."

The bishop struggled to get up. He leaned his right arm on the ornate chair. His face was redder and his chin shook with anger. "That's enough, Father. I set this interview time up for emergencies. You're wasting my time. Good day."

He turned to leave, but at the entrance to his luxurious living room, he turned to me, the anger gone from his face. "I'm going to pray for you, Father."

"Thank you, Bishop."

I put my hand on the heavy silver doorknob and watched him walk slowly through his house.

I left. Outside, I took a big breath of Lake Erie air. I felt terrific. I knew I hadn't accomplished anything practical, but I had fought an important battle that every young man must fight. My own father was dead, so I had stood up to my spiritual father. I had become a man.

And what does a man do next?

He falls in love.

*   *   *   *   *

Her name was Rose Ann, a black woman with light skin. She often seemed embarrassed by her light skin and almost apologized for it. "Black is beautiful, Father," she said, "and I'm black." She had just graduated from college, and with her friend, Carmelita, she helped me with youth groups and social action projects. All the kids I worked with were black and both women could relate to them better than I could.

Rose Ann was tough and funny, an attractive woman with a biting wit. She wanted to write a book about black women, their struggles and their glory. Carmelita was taller than Rose Ann, a professional social worker, a quiet woman who thought deeply about everything.

After our youth social action meeting the three of us would go out for drinks – and an occasional drink for me – my five-year, no-alcohol pledge for young priests had just ended. We always went to a hotel bar near Lake Erie. It wasn't on the shore but we could see the lake from the parking lot. Sometimes we caught a whiff of Lake Erie fish, and in warmer weather a cool breeze blew in off the lake.

One night we got into a discussion of what we would all be like in twenty years. Rose Ann would be a famous author and Carmelita would be in Washington in charge of Social Services. I would be a bishop.

"Okay," I said, "now that was fun. But I want to know really what I'll be like in twenty years. I mean, I've seen lots of priests who started out fine, but—"

"Like Philip Lynch," Rose Ann said. "He starts out great and opens a home for alcoholic cops and then becomes one."

"A cop?" Carmelita asked.

We all laughed. "No, an alcoholic."

I persisted, "Tell me. I want to know. Carmelita, what do you see in my future? In twenty years?"

She didn't answer right away. Her smile disappeared and she said, "I'm not going to tell you."

"Come on. I'm asking."

"No, I won't tell you."

Rose Ann said, "She doesn't know."

But I knew Carmelita. She *did* know. I began to ask myself the question. Twenty more years of loneliness, of drunken pastors or of pastors who stepped on every initiative I started. Being moved from parish to parish. I had already been moved three times in five years. Two of my classmates from the seminary owned boats and one was studying in Rome, exactly the future my mother wanted for me. I was often full of ideas and plans and I wanted to share them with someone – but there was no one.

What would twenty more years of the priesthood do to me? I already had lots of doubt about church doctrine. When Pope John XXIII started the Vatican Council, he said he wanted to throw open the windows in the church. My trouble was that I couldn't get my own windows closed.

In the seminary my best friend was a guy named Charlie. He was a big man who always fought his weight problem. In every discussion we had, he championed the left liberal side and I stood up for the conservative side. He said celibacy was a misguided idea, and I defended the church. Now in five short years I had out-Charlied my friend Charlie. We met once for coffee and I knew that I, who was way to the right of him in the seminary, was now way to the left of him. Charlie was shocked when I told him I didn't read the breviary anymore – a supposed mortal sin for a priest. "It's not that I don't read the Bible, Charlie," I said. "It's just that I read the parts I want, not what the Church says I should read. And I don't read a certain amount every day; that's too artificial."

Charlie and I were similar in one way – we were both active in civic affairs, I in civil-rights and he in the community welfare organization in Akron where he was stationed.

And children – I loved them. I could see that from my parish work. Every time I visited a parishioner's home, I ended up playing with the kids. I loved it when they laughed or showed joy at a trick I taught them. I loved them clean and dirty, even the babies with stinky diapers.

No children for me? Ever?

*   *   *   *   *

In late October, 1967, Carmelita couldn't come to a youth group meeting, so Rose Ann and I drove the kids home. Afterwards we went to the hotel bar. We talked about the social action meeting with the kids, I told her about the changes coming in the Church and she described the appeal the Black Muslims had in the inner city. I was very curious about them, because I had seen them in action – black men in suits passing out literature on the street, caring for children and helping teenage boys go straight. We talked and laughed for a couple of hours. As we were getting ready to leave, she said she wouldn't make next week's meeting because she was going to Toledo, a hundred miles west of Cleveland.

I said goodnight and drove back to the rectory. But it bothered me all the way home – why was she going to Toledo? Never in my life had I had a feeling like this – wondering who she was going to see in Toledo.

When she came back to Cleveland, Carmelita missed our next meeting as well and Rose Ann and I talked again at our late night session.

"How was Toledo?" I asked her.

"I went to see my cousins," she replied.

"I didn't ask that."

She laughed. "But you were wondering, weren't you?"

I laughed, too. Women have X-ray vision into the human heart.

"Let's talk about it," she said.

"What?"

"You and me."

For a second, I couldn't breathe. Tears came to my eyes. I finally got a word out, "Yes."

"In Toledo, I kept thinking about you. It's crazy and impossible, but that's the truth."

Again, emotion choked me. "Me, too," I said.

"It's funny," she sighed. "I talked to Carmelita about this and she and I laughed. It's a sign that there are no good marriageable males around – me falling in love with a priest."

"What does Carmelita think?"

"That it's an infatuation."

What did she mean? Was the infatuation on both our parts?

Rose Ann asked, "What are we going to do about this?"

I didn't respond. I couldn't. I didn't know what to do.

* * * * *

For the next two months I went through a torturous debate with myself – stay a priest or leave? I knew other priests who had had affairs with women, even lived with them without giving up the priesthood. I couldn't do that. For one thing, it wouldn't be fair to the woman. And I wanted to live my life in the open. How would it feel to preach one thing and live another? What would I say in confession if someone said they were living in sin and didn't want to give it up? How could I advise them if, according to the church, I was living in sin?

I never hugged Rose Ann or kissed her, yet she was always on my mind. My cold intellectual debates about celibacy and the priesthood left the theoretical level. I now had a practical problem, a very real one. I was in love. What was I going to do about it?

* * * * *

In late October I had to go to a retreat house for my annual 'spiritual tune-up,' a requirement for every priest in the diocese. We were supposed to spend the week listening to talks and meditating. Once there, we were not allowed to leave the grounds.

I had developed a cassock phobia. I had decided that the long, black cassock was a feminine form of dress that emasculated me. Back at St. Thomas, Father Lynch had been harping at me to wear a cassock. I refused and wore my black clerical suit with a roman collar. On this retreat there were forty-nine priests wearing cassocks. Did I stand out? I did – to a deluge of negative comments from older priests and a direct order from the retreat director. I still refused.

On Tuesday of the retreat, I received an emergency telephone message. I called the number. It was the campaign manager for Carl Stokes, the first black man to run for mayor of Cleveland.

"Father, we need you to give the invocation on Thursday night. We're planning a big rally in a white area – we need the white vote to win, Father."

"I'm flattered," I replied, "but you want to get a bigwig monsignor or an important pastor of a white parish, not a civil-rights activist like me."

"Ah...we've tried. We can't get anyone."

"Listen, I'll give you a few names, you try them and if they say no, then I'll do it. Just leave another message at this number and say it's an emergency, but don't say what kind of emergency. Okay?"

The man agreed and I gave him a few names. The next day I got another message labeled *Emergency*. I walked out of the retreat on Thursday evening and went to the rally. My invocation prayed, "May God's blessings come down on Carl Stokes. Like little David in the Bible, he faces a giant of a challenge in the next few days."

My prayer went on in that manner. It was a little over-the-top, but Carl Stokes won anyway in early November.

* * * * *

In my hour of crisis, I sought help from two people. The first was my brother-in-law, Tom. He was a computer engineer and a believer in social justice. In the late fifties he participated in the famous lunch counter sit-ins, where students and activists occupied segregated lunch counters. I respected Tom because he moved me from being a talker about racial justice to an actor, persuading me to participate in my first demonstration at the Granada Hotel.

In mid-November Tom and I took a long walk in a park outside Cleveland. The sun felt good that day after a few weeks of gloomy, stormy weather. The trees had shed their leaves, opening vistas in the park. As we hiked along a ridge, we could see the creek in the valley below.

After hemming and hawing for a while, I got to the problem. "I'm in love, Tom," I said, and I told him all about Rose Ann.

He patted me on the back. "Come on, Ed. It happens to us all. We meet a woman and for a day, a week, whatever, we can't think of anything else but her. But that doesn't mean we give up everything we've worked for. How long have you been a priest?"

"Over five years."

"And it's never happened before?" Tom asked.

"No. Never."

"Well, something's different now."

We walked for a while in silence.

"Have an affair with her," he said. "Maybe it'll get the whole thing out of your system." He thought for a minute and added, "Or it won't."

We walked on in silence for a few minutes.

"If you leave," Tom asked, "what are you going to do?"

"I don't know. Get a job, I guess."

"What kind of job?"

I didn't answer. He had me. I hadn't thought this through.

"Here's an idea, Ed. Go get a master's degree in something you're interested in. Then quit. Let the church pay for your education. Then you can move into a field you like and leave the priesthood. It'll only take a year or so."

Tom's advice sounded pretty sensible, but somehow it didn't fit me. Perhaps it's a failing, but I'm a *now* person. If I have a problem, I get at it *right now*. If I want something, I try to get it *now*. I was in love and that situation had to be dealt with *now*.

*   *   *   *   *

The other person who advised me was Sister Mary, a nun whom I often met at social action groups. We talked a lot about spirituality together. She was a few years older than me and the principal of Catholic High School in an older part of Cleveland. I called her on a Sunday afternoon and asked if I could come over and talk.

"I'll meet you at the school," she said.

We met in the staff lounge, a quiet room with notices on the walls and a little kitchen at the back. A pizza and a bottle of soda sat on the coffee table. Mary understood a young man's appetite.

In between bites of pizza, I laid out the problem, holding nothing back.

She munched on a single piece, sitting opposite me on a folding chair, the afternoon sun casting bars of light on her and on the wooden floor. I sat on an old couch, the coffee table between us. Visually, she was a foot or so above me, which is where I always placed her in my mind.

She had an attitude I strived for – she did as much as I did for social justice, but there was an aura of spirituality about her. She could laugh with everyone else about the foibles of the bishop, but I knew that prayer and meditation went deep in her.

When I finished the story of Rose Ann, she didn't say anything for a minute. Then, "How's the pizza?"

We both laughed. I had already eaten half of it.

Again, we were silent. She was such good friend, these silent periods felt natural to me.

"You know," she said, "you've changed me a lot. I have never met anyone to whom Jesus was more present than to you. You have made him come alive for me. I'm telling you."

She tried to camouflage it, but tears came into her eyes. "The talks you've given at meetings, our conversations, Ed, I mean it, they've made a difference in my life. . . the way you talk about Jesus..."

I knew she wasn't just saying this to keep me in the priesthood. Mary was a straight shooter.

"So you think I should stay."

"You're good at it."

I told her what my brother-in-law had said.

"Yes, maybe it is just an infatuation and maybe it's real. I don't know. But I think something else is going on – you've fallen out of love with the church."

"What do you mean?"

"After all you've been through, after all the moves from parish to parish, you've been hurt and the wonderful church you dedicated your life to doesn't look so wonderful anymore."

"You're right there, Mary."

"But bishops aren't the church and neither are the drunken pastors and white racists or whatever. The church is all of us. All of us striving together to reach the kingdom."

"I know that's what the Vatican Council says, but...."

Mary took a few more bites of her pizza and I ate another piece and thought about what she had said. We were both quiet for a while.

Mary broke the silence. "I read about a conference in Mexico called *The Priest in Crisis.*, Father Ivan Illich, the famous priest who's training priests to help the poor in South and Central America, is giving the conference. Would you like to go? Sounds like it's what you need now."

"Sounds great, Mary, but you know my finances. I've got nothing."

"You've spent it all on others. I'll give you the money."

"No, I'll borrow it."

"Okay, it's a deal."

"It's in Cuernavaca, Mexico, right after Christmas."

"Thanks, Mary."

"And remember what I said, Ed, that you're very good at what you do."

"I will."

* * * * *

Christmas came and with it a bittersweet meeting. Tom and my sister, Joy, had moved in early December to Beloit, Wisconsin where Tom had a new job. Tom and Joy returned to Cleveland for the holidays and stayed with friends. I went over to see them and my sister came down the stairs with a Christmas present for me – a new set of vestments that she had hand sewn for me. Tom had kept the confidentially I insisted on and had not told her what was going through my mind.

I thanked her for her thoughtfulness and told her about my upcoming trip and the reason for it. "Have you told Mother?" she asked. We both knew how often our mother bragged about having a son who was a priest.

"No, I haven't told her anything."

"Well, don't," Joy said. She, herself, was on the verge of tears.

"I wasn't going to." I fingered the beautiful work she had done. "I don't know what to do. What if I leave the priesthood? What should I do with these?"

"Give them to the missions. What about the chalice you got at ordination?"

"I gave that to the missions a long time ago."

* * * * *

I told my friend, Justin, about the conference and he told our other friend, Don. The three of us – the three troublemaking priests in the diocese of Cleveland – flew to Mexico City right after Christmas and spent a day sightseeing. We took a taxi over the hills to Cuernavaca, a beautiful little city nestled in the mountains to the south. We rode through this colonial city and up into the surrounding hills. Illich's school was located in a small building in a group of simple Mexican homes that he had bought to house his students.

The conference we came for, *The Priest in Crisis*, never really happened. We met Illich and he gave us only one lecture. He talked with us about his work in South America and about his ideas for society. I knew him to be widely respected, but I was dealing with a crisis in my life and I didn't want to talk about globalization or what the CIA was up to. After the talk, I went up to him and said, "Professor, I'm thinking of leaving the priesthood."

He stared at me for a long minute and then said, "Don't tell your mother."

"What?" I asked. "How can I *not* tell my mother?"

He shrugged and walked away. A year later he himself left the priesthood and I wondered if he followed his own advice.

With the conference over the day it started, Justin and Don took off to sun themselves in Acapulco. I decided to stay in Cuernavaca and think. We agreed to meet again to celebrate New Year's Eve in the town square.

I walked around the city for a day and tried to think, but no great insight came to me. I went back to the little Mexican house where I was staying. The house was just one big room. There was a bathroom in a corner and a ladder in the center to go up to a trap door that led to the roof. A natural gas two-burner hot plate was the only way to heat water or food, and the house for that matter. The stove, however, gave off the smell of rotten eggs, not a good sign for natural gas. I didn't care about the natural gas problem, however, because I had a bad case of traveler's diarrhea for the next twenty-four hours.

The next night I felt well enough to go up the ladder and sit on the roof to watch the stars. No railing blocked the view and I was far enough from the city that no lights interfered with the view. The temperature was mild as it is year round in Cuernavaca.

That night it seemed that the universe opened up to me. I was one with the stars and planets over my head. I could do whatever I wanted and be whatever I wanted to be.

I stayed up on the roof until dawn, then slept for a few hours and toured the area for a few more days until Justin and Don returned on New Year's Eve.

We spent the last evening of 1967 in the city square, drinking *cerveza* and talking. I told them about my night under the stars. "I'm on the verge of quitting," I said.

"Ah," Don said, "sex in '68."

We all laughed, but as we headed back up to our sleeping quarters, we stopped on a hilltop overlooking the city.

Justin patted me on the back and grew serious. "I've been thinking about you leaving, Ed. I'm going to miss you. You're a hell of a guy. But don't just quit. Take a leave of absence. If things don't work out, you can come back. Just don't burn your bridges behind you."

It was good advice and I determined to do exactly that when we got back.

We finished our trip by returning to Mexico City where I went into a little men's shop. Here I was, thirty-one years old and I didn't own a shirt with a collar nor did I own a single tie. I bought a white shirt, a blue striped tie and matching silver cufflinks and tie clasp. Dressed in my new shirt, tie and cufflinks, I was no longer Father Edward Griffin. I was Ed Griffin, man of the world.

*   *   *   *   *

We returned to Cleveland late at night. The next morning I sat down with Father Lynch. "I'm taking a leave of absence, Father," I said, "and it has nothing to do with you."

I was worried about him. His exterior was blunt and unfriendly, but I knew he took things very personally. His concern was what the bishop might think of him.

And here was his assistant priest, leaving the priesthood, on his watch. How would the bishop interpret that?

"Sure, sure," he said, "more protests, no doubt. You've gotten yourself into this mess, young man."

Next I visited the bishop in his mansion. He greeted me in the same unfriendly way he had before. "I hope this is an emergency, Father?"

"Well, I guess so," I replied. "I think I owe it to you to let you know I'm taking a leave of absence from the priesthood. You'll need to send another assistant priest to the parish. Father Lynch isn't doing well, nor is the dying Irish priest he took in."

"You can't just walk out on your priesthood, Father."

The phrase 'leave of absence' had been on my mind since Justin suggested it. I wanted to say exactly that, but now the bishop was pushing me.

"I'm leaving," I said. "I'm joining the hundreds of priests who are leaving the priesthood."

"What? Are you leaving or just taking a leave of absence?"

"A leave of absence."

"Well, listen Father, there is no mass-movement of priests leaving. I don't know where you got that idea."

I didn't reply but I knew many priests from Cleveland had already left and an independent Catholic newspaper, the *National Catholic Reporter*, often commented on the nation-wide exodus.

I turned to go. "Anyway, Bishop, just to let you know about the parish."

I put my hand on the door.

"Father, think of your immortal soul."

"Goodbye, Bishop," I said and left.

After I left the priesthood, I faced the entirely new problem of dating. I was a thirty-one year old virgin who knew nothing about dating, nothing about women. Once I learned to trust my own instincts, I was fine.

My mother never reconciled to my leaving the priesthood.

I met with Rose Ann just after I left, but my whole world felt like it had been turned upside down. I still wasn't used to being 'Ed.' Rose Ann did write her book about black women and teaches university English now.

I moved from Cleveland to Rockford, Illinois to establish the new Ed, and then to Milwaukee, Wisconsin. I dated lots of women. An ex-nun I went with had far more sexual experience than I did. She ended our relationship after nine months and I'm glad she did, but it hurt at the time.

After I got my master's degree in community organization, I applied for a job with a couple I knew in a poor area of Milwaukee. I went over to their house and we had a pleasant chat. I knew after a while that the job was not mine – we had differing opinions of the mayor of Milwaukee. I was about to leave when the woman's sister walked down the stairs. She was twenty-six, a beautiful woman with a New York accent. We talked and discovered that both of us had picketed for civil-rights and for the grape boycott. We both were against the war in Vietnam, we didn't like Nixon as president, and we wanted the Catholic Church to change.

That was forty-two years, two children, two countries, five careers, and fourteen cars ago. Kathy is a retired kindergarten teacher now and I still volunteer to teach creative writing in prison. I never made it to a bishop's mansion as my mother wanted and besides, bishops have sold most of the mansions. Kathy and I live in a modest home in a suburb of Vancouver, Canada. We're very happy.

Most of this account came from Ed's book, **Once A Priest***. He is the author of five books and writes two blogs,* **Writers Write Daily** *and* **Prison Uncensored***. His website is:* www.edgriffin.net

O-oh Freedom:

A Passage Toward Faith

John Ardizzone

On March 8, 1965, early one Monday morning, I received a telephone call, an invitation from a friend. He asked me to consider whether I would go to Selma, Alabama, where a demonstration about voting rights had turned into a bloody Sunday the day before.

Vocation

In 1962, ninety-seven years from the end of the civil war, Delaware was still a border state. The southern end of this small, original colony (the second smallest state in the Union) was still segregated at lunch counters, water fountains and in its color consciousness. Its northernmost city, Wilmington, where I had come to begin my life as a priest that year, was also racially divided. As a new priest, I was racially divided, too: my thinking was in the right place, my actions and heart were somewhere else. The compartments for race were easy to overlook, if you were white. Its mentality, though, if you were black or any other color and cared to notice, was racist. If you were in the "majority" you didn't talk about race or rights except privately when the fledgling Civil-Rights Movement caught your eye in the newspapers. If you were like most priests, you didn't think about race and you certainly didn't preach about it. Yet, after Selma and after Vatican II, both events dominated my mind and my work.

That string of yarn, rights (civil and otherwise), was there all along but undercover. It began to unwind later as my life unraveled. I have come to see that, at the center of the spool was not "rights," but freedom. First, it was the freedom of others to live authentically; later it became my freedom to do the same.

In 1962, I was like many white, supposedly forward-looking people; understanding and noninvolvement mixed easily, especially if you were not reminded about the inconsistency of it all for a believer. The fledgling civil-rights movement seemed far away...or I made sure it was. Bruce, my best priest-friend, was involved in some sit-ins, but that was just like him, I thought. He was sincere, but loud, liberal and prone to drama. He was also boisterous, and that made him and the Movement something I could just shake my head at.

Unlike him, at least in my mind, I was a man on the move in the local church. Roderick Dwyer, the Vicar General (the Bishop's second in command) had requested me to be his assistant pastor. I had an advanced degree in theology from Catholic University with a personal concentration in Catholic liturgy. Changes in worship were beginning to sweep the Church as Vatican II issued revelatory documents and new rules. The Monsignor was anxious to have a knowledgeable priest help him understand and cautiously address the new theology coming out of the Council. I sensed he wanted to understand more about these teachings when he advised the bishop. I felt privileged to be given opportunities to influence him and the local church through him, as long as I didn't upset anyone with what I said or did.

Accepting the strictures made sense; charging ahead seemed naïve. Why should I question my direction? Within the confines of my thinking and work, I quickly found myself helping to lead diocesan liturgical reform, and soon, the realignment of the laity and priests' roles in advising the bishop. Did I ever preach about Civil-Rights? I didn't *mention* Civil-Rights. It was too controversial, too political. Besides, I was too busy.

* * * * *

I was born in New York and raised in the nearby diocese of Paterson, New Jersey. My journey to priesthood in Wilmington was circuitous. When I first requested admission to the seminary at the end of high school, James NcNulty, the conservative bishop of the Paterson Diocese, adamantly refused to accept my application. No one used the impolite word, but, in Canon Law I was considered a bastard.

That brand on my soul was explained delicately to me by the Rector of the Minor Seminary at Seton Hall University. Since my mother was Jewish and my father was Italian Catholic, and especially since they had been married "outside the church", their marriage was "invalid." No matter that they were married by an Episcopal priest, that my mother had died giving birth to me, or that my father had married a Catholic in the Church three years later. I was a product of my father's original, invalid alliance. I was stunned.

"Do you mean the Bishop said this because of something my father...?" I asked the rector.

"Oh, my son! Jesus loves you! But ordaining you here in Paterson where you live and where people know your family (translation: "know you are illegitimate") might cause scandal." He said more. I was too stunned to hear.

He didn't tell me I might serve elsewhere as a priest, where people wouldn't "know".

I couldn't find words. I don't recall that he could either, or cared to. I clearly remember how he signaled the end of the conversation: he stood up. Oh, in parting, he blessed me.

The message was painfully clear: like the current Church practice toward gays, I was loved by Jesus, but not accepted by His Church, or, at least, not by the Church in the Diocese of Paterson. Bishop McNulty did more. At my graduation ceremony from Bayley Ellard Catholic high school in 1954, when I knelt before him to receive my diploma, he sat stone-faced and pointedly refused to allow me to kiss his ring, a gesture the class had practiced and which every other graduate made.

I wish that my reaction to that snub had been anger, as was my father's. That would have been cleaner, truer. I didn't yet recognize my anger. That would take some time. I didn't feel anger. I felt shame. I didn't only believe in God; I believed in the Church and it had decreed my parents' marriage illicit. It had decreed me illicit. I see now that the saving grace was that I felt more determination than shame.

For better and for worse, I was and remain a fiercely determined person. The parish priest who had inspired me, Jim Fallon, only shook his head when he heard about Bishop McNulty's decision. He didn't say he disagreed; he only said, "The bishop is a tough nut to crack." There was no sense knocking on that door. But I wasn't ready to take "No." He suggested that I apply to the Diocese of Wilmington, Delaware: "They need priests." Wilmington was far from upper New Jersey where I lived. The message was, "No one will know your background there." No matter what the local churchman said; I was determined to follow this vocation I believed I had received from God.

In the summer of 1956, the elderly Bishop of the Diocese of Wilmington, Edmund FitzMaurice, asked me to come to his home so he could meet me. It was a warm and very long ride from northern New Jersey to

Delaware. I remember both parents in the car, sitting in the front as they usually did, with me in the back seat. Something was different about this ride: I can't remember that any one of us exchanged a word on the way down. I think my father was still fuming at the indignity suffered from the last bishop I met at graduation. I think my step-mother was only anxious. I don't have to think about my state of mind; I know I was in knots the whole ride. I knocked on the door of a big, but not palatial, home in the city. A wispy housekeeper answered pleasantly: The bishop was expecting me.

Bishop Fitzmaurice welcomed me into his home dressed in slacks and a rumpled smoking jacket, cigarette in hand. He squinted over his round spectacles at my skinny frame. Then he squinted again. "My, my, we'll have to fatten you up." Those were his first words, not some gesture telling me to bow and bend. Not, "Now you can kiss my ring."

Fatten this kid up. Although we had a short, simple conversation, most all I could think of immediately afterwards was that warm greeting. Fatten me up? That's about feeding, about nurturing; that's about noticing the thinness barely hiding my frame, let alone noticing my fears.

Quietly: "Monsignor Taggart (the vocation director) tells me you want to become a priest."

He waited. It was my turn. It was my turn to talk! "Yes, Your Excellency..."

"Why do you want to do that? It's hard work." Hard work? Is that all it is? Is that all you want to know?

Then, "For a long time, Bishop....." and the words spilled out, spilled out all over his ash-strewn jacket, all over the floor, all over the room, I swear. I don't remember what I said; I only remember being struck that he cared to ask, and that he seemed to listen. He asked a few more things. Did I mind going to school for a long time; did I mind studying hard? I am not sure what I answered. I'm confident I wanted to say. Work? I'll work my ass off!

He stopped my torrent of words with a simple hand signal and was silent for a long moment. He stood up, brushed more ashes off his shirt

"I think you'll do fine."

That's all. It was over. No obvious investigation, no history taking, no papers, just a simple man and a skinny kid having a serious conversation about the rest of this kid's life. I left his home on a cloud. My youthful gratitude spilled over when I saw my parents. My mother's anxious voice the moment I climbed into the car:

"What did he say?'

My answer, "He looked like Santa Claus!"

His personal acceptance was full-hearted and more than a formality. Because of his generosity and my hard work academically, I was offered what my father's meager income could never afford to provide. While still in the seminary, I was given opportunities for summer studies where I chose and to pursue an advanced degree in theology. I did and still do love learning. I later recognized that the trip to Delaware set me on a journey I never expected. It offered me a more open-minded way of viewing the world and learning than I would have had in my parochial home. It put me on a scholarly course that would become a template for my life. Going to another diocese, another part of the country to study and to work was the first step in my journey toward freedom. At first, it gave me freedom to think differently. Finally, it gave me freedom to become authentic, a grace that I treasured in time, a gift that was seeded in faraway Baltimore, Maryland, at St. Mary's Seminary, Paca Street where I was sent to begin my studies.

On the first day at St. Mary's, September of 1956, going to my assigned small room, I nervously tried on a cassock and roman collar for the first time as I prepared for the obligatory first meeting with the rector. My heart in my throat, I actually wondered if they knew I was... illegitimate? Would they throw me out even as I walked in? My boyhood fear was at full throttle as I left home for the first time, still grieving my father's death some months before. Gratefully, that was eased because no one there ever questioned my belonging to this new family. The seminary and faculty accepted me fully. I found a community there as I studied philosophy, the first step then in the academic preparation of priests. At the Theological College at Catholic University in Washington, D.C. where I was sent two years later to study theology, I truly began to breathe easier. The air started to feel fresher, perhaps freer.

In the Catholic Church, freedom is not truly considered a value. Yes, "free will" is God-given. That is the official teaching. But freedom is inexplicably disconnected from the belief in free will. Church leaders would likely not say that today, but their thinking and acting is often not far from that position. The American Church hierarchy currently speaks righteously about the Church losing freedom in America, freedom the Constitution guarantees. They forget to mention that the government of the United States guarantees freedom while the Catholic Church government does not. Given the mentality I grew up with in mid-century I didn't think much about this. Only later, as I was given more freedom and as I took more did I begin to value it. At first, I was only boyishly grateful to my new Diocese.

I still appreciate the education and opportunities I was offered in Wilmington. In time, gratitude alone seemed a child's response, albeit an abused child's response. In time, my life was fueled by different values. Yet, my personal search for freedom of thought and conscience started in those seminaries. The search for fuller freedom, adult freedom came later. That quest became the yarn that knitted my life fabric together, first by holding me to the priesthood as others began to leave. Later, it released me to follow the thread in a new direction.

North American Liturgical Conference

The humble church that is Wilmington's "cathedral" witnessed my ordination to priesthood in May, 1962.

That same year marked the start of the Second Vatican council, a short-lived, but vital opening of windows, as Pope John XXII called it. The consequences of that event formed the center of my focus in the priesthood. In calling the council over the objections of the Curia, the Pope justified it by explaining that fresh air needed to blow through a musty place. For me and for many, that wind was bracing.

It hadn't always been so. The fervent passion I had for reform of the celebration of Sunday Mass, and of the Church itself began in the summer of 1957, in a hotel elevator. That year, the summer between my first and second year in the seminary, the diocese sent me to my first national conference to broaden my understanding of the worldwide movement fomenting for liturgical change. No one could know how those talks would awaken the first stirrings in me that would lead to quite a personal journey about justice, about participation in all of life, a trip that would lead to Selma.

I recall that I was surprised that week that so many of the speakers focused on the urgent need for the Catholic Church's conversion of itself first, not of others. Speakers called for a re-thinking of Catholic theology to address new questions for a change from a Latin to an English Mass, and for much more.

The call was for sensible answers to the turbulence following cultural and moral changes that were shaking mid-century America, and for lucid, relevant sermons that might engage parishioners. These pleas stirred me, but mostly in the sense that the urgency of all the talk was upsetting. I was on the edge of that mass of conservative people in the world who did not find the transformation of culture exciting. Like many who had never heard such talk or seen such fervor in their parishes, I was deaf and blind. The talks that week, the disregard for rules (What, laymen drinking from the sacred cup?!) didn't leave me uplifted, they left me confused.

What happened to me in that hotel? Returning from another unorthodox presentation on a hot summer afternoon, in the elevator I met a priest from my seminary, Father "Gino" Walsh. Father Walsh was a popular teacher at St. Mary's with a reputation as a "radical" thinker. I hadn't taken his class yet, but as music director he conducted our weekly hymn practice in chapel. I knew his large presence, his booming voice. He knew of me, but in the same distant way I knew him. On the crowded elevator, cheek to cheek, he literally bumped into me.

"John! What brings you here?"

What might have been a casual question sounded very pointed and surprised. I told him the diocese had "sent me." He asked what I thought of all this. I was hesitant at first, but honest.

"A lot of what I heard confuses me," I said. "I don't understand taking communion in a way that the rules of the Church forbid." I went on. "I guess I can see the reasonableness of the changes people want, but I don't understand the *fever* for change. Wouldn't their passion alone, let alone the disdain for rubrics, or for Church traditions, make it less likely that the hierarchy would listen?"

His eyes grew wide as the elevator stopped and the door opened. Without asking, Gino gripped my arm and just about pushed me out the door, saying a quick goodbye to his friends. Steering me to the end of the hotel corridor, we sat on the floor, legs crossed, twelve inches from each other's faces. For more than an hour he talked about many things, especially about change coming from the bottom not the top. After that, we both talked. He satisfied every question; he answered every doubt; he reasoned, he lectured and he cajoled. Six years before the start of the Vatican Council, years before the reign of Pope John, he explained what he, theologians and some bishops worldwide wanted: to offer a vibrant faith to a hungry people. He reminded me I wanted to become a priest: could I want less?

Anointing

I wasn't ordained that day. But I was unquestionably "anointed." That was where my priestly life really started. It began with me sitting on the floor in a hotel hallway. Gino didn't just lecture me. He encouraged me to answer my doubts by reading and exploring further, by traveling and meeting "people in the pew" different from the people with whom I'd grown up. At one point in that long conversation, he made a proposal.

"John, this is about so much more than changing the Mass into English or how we take communion. Since you've come halfway across the country, why don't you keep going? I know some people in Chicago who are leading a lively social movement there. I can introduce you to laymen and priests who are true leaders, who are putting into practice what the speakers here are talking about. Why don't you take a look at what is going on there? While you're traveling, go on to the parish of a friend of mine near Minneapolis? That place is unlike one you've ever seen. I know the pastor well. He'd be glad to have you."

Coming to St. John's University, Collegeville, Minnesota for this conference I had just taken my first plane ride, my first trip outside the confines of family or seminary. Like many Easterners, I thought the country stopped with the Hudson River. Gino said he would give me contacts in these places, make sure I was introduced to Church leaders who were neither bishops nor priests. He suggested ways I could persuade my diocese to give me the money and chance to do this. I agreed, reluctant about what I was stepping into. He promised he'd make those calls to Chicago and Minneapolis. The next day, he did.

In Chicago, I met social activists who spoke convincingly about the Church's need to translate the gospel message of love thy neighbor. Without hesitation, they bluntly asked this aspiring cleric to rethink the mission of priest, to not disappoint them as others had. Early on one of the mornings there, I was dropped at the gate of a non-union manufacturing plant and told to distribute pamphlets about workers' rights and social justice. "My God," I thought, "Am I turning into a socialist?" These leaders in social justice asked questions: Had I heard of Saul Alinsky's and Monsignor Egan's work in Chicago? Did I know about Dorothy Day's efforts with the poor in New York? How about the worker-priest movement in France, the Jesuit writer Pierre Teihard de Chardin who had groundbreaking thoughts about life itself, or the South American bishops espousing liberation theology and fighting for the working class? No, No and No.

In Chicago, Pat and Patty Crowly, founders of the Christian Family Movement, invited me to stay at their home. Over dinner, they and their several children had a vigorous conversation that took me aback. It wasn't about the latest TV show. It was about politics and the difficulty of living out Christian social values. From youngest to oldest, all the children were part of the conversation.

That is where the seeds of my real life vocation truly were watered and sprouted. Underneath it all, I was beginning to recognize that I could think for myself, think anew. This experience offered me a different way to frame my understanding of my mission as priest and even of the world around me. I didn't jump into civil-rights or social justice. I didn't even run. I walked very gingerly. The path before me was a new one and I felt its force. That conversation with Gino Walsh began a personal march, longer, more arduous than any other journey in my life. From a hotel floor, I began to learn about thinking freely, outside the (my) box. What does good liturgy have to do with authentic religious practice? What does a priest's religious practice have to do with a concern for anyone's freedom? Everything. I say and believe that with ease now. Yet, the transition from brain to body, from pondering to marching came slowly, even painfully.

*　*　*　*　*

Today I am a clinical psychologist and have been for thirty years. In family therapy studies (one of my areas of concentration) tracking family-of-origin culture is an important way to understand the source of adult patterns of acting and thinking. In my family religious training, freedom of choice was not a value. My Italian grandfather had only to glower and I knew what was expected of me and what wasn't allowed. His way of making a point or stopping a conversation was to raise his voice and bang the table! Freedom wasn't valued in my immigrant family or in my Church, despite its being God-given. Where would I have learned to value it? Silence, maybe shame, are still proper responses if you are a Catholic who uses birth control, or even if you support a President that the collective group of American bishops castigates openly. Plato has a story about people held prisoners in a dark cave for years. When they are freed, do they love the light? No. The light is blinding; like people coming out of a dark movie-theater, we shield our eyes at first. I did. My first experience at the North American Liturgical Week (as it was then called), my first trips to Chicago and Minneapolis did not cause me to run out of the cave. I treaded cautiously.

Liturgy and Reform

Father Jim Fallon in my home parish in Madison, New Jersey had originally inspired my vocation and encouraged me to read Scripture. I was particularly moved by the gospel passage that asked what one possesses if he gains the whole world, but loses his soul. I never understood that verse as a call to save my "soul," but to expand my life. Those ideals were on the top of my mind at ordination. However, we all have more than one motive for what we do. Taken together, they better explain us. I was enthusiastic about serving, about promoting the liturgical changes stirring the Church, about teaching a new theology, and about changing minds and hearts. For better and for worse, I also wanted to succeed, to become somebody, to achieve.

For those reasons, it meant very much to me to have a position of respect, of leadership, of status. I couldn't admit it, especially to myself, but I was pleased to be able to live more comfortably than my family. I recall being impressed as a boy overhearing Jim say he'd just returned from skiing in Quebec. Skiing? In another country? I didn't know priests could afford to do that. My family couldn't. My father was the only son of Italian immigrants. They lived and worked in the east side ghetto of New York. My father never finished grade school. My stepmother was the daughter of Depression-era Polish immigrants who needed her to go to work after ninth grade. My birth mother was the child of immigrant parents, too, Russian-Orthodox Jews. Coming from unassuming roots, my priestly status brought a sense of pride to my father's and step-mother's families. It wasn't pride based on religion; it was social. Look what I was attaining! Everyone was proud of me. I was proud of myself.

In addition, I was always a student. I was "intellectual." I loved to study and still do (sometimes, my wife teases me as "Rabbi" – the serious scholars of my maternal Jewish heritage). It isn't surprising, then, that the subject of race was introduced to me in an intellectual way in a social studies course I took at St. Mary's Seminary. By 1958, the year I took that course, African Americans seeking civil- rights were beginning to become publicly restless. In class, the Church's official position on social justice was discussed actively. I recall the teacher giving his opinion.

"There will not be equal rights for Negroes until marriage is allowed between the races."

In 1958, many states still had laws banning "miscegenation," the name itself suggesting something tawdry. I agreed with his thoughts and with the careful justification he gave implicitly supporting interracial marriage. I might bait my family with my shocking ideas, but my assent was intellectual. I backed my positions up with thinking, not with action. I stayed with rationality, with the opinion that changing embedded bigotry would take time. How long did I myself wait before I seriously thought of this again? Ten years. That wasn't so hard, was it? Not for me. For *them*, for the blacks throughout the country, was it hard for them to wait? In 1958, who asked?

After Vatican II, I wrote about, preached and lectured on liturgical reform. Church conversion of itself was always a subtext and sometimes a central theme in my talks. In quick succession, I encouraged Monsignor Dwyer to have the bishop start a Diocesan Liturgical Commission with me as the executive secretary. I became the leader of the newly formed priest advisory committee to the bishop, then president of the National Liturgical Conference (where this had all started). I thought about helping lead the local Church into new times and little else. I was achieving my two goals, meaningful ministry and achievement. On a fast track, it should have been no surprise that in the first years after ordination I got crippling kidney stone attacks, then acute pneumonia. Then came my slow estrangement from clerical life.

Then came Selma.

<u>March to Selma</u>

"Civil-Rights Marchers Attacked in Selma"

"...The first ten to twenty Negroes were swept to the ground screaming, arms and legs flying and bags went skittering across the grassy divider strip onto the pavement on both sides. Those still on their feet retreated. The troopers continued pushing, using both the force of their bodies and the prodding of their nightsticks. The police also fired tear gas at the crowd and charged on horseback..."

(Afterwards at a makeshift hospital at a church) "...Negroes lay on the floors and chairs, many weeping and moaning. A girl in red slacks was carried from the house screaming....From the hospital came a report that the victims suffered fractures of ribs, heads, arms and legs in addition to cuts and bruises..."

New York Times, March 8, 1965

Certain dates and times of the day stand out in our individual and national memories. I remember 9 AM, Monday, March 8, 1965. I had returned to the rectory for a quiet breakfast after celebration of the eight o'clock morning Mass at my parish. Still in my Roman collar, black cassock and French cuffs, I drank my coffee alone and ate breakfast, served by our housekeeper. As I ate quietly, I read the New York Times, as was my morning custom. Engrossed in the news, I was shaken by the stories and pictures of an attempted march to Montgomery, Alabama the day before by a group of Civil-Rights protestors. I read of the chaos that had enveloped a group who posed no threat, except a moral one, and whose only weapon was courageous non-violence. I was mesmerized by the story. As God' grace will work, at precisely that moment, I was called away from the table to take a phone call. It was my friend, Bruce. He asked me if I had heard about the riot in Selma.

"Yes, yes, I was just reading..."

He interrupted me, no time for a quiet conversation.

"King is trying to get clergy from around the country to go to Selma to protest this stuff. He's afraid that the young people there will erupt in violence. It's urgent to get clergy there because the press will pay attention to them. They need help to keep tempers cool."

At first, I thought he was telling me the news I had just read. I thought he was explaining his need to leave town quickly. Maybe he wanted me to cover his emergency calls. No.

In a strained voice, "John, I can't go and I am really upset about that. I have a wedding and a funeral I just can't miss. I promised...I am really beside myself. They need priests there, bad."

Maybe he was telling me what he wanted to do, but couldn't. Maybe it was a cry for understanding for his conscience-driven conflict. I tried to be empathetic to my well-meaning friend. I murmured sincere understanding. I was wrong. Bruce quickly made it clear that he was asking something of me.

"John, for God's sake, stop! Don't feel sorry for me! Let me say something! John, I know you've never done anything like this and that you agree in your head with the need for racial justice. But, Brother, I also know where your heart is. John, my friend, I know you." A pause, then, "Would you go there and take my place? Would you go down and be part of this?"

I was stunned physically and mentally. My heart was racing, but my brain was numb. If my mind wasn't open, my mouth was.

He went on, "I don't know what I am asking you to get into down there. It might be dangerous. Like I said, I don't know what I'm asking of you. People are getting beaten. Don't answer me yet. First, pray about this, will you? Then decide."

I don't remember what I said, or if I did more than stammer, "Sure, Bruce, sure... I'll pray about this."

I put the phone down, left breakfast half eaten and went into our church, next door. I tried to address God. But as much as a cry to God, I was addressing my anxiety and my conscience, both, stricken by Bruce's call. For over an hour, I agonized over my conflict of conscience. I had thought that everything I believed was synthesizing. Suddenly it was coming apart. I was frightened at the possibilities of what I'd meet and at the choice put before me. I can admit that I was also upset about how our white, middle income, border-state parishioners would view this, about how the pastor would take my request to go. I didn't have words for all I felt. I can hardly remember what I thought more exactly than I've just said. I know I was both afraid and conscience-stricken in prayer about my good intentions about race and about my inaction. I thought for the first time in eight years about what I'd learned at my first foray into liturgical studies, about the connection between participation in Mass and participation in society's needs.

When we feel deeply we can feel many things at once. Just like our motives, our emotions and the thoughts behind them can be noble and banal, selfless and immensely self-centered, all at the same time. Minutes before I had felt anguish and revulsion at the scene on the Selma Bridge. I still felt that. Now, those emotions were mixed with worry for myself and about how I might be beaten or hurt there. I was upset about how the trip would affect my reputation, my career in the Church. Was it worth losing all the influence and regard I'd earned? At the same time, I couldn't see how I could refuse to go and still keep to a faith that wasn't about words. On my knees, I decided to go to Selma.

First, I needed to approach Monsignor Dwyer. I really didn't "ask" him much, as I recall the conversation. I talked to this patron, this mentor, about the Church's mission for social justice; I talked about the priest as witness; I talked about the Church and the "Negro." As I'm likely to do when I am upset, I talked in a torrent.

"Father, how can we talk to the Negro and not stand with them?"

I know now that I didn't simply want a short leave of absence from my parish duties. I wanted approval, too. He listened quietly with few questions. Finally, he said, "I'll speak to the bishop."

I hadn't asked for anyone's understanding or permission to leave but his. The bishop? I knew that was as much blessing for this as I would get. I walked out of his office in a daze.

* * * * *

The small airport in Montgomery, Alabama wasn't crowded on that warm evening of March 10, 1965, when we arrived. There were now four people going from the Diocese of Wilmington, two young priests, myself and Ron Powell, and two nuns I didn't know. Ron was known as a firebrand, already active locally in "the movement" for racial equality. I hardly knew him, though I knew of him. We didn't travel in the same set of people. We two priests were dressed in clerical garb, black suits and Roman collars. The nuns, one young, one older (about thirty and sixty years old each) were habited in 1960's nun garb: floor length black dresses, wrist length sleeves and starched white skullcaps beneath black veils.

As the only obviously Catholic clergy in Montgomery's small airport, the four of us attracted a lot of attention...and hostility. Baggage and desk clerks sneered and barked answers to our ordinary questions; police seemed to be everywhere. Plainclothesmen avoided our gaze, but watched and whispered into walkie-talkies.

Out of nowhere, a very nervous, very young black man hurried over, whispered he was from Selma to pick us up and hurried us away. In the parking lot, he literally threw our bags into his car trunk, and told us to sit in the car, fully bent over, with our heads on each others' laps. "Don't raise your heads," he said hoarsely. "If the police see me driving white folk, I don't know what will happen." I have no idea what the road from Montgomery to Selma looks like. Doubled down in the back seat, I didn't see it. None of us did. I could tell when we got to the "Colored" section of town, though. That was where the pavement stopped.

As we got out of the car at ten that night, it was clear that we were at the heart of an organized demonstration. Shoulder to shoulder and armed, a line of police formed a barrier across the dirt road that led out of the black ghetto to the center of town. Filling the street behind them were police cars, headlights blazing into the faces of a group of black and white demonstrators. The demonstrators seemed anything but that. They consisted of a small crowd of people of all ages, mostly young blacks, mixed in with a few clergymen in full garb.

"My God!" I thought. "My God, they're SINGING!"

They were belting out the first freedom songs I had ever heard. The line of police, legs braced wide, arms crossed, expressions determined and fierce, glared in silence. It looked at first like they were just standing there, posturing.

"I'll show you to the gym of Brown Chapel a couple blocks away," our driver said. "Y'all will sleep and eat there. Everybody's pretty tired and you must be. You can stand on line in the kitchen there for some food, if you want. Leave your things on the floor of the gym. That's where y'all will sleep. You can go right now. Get some rest, if you 'all want. Or you can come back here and join the line and sing. Just be careful. You don't want to get too close to the front of the line. The police sometime shoot around people's feet. It's just to scare them, that's all. But you be careful."

Many of the next six days are a blur now. We went to daily meetings organized to inform and lift our spirits about the dire state of affairs. I think Dr. King was in jail at the time. The local police chief and Governor Wallace were intransigent about prohibiting a march to Montgomery. There was no way to know what was going on beyond this ghetto of shacks where we stayed. Telephone operators controlled access to communication. The few times I tried to call Wilmington the phones went dead after the operator heard my Northern accent.

Both organizing groups, Martin Luther King's Southern Christian Leadership Council (SCLC) and the Student Non-Violent Coordinating Committee (SNCC), were there with Dr. King's people taking the lead. I learned later that SNCC had wanted youngsters involved in demonstrations, knowing that their presence would produce stunning pictures for newspapers and TV of the urgency of repealing Jim-Crow laws.

Dr. King's group was composed of older people, parents and grandparents, who were afraid for their children and upset at the possibility that they'd be accused of manipulating little ones. Somehow, on this occasion both groups came together and agreed that young people could take part, but that they needed to be kept occupied in order not to provoke a confrontation with the police. Keeping order and getting headlines were two reasons to encourage clergy. And both groups agreed on another thing and agreed with the police: the clergy needed to be kept in the black ghetto. The townspeople were seething. It was too dangerous outside.

In a few days there were hundreds more clergy and nuns from all over the country. Famous people like Andrew Young and John Lewis spoke. We attended daily seminars on the history and practice of Jim Crow laws, on the history of the Civil-Rights Movement, on the philosophy and practice of non-violence, on how to act and what to bring on the small marches from the ghetto to the town hall.

"Lock arms and sing freedom songs. Look straight ahead; don't talk to anyone or answer anyone no matter what they say. Only take identification and a toothbrush. You don't want to have too much with you in jail." I was never personally harassed, but my friend Ronny Powell was knocked out by a policeman, and our nun friends were spit at by passing white motorists.

Brown Chapel

Two things happened in Selma that clarified my biased insensitivity to the truth that "Justice...later," was more injustice. One involved a near riot. The other concerned the opposite: an elegant, even genteel dinner just down the street.

One very hot day, I stood in the back of Brown Chapel as we got our daily update on the state of the negotiations by Dr. King and others to get the U.S. Department of Justice to guarantee safety for another attempt to march the fifty-one miles to Montgomery, the state capital. For more than an hour, we sang hymn after unfamiliar hymn and the preacher preached in grand Baptist tradition. In this sweltering place, I was bone-weary. At one point, the service stopped. The preacher announced: "There seems to be somethin' goin' on out the line. Would somebody standin' in the back walk on down there to see what's goin' on?"

My hand shot up to volunteer, eager to escape the heat and tedium. A moment later, I began to meander down the two or so blocks to the "line," the one I had seen on my first night, the one I had stood in, singing freedom songs for hours, every day.

The short journey down the street began with me strolling. It ended with me running as fast as I could. As I got closer to the line of the police and youngsters, all in their late teens, it was clear the two sides were facing off...loudly. No one was singing. Both sides were yelling obscenities. I ran to the front, a place on the side of the road looking down the no-man's-land empty space between police and demonstrators. It was a space no more than four feet wide.

I can't remember thinking anything. All I knew was that this was not the way it was supposed to be. This was not the practice of non-violence that had been taught to me day after day. I felt panic. I'm a small man, not five foot three. I was the only clergyman there, and I was about to witness the start of some kind of race riot! That was all I could think. In fact, I don't remember clearly what was going on in my mind. I only recall I felt very helpless, and very responsible.

What I did next still surprises me. I don't know where it came from. It didn't start as an idea. It wasn't a plan. Suddenly I spied a small black boy sitting on the curb on the other side of the street. I remember vividly his mouth was open as he looked up at the line of his dark brothers yelling at the police. I doubt he had ever heard a bunch of black kids shouting at white authority as defiantly as they were doing now. They didn't dare in Alabama; not if they knew their place. Had he ever seen a crew of police, batons in hand, red-faced, not pummeling blacks, but bellowing?

"Y'all wait 'til these nigger-lovers go on back home..."

That's what I heard, but colored with obscenities.

For a moment I stood paralyzed, facing the boy from my side of the street looking down the two lines. At that moment, that's all I saw. Out of nowhere, I started hollering at the child at the top of my voice above the ruckus.

"What are you doing, sitting there!!!? You're supposed to stand up for your rights, not sit down!!!"

I started down the thin space between the two lines. I strode purposefully, head up, chin out. I marched as if I were in charge, as if I felt brave or commanding. I didn't feel any of that. I only felt pulled in the direction of a wide-eyed boy, bolting upright onto his feet, gaping at me. All I thought was, "Are you nuts? You're inches away from a line of police batons. You're going to get killed!"

I can't tell you why I did what I did, but it didn't matter.

"Get up; stand with your brothers!" I yelled to the shocked boy. "SING!"

Then, I faced the crowd of older boys.

"AND Y'ALL SING AND SUPPORT YOUR LITTLE BROTHA!! DON'T Y'ALL LET HIM BE BY HIS-SELF!"

I turned my back on the police inches behind me and I faced the boys. I lifted my hands like I a conductor, the way I did when I taught my congregation how to sing a new hymn. Unconsciously, I imitated the cadence and words of the southern Baptist preacher I had just heard in Brown Chapel. With the earnestness I used to cajole reluctant participants at Mass to stop sitting silently, I found myself shouting, "Y'ALL STAND TOGETHA! JOIN EACH OTHER AND SING LIKE YA MEAN IT, LIKE Y'ALL ARE IN THIS TOGETHA!"

"....Sing to God! Sing, Goddamn it; sing something!!! Please...please...before I die here!" is what I meant.

Even if my voice was commanding, my heart was pounding. This wasn't my Sunday congregation who knew Father John. Now, I was facing a very different, but very real people of God, a different Church. I didn't think that as I faced the small crowd of black kids. I only thought, "Please, God, let me remember even one of the freedom songs I've been taught here."

I raised my hands and sang as lustily as I did in church:

"Oh, Oh, freedom. Oh, Oh, freedom.
Oh, Oh, freedom over me, over me.
And before I be a slave,
I'll be buried in my grave
And go home to my Lord
And be free-ee-ee!"

Slowly, first in a mumble, then louder, the small crowd of boys took up the song. I'm not sure why they sang. Because they believed in non-violence? I doubt these or any seventeen and eighteen year olds *believed in* non-violence. Because I was a clergyman? Because they were told to by the demonstration organizers, or by Dr. King? Because they hoped all that they were taking part in would make a difference? I don't know why. I only know they sang and that that was enough. They stopped yelling, stopped arguing and for a moment stopped the white authorities from beating them down.

For about ten minutes, I sweated far more than the Alabama spring demanded. I sang every freedom song I could remember, some twice. The kids didn't grumble, or cuss, or walk away; they stayed. Even with sullen faces, God bless them, they sang. In a little while, other clergymen drifted over from the church meeting that had finally ended.

Unaware of the commotion of minutes before, they joined and sang, too, not to quell anything but because that's what they were there for, to stand up for freedom. My legs were shaking. I sat on the curb right where I'd told the boy not to sit. I knew I'd fall down if I didn't sit down. Now! I was too shaken, too shaky, to do much more than get my breath. By that point the police were stone-silent. A few glared at me; most now stood ramrod straight in a line, heads up, arms crossed. Good soldiers.

Two days later, there was a very different happening. We demonstrators were told to gather outside Brown Chapel. A loudspeaker had been rigged to a radio. We stood in stunned silence and heard a broadcast from Washington. President Johnson, the news report said, had announced he would petition Congress to pass the Voting Rights Act and that he was doing so because he felt that the demonstrations at Selma had raised the awareness and the conscience of the nation regarding the "disenfranchisement of the Negroes" (as Dr. King would later speak of it). The crowd erupted into a whooping cheer. People hugged, laughed, sang, cried and danced. A tall, young black man lifted me off my feet and spun me around. He looked into my brown eyes, laughed and said, "Lookit those eyes! You gotta have some black in there somewhere!"

In that glorious pandemonium a different illumination came. A well-spoken black man approached me, smiling. He said he and his wife wanted to thank the four of us for coming. They especially wanted to appreciate the "angels of mercy," the nuns among us, who cleaned house and cooked and taught the little kids so their mothers could stand in line all day to register to vote. Would we accept his invitation to supper the next night? He'd pick us up.

He came at the arranged time, an older black man driving. We slowly drove through a part of Selma we hadn't seen. Here the houses were old, big in a classic southern style, wide porches facing the street. However, they and the neighborhood looked rundown. The houses were badly in need of paint, the fences around them were bent or decrepit, the yards untended and weedy. His house was one of these.

When we stepped inside I felt like Dorothy and Toto going from upended Kansas into the Technicolor world of Oz. The wood floors and furniture gleamed. So did the elaborately set table. A beautiful dinner was served by their black cook. Our host, we found out, was the black dentist in town. The house evoked a man of means. While our host was thanking us was not the time to speak of the contrast I suddenly saw between the tumult all week just blocks away and this serene dinner. As much as the demonstrations I was in, as much as the impact of my experience facing down a confrontation with police, the genteel serenity of this dinner stayed with me.

That dinner and the contrast between it and my other experiences were searing. In an instant, with no one explaining, I learned one more thing in Selma. It was something the newspapers were not headlining. Jim Crow not only made blacks feel unequal; it made black people make sure, consciously, that they *appeared* unequal. That seemed the ultimate degradation. You couldn't measure the cost of that practiced sham. You couldn't count the cost to their sense of self.

Return

I went back to unreconstructed Wilmington with a story to tell and sermons to preach about racism and the change in heart and mind we all needed. All my work was immediately influenced by my Alabama trip, to be sure. However, the time in Selma didn't change my whole direction as a priest, and I don't think it should have. I also returned to my calling to lead liturgical renewal. Yet, influenced by a growing concern for preaching the gospel in action as well as word, I became involved in efforts to stop unscrupulous realtors from scaring parishioners, pushing them to quickly leave their homes once blacks moved in and in small demonstrations. I had relearned in Selma what I was taught in Chicago and Minneapolis years before. My priesthood needed to be larger. So did my life.

I returned to face many parishioners who were upset at me for going to Selma and for strongly supporting equal rights for black people. Though my pastor cautiously supported me, his health was quickly deteriorating. Within two years of my return, he passed away. Suddenly, much of the behind-the-scenes influence I once had in the Diocese shrank.

Though I was more active and preached about race openly and often, I was never at the forefront of the local movement for racial justice. I never went to jail like priest classmates began to, never was effectively excommunicated as another seminary friend was; I never even wrote about racial equality. For the next seven years, I concentrated on expanding locally and nationally my fervent interest in liturgical reform. However, I began speaking more and more about the need for general reform in the Catholic Church and outside it, especially the need for transparency in the leadership of priests and bishops. I was never censored by my bishop, or his successor. At the same time, I couldn't help but notice that when I was twice invited to speak publicly at events where the bishop was being honored, while he didn't criticize me, he carefully avoided thanking, or even speaking to me.

* * * * * *

In Wilmington, like in many dioceses, priests were transferred routinely every five years. After my time in the city of Wilmington, I was changed to a new parish in the middle of the diocese, this time as assistant to a very different kind of pastor, a bully of a man, belligerent and angry at the liturgical changes taking place.

St. John/Holy Angels parish in Newark, Delaware, half an hour south of Wilmington, seemed a world away from the parish I left. Of course, it was hard working for someone who abhorred the changes coming out of Vatican II. Everything I thought important about the prominent new theology was pointedly ridiculed at supper and practiced grudgingly, if at all. For me, there were a lot of silent meals. Not taking the bait, I usually followed his tirade with, "Please pass the mashed potatoes."

Like many other young priests, I was given rudimentary duties (e.g., writing the church bulletin each week) without the freedom to do what was at the center of my pastoral interest and growing expertise. That was among my biggest disappointments there, and it felt very calculated and personal. The message I took from this: The young kid with the bishop's ear needs to be put in his place.

At the same time, the assignment had its advantages. I began to lose some of my naiveté. I found myself justifying bending some Church laws and ignoring others, lacing private conversations with occasional obscenity and facing down the pastor when necessary.

On one occasion, I quietly told him that I had felt the responsibility as a member of the bishop's advisory commission, to comment on the progress in liturgical change parishes were making. I said I had reported that he had discouraged parishioners from drinking from the blessed cup (a new optional custom at Mass). He had said publicly that this practice gave people the option of drinking other people's spit. He exploded. I didn't raise my voice; I didn't argue.

"Father," I said, "I am not arguing with the accuracy of what I said last night. I am telling you because I assume you'll find out you were "reported" and I didn't want you to have to guess where that come from."

He exploded. I didn't answer. I turned and walked away. Then I called the head of the committee, Monsignor Taggart, to tell him what I had said. There was a long silence.

"John, I don't understand why you...."

I interrupted. "Paul, if he finds out what I reported, he'll bully me."

A sigh on the other end, "I'll call him and tell him he has to go along with this communion practice without comment."

Of course, I was pleased that I was unexpectedly supported. More, I was pleased at myself for speaking up just as surely as I had braved a line of police in Alabama.

"Oh, oh, freedom over me, over me. And before I be a slave..."

Within a year the pastor abruptly retired saying to his favorite cadre of parishioners that the Bishop had sent me to the parish to spy on him. A new, progressive pastor was appointed who, like my first one, was eager to learn and practice all he could about the meaning of the changes mandated by the Vatican Council. It felt like release from prison; it felt euphoric. In hindsight, those years witnessed a difficult, but needed loss of childhood innocence, a stripping away of layer upon layer of naiveté.

The new pastor was a gift. He allowed me great freedom to introduce changes into religious education and into the celebration of Mass: guitar music, dancing in the aisles, swaying to the drumbeat of Latin-Jazz. He let me unpack these changes quickly in a newly instituted Sunday liturgy for teenagers. There was a clumsy beauty to some efforts, justified by the attempt to bring relevance and life to our faith-narrative.

To an older pastor who griped publicly, "They didn't have guitars at Calvary!" one friend paraphrased a wise writer, "Father, they didn't have an organ either."

Once more, I was able to institute liturgical and religious education efforts. I was given permission to spend money to revamp our children's religious education program, to build an office dedicated to the program and to recruit a dedicated staff. In that whirlwind era, as in the parish before, I was either reviled or revered. One of the reasons for my unpopularity did not center on liturgical changes; few people complained about them. Now it was Vietnam taking center stage, first on the periphery of the country's consciousness, then in our midst.

Since Selma, I had begun to see the need to tie good liturgy and good preaching to an effort to make sense out of what was erupting all around us. Drawn to its contradictions cautiously (again!), Vietnam began to erupt in my mind as it did in the world. At first my sermons must have seemed disjointed. If so, they reflected the controversy going on in my mind and heart. I was trying to reconcile what we were doing as a moral nation with this immorality.

First, my words likely only showed disappointment, then, more and more, they spoke to the horror many saw at the errors of the Vietnam War. I began counseling students at the nearby University of Delaware on how to avoid the draft. Many people were upset at me. I was quietly told by a friendly parishioner, an attorney who worked for the government, that my phone had been bugged by the FBI.

But, not everyone was angry. A lot of talented people told me they felt that Sunday morning offered time for reflection and food-for- thought not offered elsewhere. They told me they felt less alienated from current Church teaching, or lack of guidance. Suddenly, many people felt welcomed in the parish and came out to volunteer. Not a few were smart business people who taught me a lot about enterprise and management to help set up our new endeavors. These were sharp men and sharp women.

Intimacy

Sharp women? Sharp *looking* women, I began to notice. In sleepy Newark, Delaware, I woke up to more than I bargained for. I had already begun changing my views on sin based on the new theological understanding epitomized by the Vatican Council's changing the name "confession" to "sacrament of reconciliation." The meaning of sin began to change for me from stain on the soul to state of willful separation from others and from one's authentic self. With that change in thinking came personal changes, came bad decisions and behavior, and good changes, too.

I said "sharp looking." Suddenly I was looking. During that time I lived out some of the adolescence I had bypassed in my earnest pursuit of a religious vocation. Among the new full time staff I hired was a woman (a fairly new idea!) to formulate a religious education program for children and adolescents. She was eminently qualified. She was aware of currents in Christian education that followed current advances in scriptural knowledge, new music and new music modes. She understood child development and how that could enrich how we might teach about God, Jesus and a life lived in faith. She was enthusiastic, learned and had worked in parishes before. She was eager for the job.

And, I noticed, she was very attractive. Don't mistake

where this tale is going. We were never *involved*. We didn't do anything *wrong*, but while we worked together, I certainly found myself awakened, and more than spiritually. I was having the good times that hard family finances, my father's lingering illness and death and my own seriousness had not fully allowed in my high school years. It was different—planning, organizing, and having a common higher purpose... alongside a woman. It wasn't long before I realized that because she was a woman the work seemed more focused and more personally a testament to my faith.

We can have many feelings at once. After meeting this vivacious woman I had more joy, more excitement in my life. Something else happened that puzzled and disturbed me deeply. Suddenly, I felt very, very lonely. Raised in a loving family, I had felt loved and I loved in return. As an adult, as a priest, I never felt intimacy. I had sexual feelings since adolescence, and they grew stronger with the years. But those emotions are different from the straightforward gestures men and women in love presume.

Putting a hand on a woman's face, or sitting with knees touching were things I'd never experienced, or thought about once I was set upon the course of priesthood. Now that I am married, I still marvel at the surprising power that simple, intimate gestures have to bring quiet, let alone to become a signal about confidence that your touch will be understood and wanted, not just allowed. In accepting these gestures, we are accepted.

When we Catholics take for granted that our priests must be celibate we aren't paying attention to how small intimacies can enrich a man's life and imbue even his ministry with humanity. You can't know what part of yourself you lose when you are required to give up closeness. The Catholic Church doesn't know what it has mislaid in mandating that the dedicated priests it has (let alone the ones it might have) take on celibacy. By definition, and in law, if we are *required* to accept something, then we are not "choosing" it. I still wonder that priests can think they have "chosen" celibacy when they have no choice.

Soon, I met another woman, also sharp, also beautiful. We began an intimate relationship. It isn't important to describe the details; I won't romanticize it. I won't justify it, even if I was developmentally an adolescent. I was, up to then, a faithful, celibate priest. That was sin for both of us, or I think of it that way. I think unfaithfulness is sin and both of us were that. A very long time later, I shamefully told an understanding confessor the details of that interlude, along with the old-fashion list of sins I'd learned as a child to recite. That was my first sacramental confession in many years. After registering my list, I waited for his comment. A long minute of silence followed.

"Did you do anything else?" he said.

"Not that I can think of," I whispered.

He prodded. "I mean, did you ever do anything good in your life?"

That summed it up for me. More than the cleansing grace of a sacrament, his words were an example of a new teaching about sin, the one I now believed. Sure, I am a sinner. But that is not all I am.

So, I lusted more than in my heart. I can't say it bothered me much until years later. At the time, I was a puppy-dog, frolicking for the first time, taking chances, excited. I was also conflicted. Don't ask me how I justified my behavior as I went about my writing, working and preaching. I don't believe I excused myself; I simply refused to think about the contradiction between what I was doing and what I believed. I put those out of my mind the way I had put contradictions I saw in certain Church teachings, or in not preaching against Jim Crow.

This went on for some months. I never justified it as love, as if this child-like astonishment and giddiness encompassed the meaning of love. The upside of this burst of intimacy was that it allowed me to feel free in ways I never had. I had never reached for a woman's hand spontaneously, or put my arm against hers warmly, or whispered in her ear... or let myself look and look and look at her beauty. I did those things hesitantly at first, then fully. I did it more and more until my conscience and my life caught up with me. The idea of acceptance of sin in others and in myself became meaningful as I watched, often from afar, myself and what I was doing and why.

Then, as quickly as I started, I stopped. The freedom I was beginning to experience was catching up. I was finding what others much younger than me already knew. Freedom isn't free. Freedom isn't a free-for-all. Freedom involves accepting full responsibility for one's actions.

Pastoring

In June, 1972, ten years after I was ordained, I was appointed pastor for the first time. St. Mary Magdalen was a wealthy church and school. It had a modern church building, three priests and a convent of nuns on a main thoroughfare leading out of Wilmington. In this selectively modern parish, the priests lived in a handsome home that was not on the parish grounds. The rectory was in a wealthy suburb about a mile from the church. The church community largely consisted of upper middle-income, highly- educated people. I was told that seventy-five percent of the working people in the parish were employed at the nearby DuPont headquarters in management or in research. Ninety percent of those had doctorates.

The pastor before me was an athlete, a handsome man from a socially established Wilmington family. He was a horseman and free-spirited. He had a reputation as an easy-going, hands-off man who was liberal in his views and who allowed the same type of people to run the parish. I don't know the circumstances of his leaving the priesthood, but it had shaken the place. I was told he left in the middle of the night, without a word to anyone. It wasn't surprising that a priest would do that. Many priests were leaving in the same secretive way. I don't know if he was running away from some scandal; I was never told any details. Why was it without a "good-by?" Was it guilt at leaving a vocation? Maybe he left to live a freer life. No one said that either; no one knew. Not one person at St. Mary Magdalen ever spoke to me of the pastor who disappeared in the middle of the night.

As I think about the imagery now, it seems so strange. Then again, silence or concealment is part of the Church's tradition. In the coming decades, the worldwide scandal resulting from hidden priest pedophiles to hidden Vatican banking practices would alienate a generation of Catholics. Loyal parishioners at St. Mary Magdalen were left confused and upset with not a word of explanation from their diocesan pastor, the Bishop.

Why is the Church population diminishing? Some may think it's because we don't use Latin at mass or because we are too liberal. Maybe it's because we still think that a paternal pat on the head or kiss of the ring will pacify people. Maybe it's because, even in this new century, the Church doesn't have the common sense to communicate respectfully.

St. Mary Magdalen was a parish of very capable people. Their wide-open thinking was not universal in the parish, but it was the prominent approach of the parish leaders and of the priests who remained. I already had a reputation as a past president of the Priests' Advisory Committee and a liturgical leader in the Diocese. I expected I would be welcomed warmly by the liberal thinking majority. It wasn't that simple.

After appointing me, the Bishop called me in to talk. He said that, as a matter of fact, the parish was highly divided. The liberal group was eager to open the parish to liturgical changes. The chairman of the parish council, a leading executive at DuPont, was in agreement. The disparity between liberal and conservative groups was wide. One of the wealthiest and most influential people in the Diocese had left the parish, disgusted at the rancor between liberals and conservatives. The Bishop said he'd hoped I could restore some harmony to a torn community. It was a gracious conversation. More than that, I sensed that the Bishop wanted to be pastoral himself as he voiced his concerns. He did not warn me about any liberal ideas he knew I had. I appreciated that. He did not tell what not to do or say. He only alerted me about what I was facing. He hoped I could restore peaceful co-working.

I appreciated his words and his concern for unity. What the bishop didn't know was that I had already begun to have doubts about my commitment to stay the course of my priestly calling. In accepting the assignment, I felt guilty that I couldn't share my self-doubts. However, I silently resolved I would not be the next one to abandon these people. Although I had done many different jobs as a priest, I was determined to throw myself into pastoral work only, for the first time. I thought that after doing so for my five year appointment, I would know for certain where my heart and my vocation were. It should have occurred to me that commitment isn't free. It costs. Sometimes the cost is more than we can afford.

I approached the assignment with apprehension, of course, but with fervor, too. My first decision was a personal one. I chose to give up my post as Administrative Secretary to the Diocesan Liturgical Commission, and to leave the work of writing and promoting the liturgical renewal nationally and locally in the diocese. I would do one thing; I would pastor. That is where all my energy would go. I gave up the romantic relationship I had continued. In truth, *we* gave it up. And that made it easier...bearable. For very different reasons, we both saw we were adolescents and that, exciting as it often was, this rambunctious time needed to be over. Self-indulgence was masking as self-fulfillment. She changed parishes. We never spoke again. I've simplified the ending, of course...but it did end simply. Not easily, but simply.

As I had thrown myself headlong into that relationship; I flung myself into my new work with fervor. I consciously told myself that I would be the most dedicated man I could be. Now that I recall those ancillary decisions, those attempts to become single-minded, I can see how some were foolish and unhealthy. Though I intended to take care of the new parish, I was not taking care of myself emotionally. I didn't know that, of course. My work was non-stop; my sermons were more thought-provoking, offered more questions and sometimes were more strident. One parishioner told me that they were the Monday morning's subject at the DuPont water coolers. My sermons and work may have been better woven together but, in time, the lining underneath was getting threadbare. Some parishioners noticed it as the year grew longer.

"Your sermons are so negative!" one complained. They were right. The preaching I treasured so much, that I knew I exercised well, that, too, was fraying.

My growing ability to act and speak with less regard for whether I'd make enemies led me to a confrontation that expressed my growing righteousness. It added to other decisions that left me unbearably lonely.

The young priests who were my assistants had worked hard to establish liturgical reforms in the parish. Based on my reputation, they assumed I would join them. Some months before my arrival, to alleviate the ire of some powerful conservative parishioners, the Bishop had given this group permission to celebrate one Mass in Latin each Sunday. The reaction of the parish priests and their lay supporters was strong and angry. Their response? They refused to celebrate that Mass. That didn't stop the stalwart group who had petitioned for this. With the Bishop's approval, they went around the former pastor and got an older priest from the local Salesianum High School to come and celebrate this Latin Mass each Sunday in our parish hall.

I agreed with my associates' anger. I was upset, too, at what seemed a backwards step from liturgical reform and appeasement to an influential group. I decided it would be futile to petition the Bishop. Instead, I told my assistants that I did not expect them to celebrate the Latin Mass, but that I would.

"These people don't want Latin. They don't want change! I'll celebrate in Latin, but I'll preach in English!"

Soon, without forewarning, I showed up at the parish hall to celebrate the liturgy. Yes, I celebrated in Lingua Latina. However, I insisted the people answer responses aloud, even in Latin (the Vatican Council now required "participation" by the people). And, as promised, I preached in English. In fact, I gave a passionate sermon about civil- rights and about the Vietnam War.

After Mass, the leader of the group came to me sputtering in anger. He told me the people wanted the priest from the high school to celebrate. I righteously told him, as only one steeped in authoritarianism can, "I won't disobey the Bishop. But, I am the pastor here! I will celebrate, not somebody for hire!"

By the next week, the group had moved to a monastery for their Mass. Godspeed! I wish my arrogance didn't give me so much satisfaction that I had outwitted a conservative cluster. I wanted to think that this act was necessary to establish a strong leadership role. I didn't want to face how it fed my simmering anger about other departures from Vatican II, only recently adjourned, that the Vatican bureaucracy was already allowing. Yet, this brash approach to pastoring hardened me and hastened my departure, too.

I respected the majority of men with whom I ministered. Most were committed people. I trust that for most clergy who had left, the decision and journey were hard. I had come to St. Mary Magdalen determined not to abandon a community who had been deserted shortly before. They had not been left by a pastor, only, but by priests uninterested in forming a community out of disparate believers. We didn't welcome "sinners," like Jesus. In effect, we defined "sinner" as anyone who didn't agree with Church reform. We, I, could have done better. Almost forty years away from it, I look back and am at peace with much, but not all, of service I gave to those people. I am not at peace with how long I allowed my growing loneliness to fester. That did not serve anyone well.

Leaving

As I prayed daily and became more uncertain in my commitment to Church service I happened on a book. One quiet night, as I was reading "The Church," by Hans Kung, a passage arrested me. Dr. Kung was a German theologian whose ideas and writings influenced the teachings that came out of Vatican II and still rocked the Church. The book spoke of his struggles to maintain his faith and remain within this Christian community. What leapt out of the page was one statement which I will paraphrase: *Believing* and *believing in* are different. It is proper to *believe in* God and only proper because speaking of belief in that way includes a type of trust that is absolute. However, *believing* involves choice. I can choose to believe or not to believe something or someone. I believe in God in an absolute way; I believe the Church if I choose to do so.

So, one might believe some things but not others. And one might come to recognize with great clarity, but gradually, that the Pope is not Jesus and the Church is not the Vatican. One may choose to believe that Jesus is God's son, that the Eucharist is Jesus' special presence and also choose not to believe that birth control is a sin. Many Catholics had already made those choices; I became another. Yet, the special clarity I had at that moment was about more than one disputed teaching. I began to feel less connected to "Church," even as I still served it. Once again, the possibility of freedom reared up and knocked me over. From that day, my course was set, though I did not recognize it that quiet night.

I knew it some months later. Praying in the woods near our rectory very early one morning before I celebrated Mass, the words of St. Paul that inspired me and felt like a calling, years before came back to me. "What does it profit a man if he gains the world, but loses his soul?" Suddenly, I was clear. The same word translated as "soul" from Latin, could better be translated as "self." I might be well regarded, "successful" in many ways; I might still be a true servant of the people. I might preach well, or counsel well, or lead well, but what difference did it make, if I was losing my "self," my soul?

I felt deeply that being a cleric was costing me a price I could no longer afford. I didn't blame the Vatican for my decision; I had no reason to blame the bishop. I wasn't angry at that moment. I still do not blame someone else for my clean choice in that dim dawn. No one took away my priesthood. I was anointed priest and no one could take that. Rather, I believed I was letting go of the clerical life the church imposed. In the chilly dawn, I wasn't warmed by my decision or relieved I had made it. I was only certain that the emptiness I felt was wrenching. It was seeping into everything I did and did not do. In that instance, it seemed I had no authentic choice but to leave.

As a psychologist today, I ask myself if what I was feeling was depression. While I may have also been depressed at the time, my decision and my enlightenment did not come from a mental health disorder. It came from the fragments of my torn soul; a part of me that was calling to be whole. At that moment of prayer, I had no idea what I wanted or wanted to do. I only knew what I did not want. I did not want the clerical life. I did not then and have never regretted what I recognize was a vocation. But I couldn't live the tight, formal, emotionally distant clerical life I was in. I still felt a duty to serve. I still felt I ought not abandon my parishioners.

In that moment of contemplation, something else seemed more truthful: it didn't matter what I felt I do. I *could not* do this. I *would not* do this any longer. Did that insight make me feel free? Not at that moment. I left the woods to celebrate Mass with a very heavy heart, knowing I would be the next pastor to walk out on these people. Like the profoundly weary men and women I have counseled since who choose divorce because staying in a debilitating marriage is soul shattering, I was leaving for the same reason. I was divorcing "Mother

Church." I think I was choked up with every word of the Mass I later offered. I was shaken, but I was sure.

For about nine months, I told two people and no one else. One of the people I told was my old grandfather, Papa, whom I knew was dying. This anticlerical Italian had ruefully shaken his head twenty years before when I told him I had chosen to enter the seminary. I needed to see him again before he died. I drove to Brooklyn to the apartment where he and Nana spent his last days. I said I was coming to have supper with them and the two aunts who had raised me after my mother's death. When I got there, Papa looked so frail, so unlike the vigorous man I had known. As Nana welcomed me, the scene of his sitting listlessly on their worn coach was so sad. There was some small talk, and a last, vital chance to speak authentically to him.

"Papa, let's go out onto the balcony. I want to talk to you alone," I finally said.

He stared at me quietly and shuffled out. Nana stayed inside cooking pasta, the way a meal started every day of my life with them. Once outside, I lost my nerve and my voice. Neither of us said a word for a few minutes. We both just looked at the grimy cityscape below.

"I don't know how to say this, Papa..." I stammered.

Papa shuffled, looked up at me with his penetrating eyes, a fixed look I knew well. "You need money?" he asked.

At first I was shocked. But wasn't that what most of the men in my family came to Papa for? I had to find my voice.

"No, no!!!" What was he talking about! I had to go on. "I want you to know that I am leaving the priesthood."

There, I'd said it. I stopped. In fact, I had said it all. There was no more. We were both silent for minutes that seemed eternal. Here was this frail patriarch who used to shout and bang on the table. He was silent. What was his reaction to my statement? Did he even understand me? I waited for I didn't know what. Finally, Papa scrutinized me again with his typical "look." He nodded his head up and down slowly and said seven words.

"That is no life for a man."

He turned and shuffled inside. No more than that. He understood what I couldn't find words to explain. He seemed to know what I certainly didn't. His firstborn grandson was leaving to find something, his manhood. In my years of indecision and thinking I had never thought of it that way. He did. In seven words.

* * * * *

The month I decided I would leave was February, 1974, about eleven months after the day I had decided to do so. My guilt and sense of responsibility told me I had to tie things up well. Lent was about to start; a needed fund-raising effort had been prepared; I had put in place the things I could to make the transition as seamless as possible. I told the Bishop only days before my departure for fear the word would get out. I couldn't face that. I don't remember one word he or I said in those very few minutes. I do know he didn't put his ring out; he put his hand out. He shook mine. I want to think he looked a little sad.

I decided to do what I hadn't heard of anyone doing. On my last day, a Sunday, I stood up at the end of each Mass and spoke a few words of farewell. I asked for the people's blessing. I also said that if anyone wanted to speak to me I would be in the sacristy after Mass. I truly expected a few dozen people might come by to share a goodbye. Instead, after each Mass, there was a line of people more than the length of the church, spilling out into the street, holding up every Mass afterwards. People bade me farewell, thanked me profusely, and wept. Me? I cried from one end of the morning to the other end. People said many, many fulsome things. However, I remember best one remark especially that an older, tough-guy usher whispered in my ear with a grin, "Father, you got some kind of balls."

Boston

That afternoon, my car and car roof packed, I headed up to Boston where I had decided to start my new life. I felt I needed to begin where no one knew me, where I had to take care of myself and not be taken care of. How did I feel? Exhausted and very scared. I knew no one, had no job, but had saved money my step-mother had left me when she died the year before. Driving north through New Jersey I had one last stop to make.

I had invited myself to have dinner with my brother and his family. Joe actually was my younger brother from my father's second marriage to the only woman I knew as my mother. We were very different and for that reason alone we weren't really close. Joe is much like my father, a hard-scrabble working man, either ebullient like our dad, or a man of few words, not churched like his older brother. Before dinner, alone with him, I broke the news. First his eyes grew wide, then softened. I don't recall much that he said. I do remember that this guy's guy, this truck driver put a hand on my shoulder firmly and looked into my eyes, "What are you going to do?"

"I don't know yet, Joe. I only know what I won't do any more."

"You ready for this? It's a hell of a different life. Bro, you made a hell of a choice!"

A few hours later I continued north. Among the many things I didn't know that I would face in Boston was absurdity. When one's life is formally circumscribed as a priest's is, there is not much room for chance. I mean ridiculous chance. In Boston, as I learned to find the "life for (of) a man," I met instances that were truth-telling because they were absurd. Like a cop in a silent movie who chases around a corner to collide with a baker and find a pie in his face, life offered me lessons that could only be appreciated if I saw the humor in their absurdity.

Driving to Boston, I realized that first I needed to find a job and be hired where few questions would be asked. The first job I took was as a line-cook in an upscale Italian restaurant, Stella. I always liked to cook, so I thought,

"What the hell? All they can do is fire me when they discover I don't know what I'm doing." Walking the Boston waterfront, I saw a sign on the kitchen door of a restaurant. The sign said it needed a line cook. I walked in; I made up a story. Okay, I lied. I told the owner I had cooked for years in New York where I came from. He seemed pleased. I had read the subtext of the sign right: he needed someone right away.

"When can you start?"

I looked at the hand written sign on the kitchen door. I thought it looked desperate. "Tomorrow."

"Good. I'll need a reference," he said.

"Of course!"

"Give me the number of the place you last worked. I'll call right away," he said.

The place I last worked? You've got to be kidding me. "I don't remember the number," I said. Uh, I'll go home to get it. I'll call you right back."

I rushed to my newly rented studio apartment and picked up the phone stacked on one of the boxes that crowded the room. I called the event space in Brooklyn my very Italian cousin, Jimmy Conigliaro owned. Long before "The Sopranos," Cousin Jimmy's portly looks and loud, thick Brooklyn accent could have landed him a part in that TV show. I hadn't spoken to him in a long while, but a few years before I had given comfort to him, his wife, Connie, and to his son, as little Joey lay dying. Cousin Jimmy didn't forget such things, I knew... and anyway... I was blood, as they say in Brooklyn. I dialed the phone, praying he'd answer.

"Jimmy, this is Cousin John," I began. A long pause on his end, then a shout,

"FATHA JOHN!!! HOW YA' DOIN'?!"

"Uh, Jimmie, I'm not Father John anymore. I left the priesthood. It's a long story I'll tell you some other time. But, Jimmy...I need a favor... I need you to lie for me."

"ANYTIME, FATHA!" he bellowed into the phone.

I told him the story I'd made up to get a cook's job and that I was asking him to swear I'd worked at his banquet space for years.

"SURE, SURE, FATHA, WHATEVER YA' WANT!!!"

It could have been dialogue right out of a Scorsese movie. I don't know what Cousin Jimmy said to the owner of Stella. I can only imagine his lusty enthusiasm, or maybe how his Mafiosa style and connections taught him how to be persuasive in more ways than I knew. No matter. I got the job. Better than getting the job, I survived the job. The young Italian and Greek immigrants who worked alongside me were the reason I didn't get fired. These street-savvy cooks must have quickly seen I didn't know what I was doing. Without a word, they tilted a sauce pan for me at just the right angle for pouring, or motioned for me to do this or that in a certain way. One day when I was struggling to stuff chicken breasts fast enough, the young cook next to me watched for a moment and said, "You takin' too long! Ya' grab the stuff (filling) and shove it in between here (the skin and the meat)."

Very carefully, I tried to follow what I'd just seen him do.

He watched me, then said, exasperated, "What da' hell youse doin?" Ya' gotta fuck it. Fuck it!!!" and he deftly jammed a handful of stuffing into the crevice between skin and meat.

My face turned beet red. Fuck it. Of course. Some day I'd tell friends I left the priesthood to fuck chickens! Hey, I was learning about life, right?

A few weeks later, Roberto taught me another lesson, a tutorial about living without rank. Prepping food together, he and I had become buddies of a sort. Although he was many years younger, we laughed and told stories while we worked. For some reason, I had decided that I should tell Roberto that I had been a priest. I suppose I thought that this was an honest thing you shared with a friend.

As I started to tell him I found myself embarrassed, flushing more deeply than when he taught me how to stuff chicken breasts. Alone, preparing food for dinner one afternoon before the evening rush, I got up the courage to say something. I worried this Italian immigrant kid might feel very uncomfortable around me from that point, but I kept on with my resolve.

"Roberto, I want to tell you something...." I blurted it out: "I used to be a priest."

"No kidding?" He answered in a matter-of fact way, still stirring the sauce. "I used to paint houses."

I have mused about and laughed at that incident many times. How did I rank now that I left the priesthood? Just like the next guy. Not important, not special, just myself. To the degree I had been special, I was different. For the same reason, I was separate. And, again for that same reason, I was alone. Loneliness was built into anointment. From now on, I could lean on particular people if I chose, but I couldn't lean on being different. I had not only left priesthood, I had left privilege. I was learning the blessing of being ordinary. And sometimes, some blessed times, the lesson was funny.

At other times, the absurdity came in the form of prophets dressed as winos. At first, living in the city in Lent, I went to Sunday Mass. In a short time, I found myself leaving in the middle of it, aggravated at every pedantic sermon I heard. So I stopped going at all. What was the point of going to Mass and having my faith tested? But, again, as Holy Week approached, this liturgist felt the need to take part. This time I vowed I wouldn't leave at the sermon; I was there to celebrate the whole sacrament.

That Sunday I went to a church off Boston Commons. Sure enough, the celebrant preached a terrible sermon. In fact, he read a terrible sermon. I gritted my teeth and repeated the promise to stay I had made to myself. To help me remain glued to my seat I decided to consciously separate myself by analyzing what troubled me about the disquisition. It didn't take long to figure it out. The sermon offered no inkling of what this man personally believed. At the exact moment I thought that, I heard the hoarse grumbling of a man a few pews in front of me. He appeared to be a wino from the street, ragged and dirty, slouched with one hand casually over the back of the pew. I didn't recall seeing him before, but there was no missing him now. Suddenly, angry mumbling turned to shouting in a slurred, but understandable voice, "FATHA, WHY DON'T YA' SHPEAK FROM YER HEART!"

The few people in church gasped. There was absolute silence for a moment. The priest cleared his throat and once more began to read dully from his notes. Again, this time insistent and louder, "FATHER, WHY DON'T YA' SHPEAK FROM YER HEART!!!

In a moment, the ushers ran up the aisle and escorted the wino out. I was struck dumb at this man's echoing exactly what I had just said to myself.

"That's Jesus!" I said to myself. "That's Jesus talking!"

I rushed outside and saw the ushers giving the man a dollar to send him off. I got between them and put out my hand,

"I'd like to shake your hand..." I started. The wino muttered something incomprehensible and abruptly walked off.

I stood outside catching my breath, heart and mind racing. Just then a young guy came over to me. He'd walked out, too, I'd guessed.

"Ain't these winos something," he said and introduced himself. We talked awhile but never spoke about the incident. Out of that chance conversation I met a man who that day offered me a better place to stay (a room in a house he and other guys had rented) and who would become my first friend in Boston.

I've thought of that story many times. My faith started to mean more again from that moment of Jesus speaking to me through this wino. Lots of ridiculous things began to make sense: Jesus can be a wino. Certainly not privileged, not even "special." Just God's Son, that's all. Jesus might even paint houses.

After proving something to myself about self-competence, after "succeeding" at the restaurant (I got a ten cent an hour raise within two months!), it was time to move on. I left and in succession worked in management training at McDonald's, drove a cab for awhile, and then found what I really wanted to do. I started back to school in Boston to prepare for eventual entry into American University's Counseling Psychology Master's program in Washington, D.C., two years later.

While at graduate school I developed a special interest in family therapy and working with "emotionally-impaired" children. Later, I entered the University of Michigan for a doctorate in a combined program in psychology and education. Those years gave me many turbulent times of loneliness again and of confusion, but also of strange, exhilarating and not so exhilarating experiences dating seriously for the first time.

Ann Arbor, Michigan

Preparing to go to school in Michigan I fell in love. Clare and I had met years before when I was a pastor in Wilmington. After divorcing her husband, with her two year old daughter she went to D.C. where I was studying at American University. On the suggestion of a mutual friend who knew I was studying there, she called me to have a cup of coffee. Why not? Even though I was dating, I knew few people. So we met again, two people freer than before, maybe struggling more than before to make a new life. Coffee led to dating... a lot. And, for me, it began a foggy kind of love. I was still finding my way, still with much too much emphasis on self development.

One night we argued fiercely. Sure I loved her in an uncertain way, but once again I had a set plan. I wanted a degree in psychology. Was she part of that plan? I hadn't exactly fit her into it, not yet, at least. I couldn't understand how that didn't make perfect sense to her. We argued. Me, like Papa, convincing myself the louder I became. However, that didn't convince her though. Finally, I left her apartment flabbergasted that this woman couldn't see how sensible this was. She was so thickheaded. Two days later I called her. Maybe with space, she could see more clearly now. I asked if I could come over to talk.

"Let's talk," is what I said. "Let's see if I can drum some sense into your head," is what I thought.

So we talked. In the middle of another futile argument, I stopped, stymied with this frustrating female. I fumed. I said to myself, I just don't understand women!

"This is going nowhere," I said in irritation. "Let's stop the talk. Make me a cup of tea, will you?"

Arrogant? How about officious? The condescending Father? All that, I'm sure. Surprised, flustered, Clare jumped up and ran into the kitchen. I heard her banging around. A moment later she flew out the kitchen door and threw the cup at me! "MAKE YOUR OWN DAMN CUP OF TEA!!!" she yelled.

"There's something to this woman," I thought. "She's smart enough to not let me have my way..."

That's what it took to knock a little sense into my head, a cup aimed right there.

Only a year or so out of a painful divorce, Clare followed me to the University of Michigan, bringing her toddler daughter, Dona, with her. Within several months I asked her to let me be husband and father to her child. She supported me through graduate school; afterwards took a chance with me in establishing a private practice in family therapy and then in neuropsychological assessment. Along the way I became a father again, this time to an infant son, Alan, adopted from Chile.

We nursed him through a serious learning disability and, maybe less successfully, through finding his identity as an adopted person. Alan, of Mapuche Indian origin, has helped me become a bit quieter, like he is at his core and a bit less serious about myself. The funniest thing he ever said about me, the thing that struck home about my seriousness, he whispered to a friend when he was sixteen. As we argued after he baited me, I overheard him confess to the other kid, "I love to piss him off." Every time I recognize that I am getting intense, I smile and think of his puncturing comment.

I left Ann Arbor in 2005, but not without another powerful lesson, one that has been central to my spiritual journey. At the conclusion of our thirty years in Ann Arbor, when Dona was about to be married to a non-Christian, Japanese-American man, I was inexplicably (to me) beside myself with grief. I liked Mike, a successful businessman, a straightforward guy's guy like my brother, but city-savvy, too. Following his wishes, Dona had decided not to be married in the Catholic Church. Mike was not a Catholic, not a Christian even, though he had attended a Jesuit high school. He would not marry in the Church and she couldn't explain that to me, thinking I would be angry at the man she loved. Underneath my anger, I was really grieving a second separation from Catholic tradition.

I may have "divorced" the Church, but I was attached to her still. Clare sympathized with my pain, but couldn't understand the depth of it. Finally, after too many irritating, exhausting half-conversations with my wife and daughter, I decided to talk to our parish priest, Jim McDonough at St. Francis of Assisi Church. I felt I needed to hear from a trusted "man of God" what I already knew, that I needed to let this go. I explained my upset to Jim and, as I thought he would, Jim reminded me we both believed that I shouldn't pressure Dona about this. However, he said it better and more profoundly than I had ever done in my best arguments with myself.

"John, I know you. I know you believe what I do. And you're wrong here, just wrong. The most important gift God has given us is the gift of freedom, the ability to choose. You want to take that away from Dona. You want her to do something because *you want it*, not her. You want to take away a God-given gift, her freedom. That's a sin, don't you think?"

My face flushed. I was stopped. I also was embarrassed at myself. All I wanted to do from that point was to get out of there as fast as I could.

"You're right, you're right, Jim. I won't say any more to her," I said, trying to quickly get out the door. Jim looked at me and shook his head from side to side.

"That's not enough. You tried to take away God's gift. You need to apologize."

There it was again, freedom. It was okay for me to have searched and found it in a richer life. Why wasn't it okay for my child? I went to my car and cried for a long time. I went home to Clare and wept. A week later I went to Chicago to ask Dona's forgiveness. We both cried. And that apology changed our relationship forever. Today, she and Mike give Clare and me great respect and love. Best of all, she has given me her children. She has taught them generous affection and love for me and for their Nana. For the grandkids, for Mike (who struggled with what to call me after they married), for the family, like the grandfather I loved so much, I am simply 'Papa."

Chicago

Soon after her wedding, we moved to Chicago. Clare had received a wonderful job offer. I thought I might semi-retire. Instead, I was quickly offered an opportunity to cap my psychological career. I was asked to start a psychological assessment program at The Family Institute at Northwestern University, the foremost training program in family therapy in the United States. That has been an extraordinary opportunity to finish my professional life with a flourish, with intellectual challenges that are very rich. And being close to our grandchildren has easily made city-living a charm.

Being in Chicago offered me one more grace. Soon after coming, I was invited to join a group of men who had gotten together once a week for over forty years. Most of them are psychologists, but this is adamantly not a therapy group and not a "support group" in the usual sense. We tease each other, complain about aging and its effects, curse a bit and tell ribald stories. We meet at one another's homes (wives not invited, though welcome to make a "cameo appearance."). Over pizza and beer we meet to maintain friendships, to talk about important things like how to fix a leaky roof, our grown kids, or about national and Chicago politics. The men affectionately call these weekly meetings, "Beer Night."

Initially, the most interesting thing was that these men, every one of them, are determined agnostics. I haven't polled them, but they all seem to be "lapsed" something. They know I had been a priest. At first, they seemed bemused at that. Ultimately, they have usually been respectfully guarded in cussing out "religion." Their view of organized religion and Catholicism, especially, is bleak. Often their objections to faith seem sophomoric to me. Yet, they are all highly educated men, so their views can be astute, too. They make me think. Men in their 70s and 80s, they have clearly given religion serious thought.

Most times, we all laugh at the latest absurdity in the news about convoluted, conflicted, confusing Vatican doings, or grimace at the handling of pedophile clergymen. Our life experiences are miles apart. I wonder at their welcome, but it always feels authentic. I am blessed having these unbelievers in my life. They have helped me broaden my idea of grace and of hearty graciousness. They have unknowingly continued my education about Christian life. I am stirred and sometimes jealous of the free lives they have lived, however imperfectly. Like us all.

Often now as I drive home from Beer Night I think about why I have stayed in this Church. I often wonder if my friends at Beer Night ask each other how I stay attached to her. Maybe they don't care, respecting that it is my free choice; that would be more like them.

It feels like I have come full-circle in my journey toward freedom. Despite the first bishop's arrogant refusal, my determined will (free-will of another dimension) showed me a way. Despite the Vatican's initial refusal to release Clare and me from our vows, we freely chose to marry anyway in a Methodist church, yet continued to take the sacraments in several welcoming

Catholic parishes. We followed our consciences, not the pencil-pushers in the Vatican. And I stay a committed Catholic, still believing the bishop is not Jesus and his word is not necessarily God's. No doubt, it is easier to stay because I am blessed being in a congregation led by Paulist priests whose central mission is to be inclusive. This place is enough "Church," for me a locale tied to a larger one that started and continues the narrative about Jesus that still inspires me.

The Bishops' statements, actions, or lack of action often test my faith as they do others. Yet, this clumsy Catholic Church holds me and I willingly hold her in a clumsy, but faithful, way. As I say about Clare, a wife who commands my faithfulness and love beyond explanation: She drives me crazy and keeps me sane, both.

When Power

And

Religion Mix

Clark Gabriel Field

The year was 1966, on a lazy fall day with Mother Nature putting on her annual fashion show, and I was chauffeur for Bishop Henry Soenneker, Ordinary for the Roman Catholic Diocese of Owensboro (Kentucky). The bishop was conferring the sacrament of Confirmation on children in towns west of Owensboro, and he asked me to drive him. Actually, since the bishop and I were not on the same page—theologically or pastorally—I was both surprised and pleased with the invitation.

On the return trip, I said, "Bishop, I'm concerned with the actions of the court against some black residents." I had gone to court supporting a friend. Several of us were protesting the injustices inflicted on the garbage workers.

"What are your concerns, Father?"

"The police lie on the witness stand."

"Father, you are young. Take it from me. Neither a policeman nor a judge would ever lie." My first reaction was one of disbelief, but, then, I realized he was serious and believed what he was saying.

I remained in the priesthood another sixteen years, and enjoyed my twenty years of ministry. Yet after about ten years, I knew it was time for me to move on, to step out from under the protective umbrella of "holy mother church." Most of my seminary days were spent under the first bishop of the Owensboro Diocese, Francis Cotton. He was quite formal and strict, but we understood him— well maybe "understood" is the wrong word. Even though we would not agree with him, we knew where he stood.

His successor was a humble man, and at first, a real relief from Bishop Cotton. I enjoyed his informality. He would not let us go down on the left knee—genuflecting in church consisted on going down on the right knee— before him to kiss his ring, for instance. Bishop Soenneker was a large man, and he would hold our hands and tug us up as we attempted to go down. It seems so strange to me now both that we used to "genuflect on the wrong knee" and kiss a bishop's ring.

The new bishop was a farmer and had an easy, folksy approach to us priests. However, he had a serious handicap in that he never served as pastor of a parish before becoming pastor of a diocese.

* * * * *

Dad was an accountant and worked long hours in town, and mother managed the home including the finances. We were not farmers, but did contract with neighboring farmers to raise our crops – tobacco, corn, and lespedeza – for a percentage of the yield. One year, we raised our tobacco crop ourselves and that was tough. Mom almost got a sun stroke. We had chickens, a few cows, a horse, and one litter of pigs. About half of our fifty-three acres consisted of hills, trees, and "canyons," left from erosion around an old underground coal mine.

Marriage was difficult for mom and dad. They were young when they married—mom, twenty and dad, twenty-two. Their second child, Bobby, died of acute leukemia at the age of four, and my oldest brother, Booth, drowned at the age of twelve. Mother experienced amnesia for a number of months after the second death. She felt there had to be an easier way to reach heaven than marriage and so preached the priesthood as the surest route there.

One of the most important lessons my parents taught me—by their example—was to question and stand up to authority. Robert Edwin and Helen Booth, while respectful of the clergy and religious—mother was clearly deferential—did not hesitate to confront them when they were mistaken. For my parents, right was right and wrong was wrong.

For example, when Booth's teacher, a religious sister, began bullying him, mother drove to the school, interrupted class, and took my brother out of the school. When there was a crisis with one of his sons and the bishop, dad drove to the chancery office and met with the bishop to talk things over. He also wrote Cardinal Wright in the Vatican in order to support one son.

Mother was puritanical when it came to sex, and she passed her attitude on to me.

Growing up on a farm, you'd think I learned the facts of life early on from watching animals copulate. But not me. A concrete example of my naiveté, and I hate to admit this, was the fact that I did not know how conception took place.

In my second year college, I read a religious pamphlet on this topic written by Fr. Gerald Kelly, which spoke of the sperm entering the egg. The only way I could conceive of this happening was through the saliva in a kiss. Now, this seems unreal, but I tell you truthfully that is what I figured out.

Six years later, in my final year of theology at St. Mary Seminary, Baltimore, when an underclassman shared with me the innocence of a fellow seminarian who didn't know the meaning of a French kiss, I laughed heartily with him at such naiveté, but then quickly got to my dictionary.

Also, during my theology years, I read about how boys on a date would unbutton the girl's blouse, and I was shocked. And then how I blushed when reading of boys who would reach up their date's skirt.

You know, "masturbation" is a peculiar word. It sounds funny. It comes from the Latin: *masturbātio*. If I were Jerry Seinfeld, I would ask, "What's this with masturbation? It's a fine activity, but you won't meet new friends." Growing up in the fifties, we were taught masturbation was not only *A Sin*; but *A Mortal Sin.* One that would send you to hell AND for all eternity. Even if I spoke this word, I felt unclean. I preferred the term, "self-abuse." Yes, if one did "it," it meant he abused his body.

* * * * *

I wonder what genius "invented" high-school seminaries. I was thirteen when I left home with my older brother, Bill, for the seminary, St. Mary's College, in Marion County, Kentucky, which is in the central part of the state. We were isolated on a five-hundred acre farm. Life was simple; rules were strict; and we wore cassocks except during recreation and in the shower.

One strict rule—and I did not understand the rationale at the time—forbade us from visiting the room of another seminarian. To do so was punishable by expulsion from the seminary.

At the end of my third year Theology at St. Mary Seminary, Baltimore, our class was to receive the Order of Sub-Diaconate, when we promised to lead a life of celibacy. In anticipation, it was customary for seminarians facing such a lifetime commitment to run to their confessor for consolation and/ or affirmation. I figured I had best do this, although I experienced few doubts. So, I told my confessor, Jack Dede, I had been infatuated with an eighth-grade classmate, Pat, for many years. Jack did not take this too seriously, explaining that last-minute jitters were common.

However, in our conversation, he referred to her living in Owensboro, eight hundred miles from Baltimore. Interrupting, I explained she taught school in Washington, D. C., forty miles southeast. This got his attention immediately, and he blurted out, "Have you been seeing her?"

"No, I haven't seen her." Even now, though I haven't seen her in the last fifty years, I have thought of her off and on over the years.

Before each of the three major orders—sub-deaconate, deaconate, and priesthood—we were required to sign statements confirming our free choice in taking the order. Although realizing mother had strongly urged me to become a priest, I felt I was choosing the order freely and thus signed on.

I still remember a sermon by Father Albert Ruetz— "Big A" to us and rector of Saint Mary College. On the eve of summer vacation, he said:

You guys are just like hothouse tomato plants. You're protected from the hot winds of temptation—from the wiles of loose women. Here, you're spoon fed on a regular diet of prayer, Holy Mass, regular sacraments, and silence. Vacation time will test your spiritual health. Today, we turn you out. So, be careful! Remember your prayer life!

In the Owensboro Diocese, we seminarians were given some rules for summer behavior, which included the following: we were not allowed to work at a place where young women worked; and we could play tennis on public courts only if girls wearing shorts were not playing on the courts first. You get an idea of how progressive we were in Owensboro.

On weekends, my brothers and I would rise shortly after daybreak and rush into town trying desperately to preempt girls in scanty clothing on the tennis court.

The priesthood was good for me up to a point, and I believe I was good to the priesthood. Entering the seminary out of the eighth grade, in many ways I was formed by its rules, discipline, and culture. So, ordination gave me more freedom. The priest's salary was miniscule, but I had little need for money—our family was poor, at least lower middle class—so, I wasn't used to much. On May 26, 1962, my ordination day, I pledged obedience to the bishop and kept that pledge for the most part.

Following ordination, I was appointed to an eight-week summer assignment at Saint Joseph and Paul Parish in Owensboro. Then, my first regular appointment was to Saint Jerome Parish, Fancy Farm, Kentucky. For most of my four years there, I administered two mission parishes: Saint Denis in Hickman County and Saint Charles in Carlisle County.

I taught a course on marriage in the parish high school; moderated three Christian Family Movement (CFM) chapters; helped with the basketball program; attended some high school dances, along with performing regular pastoral duties.

I will never forget the senior student who asked me to dance with her. It was my very first invitation to dance in my life. Why did I not accept her invitation—I have wondered this many times since. Of course, had I accepted, it would have caused gossip in the parish, along with other complications.

I had two advantages over most of my fellow clergy. For one, my two brothers were fellow priests in the Owensboro Diocese, and my two sisters were Sisters of Charity of Nazareth (Kentucky). We were together in our views of church—enthusiastic believers and practitioners of the Second Vatican Council. So, I had lots of built-in support my fellow priests did not enjoy. And secondly, as recounted above, my parents modeled a common-sense approach when dealing with the hierarchy.

So, I guess, looking back, the Field family was a force to be reckoned with. When Father Mike Lally, a pastor in the Louisville Diocese, met our recently ordained bishop, he asked how he was doing in Owensboro. Our bishop answered, "I have three problems—the three Field brothers."

In an early parochial assignment, I could never have co-existed with the pastor, who was known for his harsh treatment of his assistants –a "curate crusher"—had I not confronted him when he treated me unfairly. I argued and took up for myself. Afterward, we treated one another with true Christian respect ... for a while. This ability to confront an older cleric, when need be, enabled me to survive as an assistant pastor. I was never appointed pastor.

One of the deficiencies in the management of the diocese was the custom of moving priests, with only a week or two notice, to a new assignment. On these occasions, I felt like a pawn on the chess board; I was never consulted concerning a new appointment. To give you an insight, let me share an unusual story. After serving at Saints Joseph and Paul Parish in Owensboro for about one year—I did a number of these one-year appointments—the bishop, on short notice, appointed me to begin serving three country parishes in Grayson County. The rectory in Peonia was about sixty miles up the road.

I took the bishop's order literally and fully intended to arrive at the rectory on the appointed day. When two of my fellow assistants realized I would never finish packing in time to make the deadline, they came into my bedroom and began placing clothes in the suitcase. This was greatly appreciated; however, I arrived at the rectory at 1:00 a.m., Sunday, missing the deadline by sixty minutes.

When Father Dave answered the doorbell, he greeted me in his pajamas and bathrobe. "Hey, welcome to Peonia," he said, "Did you find the church all right?"

"Dave, I apologize for waking you up. I tried my best to arrive earlier."

All of a sudden, he pulled a small revolver from his robe pocket. "Is it not pitiful I have found it necessary to have this," he looked at the gun. "I've been called on sick calls to vacant houses in the middle of the night. I've been run off the road at night. Someone put sand in my gas tank. I simply cannot take it any longer."

As he explained after the morning Mass, when he came to this parish, there was drinking at the school dances; so, he immediately closed them down for a time. This and other quick changes in the parish did not endear him to the parishioners.

Dave was from the city and had studied in Rome. He had a bossy disposition. The parishioners were farmers without much formal education. I was told by one parishioner they only began to understand Dave at the time he was leaving—the priesthood. Some of us figured Dave had been assigned to this particular place because those in power perceived him deficient in humility. What kind of management style was this!

* * * * *

Generally, I watched my P's and Q's regarding women. One rule in this regard was as follows: the priest shall not ride *alone* in a car with a woman in the front seat. One morning, when driving over to St. Charles School for a weekday Mass, I came upon a parishioner walking to Mass. She was the mother of several students; I stopped and gave her a ride. It must be that she sat in the front seat because this is lodged in my memory.

* * * * *

I gradually decided to transfer out of the Owensboro Diocese. I first became disillusioned with the diocese in the way we young priests were treated. The Priests Senate was divided into groups by age. The youngest priests belonged to Group VII, with Pete as our convener. We took our role seriously—so seriously we held regular meetings and came up with thirty-six pages of suggestions for the diocese. We were proud of our work and felt we were performing a genuine service.

Well, this really threatened some of the older priests as well as the bishop. When none of these folks paid attention to our suggestions, I, like the rest of our group, felt confused, hurt, and angry.

Afterward, at a Priests' Senate meeting, following a compulsory priests' retreat, some of us complained about the choice of retreat master—a retired bishop who was completely out of sync with us. An older pastor responded thus: "Well, once in a while you get a lemon."

Phil Riney, a pastor who supported the younger priests, answered, "Getting a lemon is one thing, but feeding us shit and calling it ice cream is another." We roared.

Part of the fallout happened when several pastors went to see the bishop, knelt before him, and pledged allegiance. The bishop followed by going after several younger priests—one was Pete from Group VII. It happened on a Saturday morning when Pete was still sleeping.

The bishop barged into his upstairs bedroom and began a tirade as he marched up and down the room, "Snake in the grass, snake in the grass—that's what you are! Trying to disrupt the diocese, you young priests!"

Pete was not wearing pajamas, and he pulled the sheet up to his chin. Unsure what was unfolding before him was real, he could not muster one word.

"I'm the bishop here; it is my duty to make the decisions for this diocese; and I don't need any of you whippersnappers to butt in."

Later, when Pete shared what happened, I was horrified at this abusive display of power. The whole episode left me disillusioned, and a large chunk of trust in the hierarchy melted away that day. Later on, some of us organized a Priests' Council as an alternative to the Priests' Senate. While this threatened the bishop, it gave us younger priests a welcome relief.

The U. S. bishops made a strong statement on racism in 1958. However, it lay dormant for years as the bishops refused to promote it; therefore, the priests did not preach on it; so, the laity were ignorant of the bishops' Letter to U. S. Catholics. I was stationed at the cathedral parish, Saint Stephen's, along with Jerry Griffith, who also was ordained in 1962.

We decided to pass out this statement to the parishioners after Sunday Masses.

We did not get the okay from the pastor, because we felt certain he would disapprove. The bishop later called Jerry in and scolded him, but did not say a word to me.

Around that time, I volunteered with a social service agency, along with Charles Reno, a close friend. When Charles approached my pastor to place a notice in the parish bulletin concerning our agency, the pastor told him we did not put any notice in the bulletin unless it pertained to a parish function. This was a lie.

I took this matter to the bishop and explained, "Bishop, I belong to a group which works hand in hand with the poor in Owensboro. We need support; therefore, my friend Charles Reno took a bulletin notice to my pastor, Father Tony. But Father Tony told Charles only notices printed in the parish bulletin were those pertaining to parish activities.

"Of course, this isn't true, Bishop. What makes this even worse is that Mr. Reno is black and Baptist. All he has to do to see this as a lie is to get hold of a Sunday bulletin."

The bishop responded, "Sometimes, Father, we just cannot tell them the whole story."

I replied as I got up and began to walk out, "Is that right?"

The bishop jumped up and hurried along beside me trying to explain—to this day I can't remember what he said. I was absolutely furious and closed the door behind me.

* * * * *

A serious wound to my allegiance to the Owensboro Diocese came around 1969, when the bishop pulled my brother, Bill, out as pastor of the parishes in Hickman and Fulton, Kentucky. It was a lengthy ordeal which boiled down to the issue of race. Bill did not accept the reassignment from the bishop and appealed to Rome.

102

Next, Bill requested the bishop give him a year's leave of absence. I asked for a year's leave also to be in solidarity with my brother. When I visited the chancery office to meet with the bishop, I asked for a year off to support Bill, who already had been given a leave. The bishop replied, "No I did not give Father Bill a leave of absence."

"But" I said, "you told him you would write a letter telling the rest of the clergy in the diocese about his leave."

The bishop answered, "Yes, but I'm not going to mail the letter."

I was dumfounded. My bishop reneged on his word and on such a serious matter for the diocese and for my brother. I had no idea of leaving the priesthood and staunchly intended to return to the diocese after my year was up. Then the bishop added, "Supporting your brother in a protest is not grounds for a leave of absence."

I added, "Well, I'm confused and I need a year off." While the bishop did not object, he did not approve. But I was stumped—*if I did receive an okay, how would I have any evidence if the bishop would not confirm it in writing*? Therefore, for the next three days, Jerry Griffith would strap the smallest tape recorder we could find (which was about 12"x 6" x 3") in the small of my back the first day and then under my left arm the following two days before I left the rectory.

On that first morning, when driving to the chancery with the recorder strapped to my back, I had to lean forward over the steering wheel. Inside, the bishop patted my shoulder and asked if I had parked in the **back.** I only heard the final word and panicked as I thought, "My God, he knows about the recorder!"

I taped each conversation I had with the bishop, and on the third day, he finally gave me permission for the leave of absence.

When I told mom and dad what I had done, while they empathized with my plight, they stressed I must never ever tell anyone about the tape recorder.

Ironically, the bishop did send me a letter outlining the conditions of my leave. After reading it, I placed it in a safe place—so safe I never again located it until my year ended and I returned to the diocese.

However, I must have been preoccupied when I read over the bishop's letter, because I thought it read I *would* retain my priestly faculties during the year off. This was extremely important to me; for, it meant I was still a priest in good standing and, if necessary, could function as a priest.

So, during that year's leave, I worked as an orderly in the local public hospital. From time to time a nurse would ask me to hear her confession. We would step into the linen closet and I would administer the sacrament of Penance.

Once on a weekday, as I sat in the pews awaiting evening Mass at St. Stephen's, no celebrant appeared. After several minutes, I walked into the sacristy; donned the proper vestments; and proceeded to celebrate Mass. I never found out why the scheduled celebrant failed to show.

It was providential the bishop's letter to me was lost for a year; for, otherwise that year would have been much more difficult both for me and my parents.

I was the first priest at the time to take a year off and remain in Owensboro—working there and living at home. One of the conditions of my leave of absence was that I visit my priest classmate (Father Tom Weise) in Mobile, Alabama. This came about because the bishop wanted to know my plans for the leave of absence.

I planned to visit Tom for a week or two and then I would get a job in town and live with my parents. However, as I read the context of the question, he did not want me around Owensboro. I told the bishop the first thing on my agenda was to visit Tom. Somehow he had in his mind—or at least hoped—I would stay in Mobile.

The first part of the year's leave proved most difficult. First of all, a son on leave from the active ministry and living at home was an entirely new experience for mom and dad. Once, during the night, I found mother kneeling in the dining room, praying the rosary, and crying.

Secondly, the doctor who was chief of radiology in the hospital unit I worked was Catholic and a friend of my parents. For weeks he would not say a word to me. Finally, he called me "Clark," and everything clicked between him and me from then on. Later, I discovered he just didn't know what to call me.

After the year was up and I had been reassigned in the diocese, I found the missing letter, only to discover my priestly faculties had been rescinded during my leave of absence... Where were those nurses who confessed to me!

The final strike for the Owensboro Diocese occurred when I was serving as assistant pastor of Saint Thomas More Parish in Paducah and administering St. Mary Parish in LaCenter. Father Bob Garlich pastured Rosary *Chapel*—one of the only two African American congregations in the diocese, and neither was given the status of parish. Rather, both were designated as *chapels*. Bob and I were working with the Paducah teens. Father Phil Riney gave the okay for us to organize a coffee house in the basement of Saint Francis DeSales rectory.

The coffeehouse provided African American and European American teens a safe place to recreate. Bob and I were very happy with the progress of the coffeehouse, and the teens were having a ball. One day, Phil Riney shared with Bob and me the bishop had been meeting with the Paducah pastors concerning these two young priests who were getting black and white teens together.

Phil also told us the Paducah mayor had driven to Owensboro—125 miles one way—and met with the bishop about this mixing of the races. The mayor told the bishop if he did not transfer us out of Paducah, he would run Bob and me out of town.

Like Bob, I was furious and did not want to give in to this racism. Disbelief flooded my brain—to think, a bishop would give in to a mayor on church matters! The word got around. However, the bishop waited for things to cool down before reassigning me.

By then, I knew most of the laity would not link my transfer to the coffeehouse episode including the mayor's mandate. So I accepted my appointment to Saint Sebastian, Calhoun, with a mission parish at Saint Charles, Livermore. However, I promised to myself I would never accept
another assignment from this bishop. This was not the first time a priest had been transferred out of Paducah because of racist complaints.

One evening my brother Phillip, Tim Gholson, an African-American high-school student, and I were driving down the street when I was pulled over by the police. In a matter of minutes three more police cars surrounded us. The arresting officer—once he learned I was a Catholic priest and lived in Paducah (my license plate showed a different county)—asked the sergeant, who arrived after I was pulled over, what he should charge me with. The Sergeant answered he didn't know because he was not the one who initiated the action.

The Paducah police were trying their best to separate white and black teens. Before my court date, I told a reporter from the Paducah Sun Democrat daily newspaper I would not pay the fine should the judge side with the police. My story appeared on the front page of the newspaper the day I was arraigned. I—not the policeman—had a witness, my young friend Tim Gholson.

The judge still sided against me and fined me $10. Then he added, "And it really bothers me to listen to someone who is too haughty to think he must answer to our police."

I answered, "I refuse to pay the fine."

The judge, waving his hand toward the door, said, "Take him to jail."

I learned a lot about the penal system that night in jail. The next morning, Father Tim Taylor, an Episcopal priest, came to the jail to visit me and brought a Mass kit, in case I wanted to offer Mass in jail. I thanked him but said, "Get me out of jail and I will repay you." He did and I did.

This story had a remarkable result. Some lay Catholics in Paducah, including Pat and Penny Lally, began a ministry to the jail, which later expanded to include the State Prison at Eddyville. They carried on this ministry for many years.

*   *   *   *   *

In 1973, I was loaned to the Evansville (Indiana) Catholic Diocese at my request. Evansville is 30 miles west of Owensboro—both cities lay on the banks of the Ohio River.

I wanted to get away from the pastor/assistant relationship and I wanted to work with the African American congregation of St. John in Evansville. Father Sylvester (Sy) Loerlein and I were named as team leaders of the St. John Apostolic Center.

Sy was a priest of the Evansville Diocese, ordained seven years before me. So, not only was he from the local diocese and knew the ropes, but he was seven years my senior. I had a real fear he would see me as his assistant. Therefore, before I moved in, I vetted him studiously. I remember one of my questions for Sy: "What would you do if I came into the rectory one night drunk with a half-pint in my back pocket?"

Sy, showing exasperation, replied, "I don't know how to answer that. Are you telling me you have a drinking problem?" He paused. "What do you want me to say?"

Realizing I had overdone my interrogation, I ceased, and hoped for the best. Many things about our relationship and ministry worked well. One of the joys was the community we formed with a group of Holy Cross Brothers, whose house was on the street behind the rectory and a group of Benedictine Sisters, who lived next door. The sisters ran the Marian Day School, which had formerly been the parish school. The three houses took turns monthly in hosting dinner. I found these relationships with the sisters and brothers very supportive.

Sy and I divided responsibilities, and we took turns preaching, cooking, and dish-washing. We prayed together daily. I was appointed diocesan representative on the Indiana Inter-religious Commission for Human Equality (IICHE) and volunteered for jail ministry. One of IICHE's programs was Adventures in Understanding. A local African-American minister and I became co-chairs of the Evansville Chapter, the first chapter of IICHE in the state.

Another IICHE program was named Development in Anti-Racial Training (DART), and I became a member of the DART state team. Sister Catherine Doherty and I worked with local congregations using the Inventory on Racism and Sexism from IICHE. I learned so much from IICHE and its programs and found this work very fulfilling.

As the months passed, I realized what an extremely different approach to ministry Sy and I had. For example, Sy took an active role in the Catholic, Pentecostal movement—a practice of which was speaking in tongues. I did not. I became excited with a project coming out of our Adventures in Understanding chapter, namely: taking a neighborhood census of Catholics, former Catholics, and the unchurched. Sy saw no need.

The Personnel Committee of the Priests Senate came to the same conclusion and told me they thought I should stay at Saint John's, and they would look for another parish for Sy. I agreed. Bishop Shea asked us both to write up our recommendations for the future of St. John Apostolic Center. I recommended it become a National, African American Parish. Sy wanted it to remain as it was.

As time went on, I began to read the handwriting on the wall, which said Sy would stay and I would go. Looking for an alternative mission—"Plan B"—I decided if I was moved away from St. John, where I loved the people and the mission, I would seek the nomination in the Democrat Primary for the Indiana Eighth District of the U. S. House of Representatives.

The bishop chose Sy to remain at St. John; however, he explained he agreed with Sy that St. John would become an African American parish. Since that was my suggestion and not Sy's, I realized the bishop was operating out of a different agenda. Sy, at the time, felt uncomfortable living in the neighborhood—I overheard him speak of his fear. Later, I told the bishop this was a racist decision.

The bishop told me, "Clark I know your interest is in peace and justice ministry, but I have no place for you."

I replied, "Bishop, I want your permission to run in the Democrat Primary for the U. S. House of Representatives."

He was taken back and said, "I think I'm supposed to say No."

I countered, "Bishop, I'm not asking you to endorse me. But as a citizen do I not have the right to run?"

He thought for a moment and then reasoned aloud, "Well, you still belong to the Owensboro Diocese, so if the Owensboro bishop will permit this, I will go along."

Feeling the media would want to know if Bishop Shea had given his permission, I asked him to put this in writing, which he did. Next, I jumped in the car and hightailed it to Owensboro and asked the bishop for permission. He reasoned in a similar way as Shea, and said, "Since you live and work in the Evansville Diocese and since Bishop Shea will give you permission, I will also."

I said, "Bishop will you put this in writing?'

"Yes, I will."

"Would you write a note to this effect now—I can wait."

He answered, "No, but I will mail it to you." He never did.

I got in the race at the last minute. As far as I know, no other priest has ever run for Congress in the Indiana Eighth District. Six of us ran in the Democrat Primary; I came in second; but lost by over twenty thousand votes to the person elected in November. My consultant had told me, if I carried the African American vote and the Catholic vote, I could win. I carried the Evansville African American vote, but I don't believe there was a Catholic vote.

When Bishop Shea gave me no assignment, Ted Tempel, pastor at Saint Anthony Parish in Evansville, invited me to live in the rectory and run my campaign from there. A few months after the election, Bishop Shea assigned me to Saint Anthony to help out on weekends; continue my jail ministry; and carry on an inter-racial ministry in the diocese.

I received some real blessings during the following five years. I became friends with Sister Alice, a Daughter of Charity, who was principal of the parish school. We did jail ministry together. I witnessed the school children hanging on and around Sister Alice during recess—in all the schools with which I had been associated, I had never seen such a relationship between students and principal.

Also, the diocese bought into Father Vince Dwyer's program for priests. Father Dwyer, a former Cistercian priest, came to Evansville and taught us priests the benefits of forming support groups.

Ted Tempel and I joined with eight other priests; we hired a female psychologist to lead our group; and we met monthly for overnight sessions. After a few years, we invited several Benedictine sisters to join us.

Loneliness is a common problem for priests. Once, many years ago in Kentucky, a Father Lawrence Durbin was appointed pastor of Saint Denis parish in the far western part of the diocese on a gravel road. After a time, he traveled to see his bishop—it was the bishop of the Louisville Diocese (about two hundred and fifty miles east), as the Owensboro Diocese had not yet been established. He said to the bishop, "Bishop the loneliness is killing me and I can't take it any longer."

The bishop answered, "Father, you have Jesus in the tabernacle."

Well Father Durbin left the area with a young woman shortly thereafter and became a postmaster out west. However, he did return to his priestly ministry in the Owensboro Diocese several years before he died. In fact, I ministered the sacraments to him in Deaconess Hospital on his deathbed.

The Vince Dwyer support group gave me much-needed help. For a number of years, I had been open to leaving the active ministry. As related earlier, I enjoyed platonic relationships with a number of women with whom I worked or was associated. With several, I engaged in some physical intimacies, but never intercourse.

One of Vince Dwyer's tenets was we priests had been taught only to have a personal, vertical relationship with God. However, according to him, we also needed to go to God through horizontal relationships with people, and priests needed to have healthy relationships with women.

Once, when I joined with the Church-Mouse Collective in Philadelphia for a two-week presence there to protest global torture, a female participant told me she wanted to make love to me. When I later shared this with my priest support group, one or two of my brother priests asked why I did not accept her offer. This really surprised me, but showed the non-judgmental attitude of the group.

For all the above reasons I was open to resigning from the active priesthood; however, three ranked at the top of the list, namely: sexism in the hierarchy highlighted by the refusal to ordain women; racism in the church; and the lack of leadership in the hierarchy. It seemed to me the leadership—or more aptly, the lack of leadership—was allowing the church just to float along.

A couple of friends gave me a shove toward leaving. Ishi, a close friend who now lives in India, shared that the priesthood was holding me back from becoming the free spirit I was destined to be; I listened. A woman friend challenged with, *how do you reconcile working for the largest sexist organization in the country?* She made me wonder if I were a fraud.

So, in 1981, I took a second leave of absence and opened the *Branching Out Counseling and Consulting Center*. I figured with my Masters degree in counseling I could make a living. After a few months I was broke, and chose Plan B: I drove a taxi. If Father Groppi, who had driven a cab in Milwaukee years earlier, could do it I reasoned, so could I. The pay wasn't great—$2.01/ hr— plus tips. However, it soon became apparent most of my customers were unaware of the custom of tipping the cabbie.

I enjoyed the priesthood and felt by serving the people I was making a difference. As the years rolled on, however, I felt it was time for me to move on. While restricting my freedom in many ways, the priesthood did allow me certain opportunities. For example, I accepted an invitation to serve on the War Resisters League National Committee, which meant I attended meetings and conferences in different parts of the country.

Also, for a short time, I served on the national committee of American Christians Against Torture, (ACAT) which met in Philadelphia. I also, as mentioned earlier, served on the IICHE Board. Had I then been married with children and job, I doubt I could have served with these groups.

Both of my brothers had already resigned from the priesthood and married. I tried to get them to tell me how things were on the other side, but they were tight-lipped. All of us were worried how mother would take it if her third son left the ministry—dad had died in 1973. However, mother seemed to take my leaving in stride. Thank heavens!

In 1982, I resigned from the active priesthood, and in 1983, I married Alice. We adopted Phillip Kevin in 1988 and brought him home from St. Francis Hospital, Beech Grove, Indiana. He was five days old, and the moment I looked into Phillip's eyes I felt this tiny baby is wiser than I. These past 29 years I've been very happy.

When folks inquire, I answer, "I used to be an unmarried father and now I'm a married father." Or I might explain, "I used to live in homes for unwed fathers, but now I'm wed."

You may reach Clark Gabriel Field at:
fieldandserr@gmail.com or visit his website at:
www.clarkgabrielfield.com He lives in Evansville, Indiana.

"First Seek the Kingdom

And All these Things

Shall be Added unto You"

John Raymaker

In the Our Father (Matt 6:10) Jesus has us pray "Thy Kingdom come". Shortly thereafter (Matt 6:33) he urges us to first seek God's Kingdom. The Kingdom signifies the reign of God's justice—a central element of the Sermon on the Mount. Seeking the Kingdom means cooperating with God's grace in spreading the Good News. It means being more concerned about the message of Jesus—living it and spreading it—than being focused on preserving Church structures. It means not rejecting the Church in these difficult times but calling it to live a more authentic spirituality.

Earliest Influences in my Life: the Gospel's "Good News"

I grew up in Brussels, Belgium during World War II and witnessed Nazi terror. Toward the end of the war came the allied bombings. In 1947, our family rejoined an aunt and cousins in Richmond, Virginia. During all these events, Jesus' Good News and his urging us to work for a just world remained the central element of my faith. Little did I know as a boy that the stage was being set in my life to let love and God's justice become central elements of my faith in my later life's struggles. Jesus had warned us that the rich of this world (and their lies) are "wiser" than those who seek and live for God's justice. Even those at the top or apex of the Church in bishops' residences and in the Vatican are not free from human frailties.

Early on in life, both in Brussels and in Richmond, I had been impressed by the majesty of Church buildings and the celebration of the Eucharist. A sermon on the love of God I heard in Brussels at the age of nine remained engraved in my mind. "Love conquers all", the priest said; he illustrated that with Damien the Leper who had volunteered to care for lepers in the remote island of Molokai. Eventually, Damien had contracted leprosy made famous when he said "we lepers...."

In Richmond, our parents sent us to Cathedral High School—a small struggling school in a southern diocese where Catholics were barely tolerated. Our freshman class had no more than 25 students but the priests of the Cathedral and the nun teachers (the Sisters of Charity from Nazareth, Kentucky) had a deep faith which impressed me and many of our classmates. Of eleven male students, four of us elected to go to the minor seminary at St Charles College in Baltimore. Two of us were eventually ordained.

Since my theme is "First Seek the Kingdom", I want to put into relief the role of three priest canon lawyers both in my life as a student and in the lives of not a few of the faithful. When named bishops, two of these canon lawyers tended to use canon law to preserve Church structures; the third,[1] chose to emphasize the primacy of

---

[1] Two of these three priests worked in the Richmond chancery and were assistants at the Cathedral. When later, one of these, Father

Kingdom values in the Church as interpreted by Vatican II. Lest I get ahead of myself, let me backtrack a bit so as to put things in perspective.

The Path toward Ordination in a Tumultuous World

It was the intellectual Father Ernest Unterkoeffler, one of the curates at the Cathedral, who most influenced me to study for the diocesan priesthood. From 1952 to 1956, I attended St Charles College in Catonsville, Maryland run by the Sulpicians. Upon graduation, I changed my mind as to studying for the priesthood. In 1958, I decided to join the Missionhurst fathers—a missionary group known in Belgium as the Scheut Fathers.

During our novitiate-training year at Missionhurst in Arlington, Virginia, Pius XII died to be followed by the "good" Pope John XXIII, a seasoned historian and pastor, who saw the need to bring the Church into the modern world with his call for a Second Vatican Council. My six years of seminary at Catholic University witnessed the complex dynamics affecting life in the Catholic dioceses, in religious and priestly life and in the seminaries. All this was "provoked' by the Church renewal Vatican II was undertaking.

The sixteen documents that Vatican II eventually produced were all compromises between the progressive bishops and their theologians who had welcomed the

---

Ernest Unterkoeffler became the bishop of Charleston, South Carolina (1964-1990), he was embroiled in disputes with some of his progressive priests who had a different view of what Vatican II meant. Although an advocate of civil-rights during the 1960's, he applied canon law in a strict sense when dealing with priest dissenters. Walter Sullivan, on the other hand, when he became Bishop of Richmond (1974-2003) was known as one of the most progressive bishops in the US. He listened intently to his priests and was much involved in Pax Christi and served as its president. As bishops, these two canon lawyers interpreted Church law, Church tradition and the roles of diocesan priests and laity in quite different ways. The third was the later Cardinal Jan Schotte, a close associate of Pope John Paul II.

Council and their conservative counterparts who had resisted it. The progressives tended to be oriented toward the study of Scripture and a clearer reinstatement of the primacy of the Kingdom in the Church rather than the strict rule of canon law.

In reality, Vatican II led to divisions in guiding a world-wide Church. Vatican II had opened many new paths. A stress on the rights of all believers and humans as outlined in the "Declaration on Human Freedom" and in "The Church Today" became for some a heady wine.

This led to a massive exodus of priests from active ministry and of nuns from their convents. Some pastors felt threatened by parish councils. It was Paul VI's task to keep the Church united during these difficult years. Ecumenism and interreligious dialogue flourished but the Church was faced with internal tensions.

Let me briefly touch on how all this played out in the Missionhurst residence-seminary near Catholic University in Washington, D. C during the Council years. The euphoria of Vatican II had opened the eyes of many young American men some of whom decided to study to become missionaries with Missionhurst which has had missions in all continents of the world.

From 1959 to 1965, life at "Catholic U." and in our Missionhurst seminary-residence reflected the complex dynamics initiated by Vatican II. Most professors, both in philosophy and theology, were of the "old school". Fortunately, some, especially in Scripture classes and in moral theology, were more open to the new. Within our residence, we started with six seminarians. By the time I was ordained we had close to thirty. We had outgrown three houses and had to build a new building large enough to house all.

Ordination and my Relations with Some Bishops

I was the oldest seminarian in our residence and for six years I tended to have a leader's role. During my last three years in the seminary, our residence director was Fr. Jan Schotte—the later Cardinal, head of the Synod of

Bishops whose role was to edit the documents produced by the Synods so as to fit John Paul II's wishes. Schotte, a canon lawyer, had in the 1960's been assigned to the missions in the Philippines but was given a year in the States to improve his English. In the meantime, he had been persuaded to become head of our seminary-residence. Schotte was a genial man and he appreciated my role as a mediator in many issues that arose in seminary life during these turbulent years.

My final years in the seminary were indeed busy ones as I studied Japanese since I had been assigned to that mission. I had become vice-president of the Union of Seminarians around Catholic U. In 1964-1965, I had to help raise funds for Missionhurst and my new mission while working to pass my Licentiate of Theology exams.

When it came time to be ordained in 1964, my first choice for an ordaining bishop was Bishop Unterkoeffler who had been one of my spiritual guides when I was still studying for the diocese of Richmond. He refused on the "ground" that I had left studying for the diocese so as to become a missionary. This was a shock to me and to Jan Schotte. Did not Jesus enjoin us to preach the Kingdom to all; why restrict it to a diocese?

The Realities of Life for me in Japan amidst Church Turbulence

During our training at Missionhurst, we had learned how to make a daily meditation based mostly on Scripture and the lives of the saints. The daily meditation, based on St. Ignatius Loyola's method, had to result in a resolution for the day which was to be renewed several times so as to keep us on a spiritual path. Meditation and its inbuilt resolution later proved to be my redemption as I eventually had to face the turmoils that unexpectedly became my daily fare for many years to come.

My problems began in January 1966 during my period studying the Japanese language—a period which I had greatly anticipated and should have been a great joy.

Missionhurst in Japan had its language school on a farm in the countryside of Himeji. The residence had eleven Flemish priests including the director, language instructor and students. The problem for me was that seven of the priests spoke West Flanders dialects and the Japanese locals tended to speak the local dialect.

Let me throw some light on that for those not familiar with dialects (which is the case with most Americans). I now live in Germany, in the Saar region which has its own dialect. Bavaria and Northern Germany have their own. Residents of these three regions cannot understand one another unless they speak standard German. It seems that people in such cultures as Flanders, Germany and Japan love to speak in dialect with family and friends. It makes them feel at home. Some people with little education in these regions do not even know how to speak the standard language correctly. As for me, in the fall of 1965, caught between dialects I could not understand and not wanting to be a "party-pooper" for those relishing in dialects, I sort of retreated into myself. But, in ways I could not fathom at the time, this frustrated retreat into self left me vulnerable and in an abyss of incomprehension.

After three months of that diet, during the Christmas vacation there, I had a crisis which led me to "overdo it". I had a type of nervous breakdown—not as to my rational faculties but in my nervous system which led to my inability to concentrate as needed. The result was constant fatigue. One symptom of that fatigue was the appearance of blisters on my hands and most of my fingers—a condition which no doctor or hospital ever properly diagnosed for me. The provincial decided to send me early to a parish where I survived for four years under strained, marginal circumstances. That is, I became "half or less" of my real self. I had not fully learned the language but was expected to communicate with the Japanese. Before coming to Japan, I had learned the 2000 Chinese characters that graduates of a Japanese high school have to learn. I was ahead of the game but what I had to do was learn to speak and write. This I could no longer properly do.

The irony is that our language class of two was the last one assigned to the countryside of Himeji. From then on, the diminished number of young Missionhurst priest students were to study Japanese in Tokyo at the Franciscan Language School. But it was too late for me. If I had been sent to Tokyo, as happened with the next class, I would not have fallen into that abyss of incomprehension whereby my seemingly normal self could not function normally. I thus had to cope with the strained marginal circumstances of being considered dysfunctional or "out of it". I knew I could still function but now as a type of wounded healer who could only retreat into smiling, into spirituality and, yes, into an ever deepening appreciation of the fairer sex.

"To Leave or Not to Leave"

From then on, "to leave or not to leave the priesthood" became for me *the* existential question—a question of survival and constant *Angst*. I wanted to be a priest and knew that I could be a good one. Yet, functioning as the priest I wanted to be was now impossible. I had to function in second gear, knowing that I was now "written off". Somewhat like what Jesus says in his parable of the unfaithful steward "to beg I was ashamed"; to dig, that is to learn a new profession, was at the time out of the question. I just had to hope against hope and to "hang in there."

Tottori, the city to which the provincial assigned me, is, a city on the Japan Sea facing Korea. The pastor there knew English well; he was a very genial man (it later turned out that he, too, left the priesthood—a decision which cost him dearly because he had renounced his Belgian citizenship to become a Japanese; when he did marry he was left with no pension to provide for his old age)[2]. In this parish, during the restless 1960's, there was a young Spanish sister who began to teach me piano.

We confided in one another and fell in love. I was now confronted with a further dilemma. I shared my dilemma with a Canadian nun who lived in a neighboring city. But wouldn't you know it? She betrayed my confidence by going to "snitch" on me to the provincial! The young Spanish sister and I were dedicated idealists. Nothing untoward of a sexual nature or even improper touching ever happened; what did happen WAS that two people faithful to their religious vows—she and I—wound up with broken hearts and a lesson in ecclesial realities.

As a young man, I was "dark and handsome". At six-foot two, I easily made an impression on Japanese women as illustrated in the following episode. One of my tasks in Tottori was to instruct two young Japanese men for baptism. Upon visiting one of these young men in the countryside, I met his sister, a beautiful woman (let's call her Kimiko). She made a point to contact me again and before long we had the hots; we also respected one another. I seriously thought about marrying Kimiko, but realized that if I did so, I would be "condemned" to teaching English in Japan to the neglect of the academic ambitions. That's mainly because, my tiring problems made study difficult; more on that later.

Although, I seemed to thrive with parishioners in Tottori and with students to whom I was teaching English both in a local high school and at the University of Tottori, I was in reality in a pickle. An unmistakable sign of my nervous exhaustion was the appearance of small blisters on my hands whenever I overdid it even a bit in my various studies. As a result of the above "snitching" and a bit of a run-in[3] with the genial pastor,

---

[2] Not getting a pension was what I wanted to avoid at all costs. The fact is that many who did leave the active priesthood were later denied a pension and some are, needless to say, greatly handicapped by this.

[3] The pastor in the goodness of his heart wanted to establish a home for handicapped children with what seemed questionable

the provincial then decided to send me to a parish in the large city of Osaka where I would live with a native English-speaking Canadian priest while undergoing some electric shocks at a local therapy house run by German brothers for "troubled" priests. How I still recall Kimiko's visit to me in the Osaka parish —a forbidden fruit ripe for the plucking! I could see in her eyes that she longed to be embraced and I wish I could have indulged. But I knew better. We parted, both sad; but I had kept my vows.

Not Leaving the Priesthood yet because of my Life Dream

At Catholic U., I had become aware of the great Jesuit, Bernard Lonergan whose book *Insight: A Study of Human Understanding* I so much wanted to read— hopefully with a view to get a doctorate in the methods of theology and philosophy. When I came back to Virginia in 1970 in a state of exhaustion, I was told that I would not be going back to Japan but instead to the Dominican Republic. I was also refused—and perhaps rightly so in my circumstance—to study Lonergan. That was the turning point for me. I had earned not a little money in Tottori by teaching English and had turned in every penny. The religious vows of poverty, obedience and chastity which I had kept could have their hard edge as I now understood. The blisters, an unfailing sign for me, kept on reappearing but no one could account for such a state. It was "my problem". Still, I could and would smile to keep up appearances. Chastity became ever more problematic for me in my condition I still held on to it as best I could. The reality is that sexual release was, in my condition, a type of cure to alleviate the

---

funding. Some of the parishioners judged that the parish could not afford this. They consulted me and I took their side. As we saw it, the Belgian brothers he was counting on to run the establishment were not in reality (it seemed to us) able to undertake this without sufficient knowledge of Japanese and under the strain of diminishing vocations.

nerves but such a rationale did not figure in the official clergy books—nor could I communicate this with those who want proof. Still, the history of concubinage in the Church (in many of the continents) shows that there has been a silent "underbelly" reaction to the official position.

"Being a Problem" and Finding Vatican II's Larger Horizons

I had become a problem both for Missionhurst and for myself but had begun to realize that I had to fend for myself—which I began to do. I had no money for studies, but Missionhurst did allow me to work in parishes in Virginia. I saved every penny from a meager salary for two years which was enough to get into the School of Theology at Marquette University in Milwaukee. Before I get into my studies at Marquette (1972-1977), I want to briefly touch on the difficulties of parish life in a now-divided post-Vatican II Church and on my initial encounter with the Federation of Christian Ministries.

In 1970, the bishop of Richmond was glad to have an extra hand. He sent me to several parishes, all of which had problems of one kind or another. In one parish, in the western part of Virginia, the pastor was accused by one vocal parishioner of sleeping with his housekeeper. As I "took over" that rectory for a month, I was amazed to discover pornography all over the place. I never shared this with anyone, not even the bishop. Perhaps I should have but I felt sorry both for this priest and for the parishioners who deserved better. I was only a transition priest and felt the next pastor could best deal with the situation. Why do I even mention this? Because in the light of both the all-too often brushed-under-the rug history of concubinage in the Church and of the recent scandals of sexual abuse by priests, one should be realistic as to celibacy.

The two most telling of said assignments were one, in a large parish in Norfolk and another, in McLean, both in Virginia. In Norfolk, there was a revolution of sorts going in a large parish where one of the assistants had been transferred for helping a group of parish council members in their efforts to get a layperson to be chair of the Council.

The pastor, a good man, tended to be dominated by his mother Julia. It so happens that the parish secretary, the director of religious education and the director of music were all named "Julia". Enough said! It became my role to carry on the struggle to get a lay parish-council president.

The principal event in this struggle led to my visiting the genial Bishop John J. Russell of Richmond along with six affected Parish Council members. This visit with the Bishop led to his dispatching his auxiliary bishop to the parish. Within a short time, Bishop Russell informed the pastor that a lay person would become the head of the parish council. We had succeeded in our mission, but a week later, the sister-principal of the parochial school asked me: "Why didn't you tell us you were being reassigned?" I asked her what she was talking about. She told me she had just read the news of my reassignment in the local Catholic newspaper.

Upon reflection, I must admit, yes, I had hurt this decent if mother-centered pastor and he retaliated. He was particularly hurt that I, a non-diocesan priest, had engineered this small coup. Since then, the Vatican has mandated that the pastor is *ex-officio* the head of a parish council; this later mandate is another indication of how the Vatican bureaucracy had begun a massive scaling back of some the Vatican II's implications.

As for me personally, I had made many friends in a short time but had to leave them behind—another example of what a priest sometimes has to put up with. Bishop Russell then sent me to a large parish in McLean where more or less the same type of discontent on the part of parish council members against the pastor was brewing. I had had enough.

A Turning Point on the Road to Leaving the Active Ministry

In the meantime, a turning point happened in my life. As part of being a priest in the port city of Norfolk, a chance was offered me of serving as chaplain on a commercial cruise from Norfolk to Bermuda. We embarked on June 17, 1972—the day of the Watergate break-in as well of Hurricane Agnes (at the time the costliest hurricane in the United States in recorded history)! On the cruise, I met a widow, Bernice. I toured Bermuda with her as I drove a motorcycle with her in the back seat. We hit it off but she was very discreet. She later invited me to her apartment in a large city and the inevitable happened. I realized the saving power of a woman's arms and care. Still, I kept on harboring my dream of writing about an encounter between the religions and cultures of East and West—a dream I eventually realized in such books as *A Buddhist-Christian Logic of the Heart*, *Empowering the Lonely Crowd*, and *Steps toward Vatican III*.

The "Luxury" of Going Back to Studies and the Hell of Coping with Fatigue

I had by then saved enough money to go to Marquette U. which is what I did in 1972. There, I had the great opportunity to be guided by Fr. Matthew Lamb in my dissertation on Bernard Lonergan and social ethics. I will not get into the particulars of my five-year stay in Milwaukee except to mention some of my broadening horizons in the role of ministry in the Church and in my realization that my state of fatigue could be attenuated by contacts with women. I again began to think of marriage—but that "state of bliss" had to wait for some thirty years in my case for I did not want to sacrifice my priestly ministry nor the opportunity to first earn a doctorate in Lonergan studies. I was able to "pull off" the feat of earning a PhD while coping with fatigue by doing what I had done in Japan to keep on learning Japanese—

listen to tapes which was less tiring. For me, ever since 1966, the blisters on the hand were an unfailing reflection of the extent of mental, nervous fatigue—that still undiagnosed condition which meant I had to take it easy for a few days until the next episode.

The Federation of Christian Ministries—an Alternative to Leaving

In 1973, I had become acquainted with the work of what is now known as the Federation of Christian Ministries (FCM). I was impressed by FCM which was originally comprised of married priests who despite it all wanted to continue as ministers of the Gospel. My studies at Marquette and my association with FCM both led to sharpening my understanding of one of the issues that divides the Church—that of a possible role for married priests in the Church. I believed and still do that the Vatican fears that if priests were allowed to marry, it might present difficulties in the process of naming bishops free from family considerations.

But a system of optional celibacy which would prevent married men from becoming bishops might very well result in a system whereby many of the ablest priests would be unable to become bishops. But the present system—developed by John Paul II and Benedict XVI—whereby only conservative "yes men" are ordained bishops has resulted in the present reality that some of the ablest priest leaders in social justice issues have no chance of becoming bishops. Because of such imbalances, FCM has become a refuge for married priests still willing to serve as ministers of the Gospel. Lately, FCM has broadened its appeal by encouraging women to seek ordination; it has been a constant advocate of Small Christian Communities on the margins of the official Church—as addressed in "*Steps toward Vatican III: Catholics Pathfinding a Global Spirituality with Islam and Buddhism*" (UPA, 2008), a book which I co-authored with my long-time FCM friend Gerald Grudzen, an ex-Maryknoll married priest.

Such issues, as I see it, touch in large part on whether one makes the Kingdom and its values one's first priority or whether one chooses to focus and comply with the demands of the Church as an institution. I'll lay my cards on the table. In the rest of this article, I shall argue that, beginning with John Paul II's naming of only conservative bishops, the Church has been highjacked by the Vatican. The conservatives now run the Church; they intend to keep it that way. Still, the Vatican cannot highjack the Kingdom nor its values. Nor can the "official" Church completely undo what Vatican II wrought. The bishops and the Vatican cannot silence such publications as the *National Catholic Reporter* or *Commonweal* which reflect the views of a "loyal opposition". FCM mirrors this type of loyal opposition; it wants to prioritize the Kingdom and its justice as well as the rights of all the faithful. It is attuned to a phenomenon manifested in the lives of many today, namely the turn to spirituality rather than a kowtowing to organized religion.

My Return to Japan and Studying Buddhism

I believe that Missionhurst is a very good missionary order. I have nothing to say against it. I praise it. Its vocations now come almost exclusively from the Third World. Missionhurst, like many religious groups today is also torn between progressives and conservatives but the former still tend to prevail within Missionhurst which is very much concerned about justice issues and about minorities throughout the globe.

Let me put this in a larger context. It is well known that Joseph Ratzinger changed from being a progressive to being a conservative as a result of the 1968 student uprisings in Europe and in the States. Two of my personal friends and mentors, Cardinal Schotte and Matthew Lamb also moved from "left to right".[4]

After earning my doctorate, in 1977, I was offered a teaching job in Lonergan studies but knew I could not do that in my exhausted state. So I applied to become an Army chaplain. It was not Missionhurst which sent me back to Japan, but the Army. After two years in Fort Hood, the Army honored my request to send me Camp Zama, south of Tokyo.

These four years in the Army were another period of personal conflicts in which women would play a redeeming role. Both at Fort Hood and in Camp Zama where I served, I was able to socialize with—even date— women but always the same problem surfaced. I wanted to apply Lonergan's ethics in scholarly and in social transformative ways. But being married would undercut

---

[4] As to Schotte, let me quote from an obituary on him; "On the papal flight to New York in October 1979, Fr. Jan Schotte gained the favor of Pope John Paul II. Rashly challenging the veteran Vatican foreign minister Cardinal Agostino Casaroli, Schotte—a mere junior official in the secretariat of state—told the new pope he should not cut criticism of the repression of human rights and religious freedom in the Communist world from the spoken text of his address to the United Nations General Assembly." See http://www.independent.co.uk/news/obituaries/cardinal-jan-schotte This laudable action on the plane should not blind us to Schotte's later role in keeping a firm grip on the scope of final documents of the triennial Synod of Bishops in Rome. He is said to have edited the documents to be in line with John Paul II's official conservative ecclesial views. It is to be remarked that, more than Benedict XVI has been, John Paul II was more attuned to realities beyond Western theological contexts. Bishops, too, have conflicting priorities. Unterkoeffler had refused to ordain me because I had left the diocesan seminary to join a missionary order. At my ordination, Schotte, still a priest, was the master of ceremonies. When in the late 1980's, I visited him in the Vatican, Schotte, then an archbishop but not yet a Cardinal, was concerned that the Japanese bishops were not attuned enough to the pope's priorities. Bishops, too, have conflicting priorities.

my scholarly commitment since I had to pace myself and could not cope with academic politics.

Missionhurst runs the Oriens Center for Religious Studies in Tokyo and in 1983, after leaving the Army, I was appointed to its staff. There I began to study Buddhism. Eventually, this gave me the chance to write books on Christianity and Buddhism in which I claim, along with many non-western theologians, that the Church in Africa and Asia must "inculturate" that is, learn to implant Gospel values in the light of traditional African and Asian cultures.

The Kingdom and its Justice
in the Light of African-Asian Values and Cultures

Let me cite two examples of the official Roman Church shooting itself in the foot due its ignorance. In 1704, Pope Clement XI condemned the Jesuit practice in China of using the Chinese Confucian Rites among baptized Christians. Not sufficiently educated Franciscans missionaries misunderstood this practice and denounced the Jesuits in the highest places of the Vatican. The Jesuits had understood that you can only proclaim the Gospel and its values from within a believer's cultural perspectives; they had realized that the Chinese rites were a matter of respecting the ancestors, not worshipping them.

When the Chinese Emperor Kangxi who had been receptive to and influenced by the Jesuit approach learned of Clement's condemnation of the Chinese rites, he forbad Christianity and began persecuting it. This ended the possibility of preaching the Gospel and establishing the Church in most of Asia. Only the French in Vietnam and the Spanish in the Philippines avoided this plight—by intermixing Church and state "cooperation".

Disregarding and being possibly ignorant of this historical lesson, the then Cardinal Ratzinger, Prefect of the Congregation for the Doctrine of the Faith, in 1990 issued his "Some Aspects of Christian Meditation" in which he warned against Eastern forms of meditation such as Yoga.

Again, a Western theologian had shot the universal Church in the foot; the 1990 "Aspects" foreshadows why the theologian Ratzinger, as Pope, misspoke in Regensberg, Germany (2006) provoking the ire of Muslims.

In his 1990 ruling, Ratzinger claimed that Yoga and Buddhism are incompatible with Christianity. He had, in my view, failed to understand what Zen Buddhists mean by disciplining the self or what Yogins mean by meditation. Moreover, he had failed to sufficiently consult Asian bishops and theologians before issuing his "Some Aspects".

I and a few other theologians reacted strongly against this grievous mistake. In my case, the result was that the Vatican: 1) sent its Legate to Japan to visit Oriens; and 2) approached the archbishop of Tokyo who strongly came to Oriens' defense. Instead of provoking the ecclesial authorities in Japan to rap Oriens on the knuckles, the Vatican had to content itself with unsubscribing to *The Japan Mission Journal* of which I was a coeditor.

One may say that Pope Benedict XVI is a brilliant theologian and a genial person but his knowledge seems to be confined to Western theology. Westerners cannot dismiss other spiritualities in token fashion. One must first study them so as to put them within Jesus' Kingdom perspectives in order to best evaluate the priorities of our global Church.

Gifts of the Spirit and the Challenge to Transcend Parochialisms

Faithfulness in our troubled world is a virtue. One cannot but praise the Church for asking her faithful to be (in principle) true to the virtues and to Kingdom values. But, in fact, the official Church—since it has digressed from Vatican II priorities—must now guard against pursuing its present all-too-narrow agenda. It must relearn how to prioritize Kingdom values such as the rights of all and the freedom of conscience.

The abuse scandals on the part of priests in so many parts of the world and the papal butler's Vatileaks (2012) coupled with the Curia's lack of effective leadership now call for a renewed assessment of what faithfulness to Jesus and his message means.

The Influence of FCM in my Life and my Decision to Marry

Here, I want to briefly assess the work and influence of FCM in my life as I began to realize during Pope John Paul II's papacy that, while he charismatically reached out to so many non-Catholic entities in the world, he systematically began to do all he could to lead the Church back toward its erstwhile authoritarian, Vatican-centered way of doing. Cardinal Jan Schotte, as head of the worldwide Synod of bishops, played a key role in recentralizing the Church.

The Pope and Schotte collaborated in restoring to the Curia much of the influence it had lost after 1965. The process was rather "simple". After each triennial Synod of Bishops' convocation, Schotte reedited the bishops's text so as to confirm to the Pontiff's wishes; he was doing administratively what Ratzinger was doing theologically, that is, attempting to ignore the Vatican II call for global renewal.

As for myself, while many of priest friends and associates had gotten married, I put off what I knew would probably be my inevitable decision once I had found the right woman. I am proud of all the friends I have found over the years in the seminary, in parishes and among people of many parts of the world. I regret that upon hearing of my marriage, many of my Catholic friends stopped communicating with me.

As a member of FCM and as a promoter of small Christian communities, before and after I got married, I have found compensating friendships with people in many walks of life and in various countries (such as with a marginalized tribe in Mindanao in Philippines) where my desire to put the Kingdom first led me to "act". My study of Lonergan had led me to become a social ethicist trying to help implement a global ethics inspired by Vatican II's message.

Lonergan has explained that all persons' experience has to be correctly understood so that we can make proper judgments and decide in ways faithful to God's love. I found it challenging to serve in the little ways I could. Jesus' Good News call us to reach out to people in the world who are truly suffering. Bernard Lonergan has for me been my constant inspiration. His method is respected by many but it is hardly understood because it can get complicated when applied. Among Lonergan followers, only a few try to implement his method effectively.

In 2003, I decided that, having found the right woman, Christa Hussong, a German, I would leave the active priesthood. Christa's life has been dedicated to caring for severely handicapped children. We had met through the Internet. Missionhurst had promised me that it would honor their promise of a pension. For me, marriage has meant the freedom to write about the challenges of the Kingdom rather than to be at the constant disposal of people in parishes. The latter, of course, is a great value, but in my case I have seen the limits of parochialism in all too many dioceses and parishes. In some cases, parishes tend to become ends in themselves. Under the last two popes, the Church also risks to again become an end in itself—missing out on the spiritual renewal that is going in the world. This renewal often takes bizarre forms; still it is a renewal in an ever-changing, globalized world which the Church cannot ignore.

The Spirit calls us to transcend parochialisms by first seeking the Kingdom. The Church is now—as it always been—caught in this dilemma. It must preserve internal unity while preaching the Good News. For me, since 1973, FCM has been a key way of resolving the dilemma. At the center of FCM's vision and practice is the fostering of small Christian communities in ways that are not contradictory, but also not subservient to Vatican-beholden bishops.

It is part of the Catholic genius that it has room for internal developments. The present state of a myopic Vatican bureaucracy calls for deeper meditation on the part of all Catholics so that the real evils and looming dangers of society and the planet may be addressed by fellow believers in effective ways. Jesus compares the Kingdom to the work of "yeast". FCM and other groups who insist on holding on to Vatican's II's priorities are part of that yeast. Such groups may all too often be relegated to the margins of the Church; in fact, they are trying to get the Church to focus again—as did Pope John XXIII—on needed renewal, on Kingdom rather than on churchly priorities.

For me, being Catholic means respecting the four Marks of the Church. It means: 1) seeking *holiness* by 2) being *united* with all in prayer as John Paul II did in Assisi (he prayed publicly with believers from various religions but also "privately" with fellow Christians; 3) the third Mark of the Church, *Catholic*, challenges us to go back to scripture and its 4) *apostolic* message of spreading the "Good News" in our ever-changing societies. I have had to live on the margins, but Kingdom values seem to permit some of that. In a way, one has to be on the margins to realize why the Church's "yes-men" bishops are in danger of becoming all too irrelevant to pressing global issues—the fate Vatican II sought to avoid.

Under John Paul II and Benedict XVI, the Vatican has kowtowed to rightist movements within the Church such as Opus Dei which has been given a status independent of the world's bishops. Being on the margins in the Church gives socially-committed groups the chance to listen more closely to Jesus' own words and his commandment of love. Jesus tells us to give to Caesar what is Caesar's and to God what is God's. Hopefully, those of us who left the active priesthood can help remedy what is lacking in the present Church's favoring its traditional structures over the Kingdom-centeredness promoted by Vatican II.

Secularism and atheism are indeed problems—as the present pope Benedict fears. In my life, I have found that Lonergan's prioritizing love in our encounters with God and with fellow human beings is one way to dialogue with other religions thereby putting secularism and atheism in their place.

The Word was

Celebrate!

Carl Roos

Introduction

Many roads come together in this account, much like the spokes of a large wagon wheel. They are all tied to the hub, and give added strength to the person I am. Events and experiences described here reflect the issues of what was happening in the Church, society, and to me personally.

My parents married in 1930 during the Great Depression. I was born during World War II. What followed was the struggle for human rights and for basic rights for women in our society. With Pope John XXIII, came exciting times and significant efforts to refresh the hearts and minds of the Catholic Church. There were mighty efforts to implement Vatican II's directives. Many theologians attempted to make sense of the changes proposed, however some were silenced. It seemed a sad commentary that no real dialogue was established. What is written here reflects my understanding of my journey and, hopefully, choices that led me to a Christ I sought, fully human and fully divine.

The Roots of Faith

As far as we know, almost all of our ancestors came from Germany, emigrating to the U.S.A. in the middle years of the nineteenth century. For the most part, they had a Roman Catholic background and tended to settle in areas that were predominantly Catholic.

My maternal grandfather, Conrad Joseph Schnell (affectionately called "Coon") was born March 12, 1881. His family of thirteen lived on a farm near Celestine, Indiana. No real tales came out of his early years, but by 1906, he had married Josephine Miller. Their beginning years of marriage were ones of hardship and struggle. Their first child, Andrew died early due to complications when a roof leaked over his crib. Their first daughter, Veronica, my mother was born on January 19, 1910. Her early years were filled with laborious farm work. There was no electricity, and of course, only a path to the outhouse. Veronica, called "Frony", remembered that she was "Coon's favorite", but could no longer sit on his lap after she was eight. German families found it difficult to be affectionate.

Conrad was rather severe and controlling. At the church picnic, no one got any cash to spend. He was frivolous enough to buy a one-cent cigar! The lifestyle took its toll on Josephine who became physically and mentally exhausted. She spent several years in the Evansville, Indiana sanitarium. By 1940 she had died, but her goodness, kindness, and gentleness lived on in the memories of her children. Veronica tells a tale about seeing a white dove ascend as her mother died; the significance of this story made a strong impression on her family.

Coon had a bit of religious fanaticism in him. He told a sister, Theresa, that if she would stand within a chalk circle drawn on the floor—that her salvation would be achieved. A brother, Joseph, was told that if he knelt for an hour on kernels of corn strewn on the floor that he would be saved. Joseph declined the offer. Conrad did read from the Bible each day and was proud to be an American. After his wife's death, Conrad did the cooking; he would fix biscuits once a week and keep them in a big tin container. What he fixed in his pan was all mixed together because, as he said, "It is all going to the same place anyway."

My paternal grandparents were Paul and Theresia Roos from Dale, Indiana. They were known for their gentility and hospitality, and were called Mama and Papa Roos. Theresia was kind and gentle. Paul sang in the church choir and worked on the railroad. Harry was born on March 12, 1906. His life and schooling were normal until he got sick as a sophomore in high school. At sixteen years of age (1922), he dropped-out of school and worked on local farms and with his dad on the railroad. Veronica completed eight years of grade school; but then, it was on to the wonderful world of work at Jasper, Indiana. She worked at the Stewart Hotel as a maid and cook.

Harry met Veronica one Sunday at a dance in Huntingburg, Indiana (seven miles from Jasper). He relates in a letter to his son, Paul, "Your mother invited me to a birthday party. After that, it was a regular occurrence to see me at Jasper on Sunday." They were married on September 30, 1930 in St. Joseph's magnificent church. The priest, Father Basil, asked dad for five dollars since he thought Veronica was an exceptional girl. The usual fee was only two dollars!

After a short time in Dale and Celestine, Indiana, they moved to Jasper where Harry worked in a wood factory, The Hoosier, for 45 years. Along the way, eight children were born: Lillian (1931), Marie (1932), Paul (1934), Anne

(1936), Leona (died at birth, 1938), Victor (1939), Carl-me (1942), and Richard (1945).

Harry and Veronica had a great love for their family and church. They wouldn't miss Mass for anything. St. Joseph's church was truly magnificent; it accommodated 1500 people. It held 12 tons of bells in its steeple which rose up to 112 feet. The pillars contained sixty feet tall poplar trees. German mosaics filled the three apses in front. As a child, I could only be amazed at the Trinity depicted there, surrounded by myriads of saints. Thus, in that milieu, it was no wonder that deep religious sensitivities grew within our family.

The Call: Seminary Life

The parish fostered that piety. There were approximately twenty-five Sisters of Providence from Terre Haute, Indiana who taught there. They were mostly kindly and gentle. For me, there were no memorable conflicts; all the Rooses were very good students. By the time I was in first grade, brother Paul decided to enter the seminary. The nuns there would ask quite often "Who is thinking of going to the seminary (or convent)?" Three of my sisters, Lillian, Marie and Anne entered the high school/college novitiate at St. Mary-of-the-Woods, Indiana. Lillian was there about three and one-half years before leaving to eventually marry at age twenty-two. Marie and Anne were professed as Sisters of Providence and spent about twenty years there, and on teaching missions.

My grade school years bring back thoughts about singing in the men's and boys' choir. We sang *Stille Nacht* (Silent Night) at midnight Mass in German. Another vivid memory was of a kid who was messing my hair from behind me while we were singing. I turned to tell him to quit—with a deft punch to the gut. He tapped me on the shoulder and applied a resounding blow to my nose, a bloody nose resulting! The choir master wasn't too happy!

I remember the priests at St. Joseph's as remarkable and friendly men. I once helped the pastor, Monsignor Wernsing, clear out cedar bushes near the church walks. I was paid big money then, a whopping fifty cents! The priests who were associates often came out of church after Wednesday evening services. They would talk with the seminarians or go for rides for ice cream, treats and other community building activities. Over the years, it was a Jasper phenomenon that for fifteen years running at least one young man was ordained to the priesthood.

My brother, Paul, had been in the seminary seven years before I finished eighth grade, and I asked him what he thought about my going there, too. The answer was, "I don't really know, it is up to you." I asked my parents, my pastor and my eighth grade teacher, Sister Francine, and the answer was the same, "It's up to you." I liked what I saw when we visited my brother. They had wonderful sports fields and gyms. To me, Paul was a hero and already there, so I thought I'd try it out.

Seminary life really didn't seem that difficult. Studies were demanding, and we were ranked each semester. I was usually in the top twenty and occasionally even better, as high as eighth a time or two. I loved the sports and singing. After three years, my brother Richard also made the scene in 1959, so three of us were there. There were lots of rules; demerits were doled out freely. Study hall time was monitored especially closely. Father Damasus was a master at maintaining silence. All he had to do was slightly pull on the side of his scapular (his notepad was there) and look at the person. Instantly, he would get good behavior.

There were about 350 students of high school age at St. Meinrad Archabbey Seminary. When we were ready to depart for summer vacation, we would get the infamous summer deportment spiel. The spiritual director would tell us in chapel that if we went home and dated girls, and liked it—not to return, since this proved we were not fit for the priesthood. If we were to date and didn't like it—we were not to come back because then we were not normal! A healthy sexuality was not discussed. Throughout the seminary years, the Latin phrase was repeated, *Numquam solus cum sola*, "Never a male alone with a female."

It was never really clear to me how I was to handle the sexual part of life, except to leave it alone. For example, to allude to a female was prohibited.

As sophomores in high school, each of us was to pick a song to sing in a class competition. Rather innocently, I chose *Casey Would Waltz with a Strawberry Blond*. After a preliminary presentation, my song was changed to *I Got Shoes, You Got Shoes (All God's Children Got Shoes)*... The song must have been too threatening to our young minds. Any thoughts of girls were to be avoided. We were to avoid visiting Sundays and walking around the terrace checking out the pretty sisters of other students. It seemed as if that was a major part of the fact that out of one hundred five classmates entering in 1956, only five were eventually ordained. I often wondered, *Why me?* How was I able to withstand their charms?

Why? Part of the answer came from our family life. Life was occasionally difficult at home. The hard years came from about 1947 to 1963. Our mother controlled the roost, perhaps reflecting the style of control of her father, Conrad. Basically, mother would control things by pulling from her memory banks her perceived peccadillos of our father. We dared not take his side. I was a lost child, never really opposing her. I was obedient and silent. I was a survivor and that set me up for surviving in the seminary. The adversities of home life formed my ability to adapt and persevere in the seminary.

Little did we know that Mom's mood swings were also due to diabetes, headaches, and paranoia? Since mother always got to a point when she couldn't stand the neighbors, we moved a lot from 1953 to 1955. In my seventh grade year she simply came to school, got us out, books and all. In 1955, my parents met a farmer while they were hunting medicinal plants to sell. In February, we moved to his farm near St. Anthony, Indiana, and finished the school year by April. We had one room at the farm for five of us. The man, John, was a tyrant; we followed his rules. By the fall of 1955, we had moved again to a small house in Jasper along with John, the proprietor. There were five more moves from 1955 to 1963, when John died.

Understanding a healthy sexuality was a challenge. We were a typical German family who cared for each other, but didn't show it overtly or very well. Any real expression of sexuality was forbidden, but the forbidden was enticing. I was a very visually oriented fellow. There was a great desire to *see* the female form. At the age of ten, a neighborhood girl offered to show the boys her wares, but only if I wasn't there. Maybe she knew I couldn't handle it!

However, we shared magazines and stories as young boys do—to see if the rest would get excited. In eighth grade, talk turned to masturbation which was a mystery to me. By sophomore year in the seminary, I knew more and understood why, in the morning, there were lines of us in front of the confessionals! Of course, we were told masturbation was a mortal sin, to be forgiven A.S.A.P., lest we die before confessing and thus go to hell.

To Innsbruck: Theology Years

Amazingly, in 1964, I was chosen by the Diocese of Evansville to go to Innsbruck, Austria for theological studies. I wasn't very sure about going, or perhaps afraid to go. However, a classmate assured me that I could do difficult things. The choice was made. Innsbruck brought a much greater freedom. All classes were in German or Latin with a smattering of other languages distributed in the professors' notes. I learned even better, how to survive in difficult circumstances.

The "sexual conundrum" of healthy male/female friendships remained. I wondered why two men who had reached their last year could leave the seminary. However, over my four years there I began to understand. There were no real relationships with any particular women, but they still remained mightily attractive. The doubts about the celibate lifestyle continued, and questions about myself remained. The church seemed to say that women were the danger, the temptresses—to be avoided—*numquam solus cum sola*, repeated by spiritual directors there.

There were a significant number of times when I went to sleep intending to leave the next day. At daylight, things didn't seem so bad, so I stayed. I believed that I could be a good father, and if so, that was a good sign that I could be a good priest. The roots of celibacy were never really dealt with or understood.

In 1967, a fellow Jasperite, Kenny, celebrated his first Mass in the small German village of Reute. He had relatives there, and there were families who had relatives in Jasper. They took us in at holidays and at times in the summers. The matron there was Clara. Clara had a bakery and store in Reute. (Clara's husband and two brothers-in-law had died in World War II.) The town was bedecked magnificently for Kenny with banners stretching between decorated gates over the streets. A procession led him to the church for his first Mass. A great banquet was held at a local restaurant with family, friends, and townspeople attending.

A year later after my ordination, Clara welcomed me and my family at her home with, "Carl, du bist heim." ("Carl, you are home!") Except for the banners and gateways, the scene was a wonderful repeat of the previous year. My sisters, Anne and Marie, and brothers, Paul and Rich, were honored guests. A sister of a seminarian from the U. S. A. was also there. She was friendly and attractive. We had a moonlight walk; it was cool, and I slipped my hand around her shoulder. That was all! However, I did wonder, I was just ordained, and yet, here were those wonderful feelings for a girl I barely knew.

I did know two families in that village, and they supplied the Braut and Brautigarm, the bride and groom (a custom in the German church at a First Mass)—which all seemed ironic. It seemed a strange sign for a man who was never supposed to marry. The grandmother in one of the families I visited wondered one day, "Why should a man trod the earth alone?" Many times, I wondered that, too.

Priestly Life

Life in the seminary for the twelve years had built up a certain momentum, and spiritual directors spoke of a leap of faith. That is what I took. I returned to the U.S.A. with the hope and intention of being true to the celibate life. There were sexual dragons to be controlled; although in my heart, I didn't believe it was necessary. There was a goodly tension between what I believed and what the church said I must do. One priest told me never to forget the status I had achieved. People expected a warrior, a pied piper to follow, or a jokester with a quip for the moment.

It seemed that people wanted me on saintly pedestal. I felt uncomfortable on any pedestal. I felt I was simply a good human being who was looking for and obedient to a "God with skin on". I found some of that as I taught religion in grade school. One of the joys of my day was to be available to the kids at lunch and on the playground. There, Christ seemed incarnate. On one glorious day, a second grade boy came to the rectory's back door and asked the housekeeper if "Father Carl could please come out to play!"

In the first three years at my first parish, the rock opera, *Jesus Christ, Superstar* came out. It was very attractive to the youth of the parish and to me, since it presented Jesus with a much clearer human face. In the process, we fashioned a liturgy with music from the opera. However, the winds of rumor brought it to the pastor's attention. In a sad moment, he forbade me to use the music in a Eucharist. There seemed to be a growing sense of law *vs.* grace. The pastor opposed what he called "protestant" music. The new Eucharistic prayers he thought were heretical. He was proud that he had never touched the host with his teeth (in 37 years of priesthood)!

The church itself was moving away from times when eating meat on Friday was a death-dealing-sin. I remember some nights coming home late with my brother, Paul, ordained in 1961. He would stop beside the road before midnight to complete his prescribed breviary prayers by the light of the glove compartment. Missing Mass on Sundays was mortally sinful, as was masturbation. The tug of war between the grace-filled choice and seriously violating the law was always there. That was part of the struggle within me, too, as I dealt with celibacy.

Also, I struggled with a sense of self in the priesthood. It seemed that whatever was lacking in seminary preparation would be covered over by God's grace, or even more, the church's simply saying the grace was there. Without teacher preparation classes, I was assigned to teach in grade school and in high school, however, I did not feel adequate to the job. I did back off of high school teaching but continued to teach in the grades. The struggle, for a greater sense of self, was heightened by the expectation that there was a certain mold for all priests.

My rebellions were simple. I bought a ring since my perception was that priests do not wear them. My hair grew to shoulder length in order to proclaim that even with long hair and a beard; I was still the same person. Wearing the collar everywhere didn't seem necessary since it might make others uncomfortable. The use of title was not insisted on, as I was comfortable just being called "Carl."

Part of this desire to express my individuality was influenced by a polarization between older and younger priests in the 1960's and 1970's. Vatican II had happened! Many of the younger priests had experienced their theological training in Innsbruck, Austria, with the freedoms it provided and encouraged. Some professors were men like Hans Kung, Karl Rahner, and Piet Fransen.

The older priests seemed to stress a cherished style of gathering for the closing of 40 hours of adoration and time-honored Stations of the Cross, printed on cards forty years old. I thought it possible to introduce new possibilities by using the Stations of the Cross to center on a theme that said, "When we hurt others, we crucify Christ again." Afterward, my rector spoke with me about a call from a lady who was left in tears because her beloved style had changed. At any rate, I was relieved of doing that particular parish function.

Life in the Diocese

When I returned from my studies in Austria, before my first Mass at home, and even before I was assigned, I was met on the church parking lot in Jasper, Indiana by a priest who presented the idea that further dialogue be encouraged on the new encyclical, *Humanae Vitae*, concerning birth control. Dialogue seemed like a good idea, so I put my name to the intended letter. That priest wrote his own rationale, which I didn't embrace fully, but thought further discussion would be beneficial. I let it stand, but I was branded as a heretic by my new pastor, even before appearing at my first parish.

In my first assignment of three years, I did have the good fortune of living next to Bishop Paul Leibold. Occasionally, he would invite a friend, Mike, and me to an evening meal. It was refreshing to find a bishop who was so friendly and embracing. It seemed good to be able to relate to him simply as a truly good human being. At one meal, conversation centered on marriage work. I showed some interest, and sometime later, and to my great surprise, he asked me to be Commissioner of Family Life, a diocesan wide position. I accepted, although I did not believe I was especially qualified.

We had a Diocesan Council, of elected and assigned clergy and laity, which functioned well at the time. After attending Diocesan and national meetings, I felt I needed further education in marriage matters, so I wrote a rationale for it and passed it on to whoever I thought might be involved or interested. Oddly enough, the letter became something of a source of merriment; one priest commented that I had sent the letter to everyone in the diocese. By then, Bishop Shea had become bishop. I had mentioned teaching Marriage in high school and going for further training, but a more conservative directive was given to me. I was asked to go teach high school theology at Rivet in Vincennes, Indiana, but not to do marriage work at all, not quite what I had in mind!

The trust I felt from Bishop Leibold was gone, and soon thereafter the whole Diocesan Council was gone. Cooperative dialogue was not needed by the new bishop. The bishop said, if he wanted to know something from anyone, he would simply ask them. It seemed to me that we had established a very valuable process of communication. I was sad and disappointed that it ended so abruptly.

In that process, every parish was to have a parish council which in turn related to the Diocesan Council. Many parishes instituted it, but others held back. At a meeting of all diocesan priests, I had the temerity to suggest a system for compliance. I proposed that the diocese appoint a "Diocesan Bouncer" who would visit all the parishes in the diocese to see about their progress. If nothing had been done, the visitor would simply tack the Ace of Spades to their door, which meant that they had a certain amount of time to comply, or he would return!

Perhaps the other priests thought that I wanted to be the Diocesan Bouncer. Shortly after my statement (which I meant to be taken lightly), I got a reputation as being a belligerent bully, a complainer, a not very dedicated priest, and one who thought only of himself. I had always thought of myself as a good, kind, gentle, and caring person.

In those days, there was a Diocesan Retreat led by a wise Trappist priest, Father Vince Dwyer. He told a story about how the Trappist monks loaded their manure. Their wondrous system had the cows living on the upper story of the barn. All the manure would be piled in the center over a trapdoor. When it was time to load, they would simply back their wagon onto the lower floor.

They would pull the release on the door, and presto, the manure would fall on the wagon. His point was that people were mostly negative toward one another, and unloaded on each other.

However, there was often a point in their lives when they felt good about themselves, but they couldn't stand it, so they pulled the release on themselves. It seemed odd that priests who had so much to be positive about often dumped on each other. My hope was to learn not to dump on others, or let myself be dumped upon. There grew within me a desire to find some balance in this celibate lifestyle.

Over the years, some really good and valuable men had chosen to leave the priesthood. It seemed a shame to me that the church considered their state a sinful one, as though they were traitors and had abandoned their calling. I knew them basically as good and talented people whose loss was saddening and tragic. One of those who left was my younger brother, Richard. He was ordained in Rome at Christmas time, 1970. He was a free spirited young man who brought a great deal of energy and creativity to the priestly life style. He did not fit the priestly mold at the time. He did have a significant relation with a young woman. By 1972, he had decided to marry her and needed to exit the priesthood. There was no longer room for him. He had taught at a high school for a year, but even his salary was withdrawn from him.

Again, it seemed to present the battle between law and grace.

In 1974, a number of priests and laity formed a study group in the diocese to discuss the problem of so many priests leaving. A working paper was fashioned concerning the face of ministry at the time. Two significant conclusions were reached. First, that we continue to recognize those who had left as our brothers in Christ, and work to restore them as valuable members of the church. We hoped to invite them back to work in the priesthood. The Priests' Senate did approve the study, and set a time to review it at a priests' retreat.

My memory is that the study was well received. In fact, a priest in his nineties found no problem in inviting them back. However, nothing came of it. The second conclusion was that the women of the church were valued members of the church, and that we needed to work toward the possibility of their ordination. Again nothing really came of this.

Each year when the personnel committee would meet, they would go over a demographics sheet about our issues. We called it a "dream sheet". It contained the hopes and desires of the priests about their future. By about 1976, I had become convinced that the church needed to take a fresh look at the whole idea of mandatory celibacy. Personally, I expressed a desire to dialogue about the whole issue. I believed that celibacy was a true injustice for many and that it needed to be faced more directly. No one ever came to me, or called me concerning my expressed doubts.

It seemed that the topic of celibacy was not to be dealt with. I remembered a little vignette about a diocese where a priest would be suspended if he skied from a boat in which a woman was riding, and he was also suspended if he rode in a boat from which a woman was skiing. We were never to ride in a car with a woman unless another person was there, and the woman was to sit in the back seat. The history of celibacy seemed questionable as a viable lifestyle.

Early in church history even with St. Jerome, to remain a virgin was the highest road to perfection and thus to heaven. By the 12th century, married priests were gone, perhaps largely due to church properties being inherited by their children. Church theology tended to say that there was one road to follow. St. Augustine saw the issue as a battle between good and evil, between the flesh and the spirit. The flesh lost.

Even Thomas Aquinas said that loving someone physically (love making) was a permissible venial sin since the good that it could produce was the creation of another human being. It seemed to me that there still could be a choice to make.

I wondered if celibacy was a burden simply to be accepted. I wondered if obedience simply meant—to give in blindly to celibacy, or if we didn't have a right to follow what we deemed as *reasonable*. Was loving another person a "good-conscience" solution that we could make and not be condemned for it by Christ?

In doing some marriage work as a parish priest, I had dealt with those I considered "salt-of-the-earth" kinds of people. They were good and simple, holy types caught within the marriage laws of the church. With one good man, I discussed the good-conscience possibilities, that if his conscience was clear, even if the church could not give him a dispensation, he could attend Mass and even receive communion. He had absented himself from the Eucharist for many years as not worthy.

Another man had been denied three times by the marriage tribunal. He was in a fourth marriage, and as I listened to him, it seemed as though he had as good a chance as anyone to get an annulment. We refiled his case, and thankfully he got his annulment. It did seem true that God's first and greatest response to us is mercy.

As I lived out my priesthood, I did feel a bit like David appreciating the beauty of Bathsheba from afar. I did admire many women and had good relationships with them along the years. In each of the relationships, I did care about them and love them. I had witnessed my brother's marriage and family life. I knew him to be a man of great goodness and integrity. Surely, God knew him and loved him as much as anyone else, married or not!

I believed that I need not deny the truly human side of myself. Sexuality was not to be faced with fear, but embraced fearlessly. A short story is told about a monk who was given the task of translating their ancient tomes. He worked faithfully for years by dim candlelight. One day another brother came to see him, and found him weeping copiously. He asked, "Why the tears?" The little monk sighed, "The word was actually *celebrate!*"

It seems to me that I was looking for a wholesome, holy style to celebrate my life joyfully, to celebrate it within the Roman Catholic system, but never found the life I needed. Also, I did not see any real empowerment in the priests around me. I did not see the joy I thought celibacy should bring. I did begin to understand priests much more compassionately. We were all limited human beings trying to do the best we could with what we had.

There were those priests who did struggle with my issues. There was especially a "fearsome foursome" who played lots of golf together, or who met for Monday Night Football. They did understand my desire for a close relationship. We struggled with church attitudes, and even the suggested prohibitions that we have no dealings with our brother priests who had left. Since my brother was one of them, I felt I could hardly comply.

One day I did share with my golfer buddies that I intended to write Bishop Shea about my desire to leave and marry. I did mention how difficult the lifestyle had been over the sixteen years (eventually nineteen). My brother priests tried to persuade me not to send the letter, as it would be used against me. However it was sent, and in a conference with the bishop, he mentioned how I had been "sitting the fence for sixteen years". He stated that my real trouble was that I was just selfish. He did seem to say that he knew better what I needed for my life, and that he would, "ask a friend of mine to pray for you." He also said that her prayers were almost always heard.

However, I still found the need for a close relationship to be paramount. There was a great need or desire simply to be close to someone, to be held by someone. That person, Michelle Kate Johnson, came into my life in 1984, just before she went to Panama, as a mission volunteer, and I went to Indiana University to work on a degree in counseling. A time with the military chaplaincy followed, as I was a Captain (chaplain) in the Indiana National Guard.

We maintained some contact by letter, and had our first real date in the summer of 1985. I did find Michelle to be all I hoped for in a spouse. Our relationship developed over the next two years. I resigned my pastorate in July of 1987, and we were married at St. Philip's Episcopal Church in Indianapolis. My brother, Richard, witnessed the vows on October 17, 1987. Over the last twenty five years, I have, indeed, found the embrace of a loving God in and through Michelle, and through our son, Carlos, adopted in September, 1997.

Wrapping It All Up

In conclusion, these are my experiences of a search for truth in life. Each person has their own truth, how they see life. There are simply many understandings. Others, no doubt, see all this differently. This past summer, my sister, Lillian was at a garage sale in Jasper, where she met a man with connections to a wealthy family. She told him who she was, Lillian Roos. He commented, "Ah, yes. I know the Rooses. They were dirt poor!"

That was his view or assessment from afar, but if he really knew our family, he would also have realized the vast riches we represented. Certainly, we began with no great wealth materially, but we achieved a lot, as the talented and creative individuals that we are—even amazing ourselves in the process, a group of well-read, widely traveled and educated siblings.

Lillian was always an excellent student. She left the convent as a college junior, and married a local army veteran and farmer. They had thirteen bright and healthy children. Lillian, herself, has been a good, loving, and faithful mother and Christian person. Her wisdom and wealth is far beyond calculation.

Marie also entered the convent with Lillian, and was professed as a Sister of Providence. She taught faithfully for twenty years. After she left the "Woods", she achieved a Ph.D. in Education, and taught as a Teacher-trainer for thirty years in colleges around the country. She is a gracious, gentle, and multi-talented, good Christian woman.

My brother, Paul, had the nick name of *Rock*. He was a rock of faith for us all, and a most gracious and faithful priest of forty-four years. He completed his Masters in Theology at St. Meinrad during the summer of 1972. He died a holy death in 2005 with his arms raised while speaking what sounded like the word, "heaven".

Anne is four years Marie's junior and was persuaded by her teachers to go to the Juniorate at St. Mary-of-the-Woods. She was also professed as a sister and taught for twenty years. After she departed the "Woods", she taught for another twenty-five years with a Masters Plus Thirty designation. She was once named "Teacher of the Year" in the Indianapolis (Indiana) Perry Township Public Schools. She is also a dedicated, creative, joyous, and faithful Christian.

Victor found his niche in sports with All-State honors in high school, and little All-American honors in college. He was named to a national All Star team. He was invited to two professional football camps. He also earned a Masters Plus Thirty, and taught in high schools for forty-one years while coaching football, wrestling, and golf. Along with his wife, Betty, he has been a good servant in the churches he attended, as well as a loving father to his two children.

Richard excelled in his studies, especially at St. Meinrad Seminary. He was asked to complete his studies in Theology in Rome. He completed the Licentiate there. He even tried rugby and excelled enough to be acclaimed, *Roccia (The Rock)*. He returned to the Evansville, Indiana Diocese, and taught for a year before deciding to marry in 1972. One of the issues for me was that I knew him to be an extremely intelligent, holy, wholesome, and talented priest. My family and I could certainly not understand how God would no longer love him, or condemn him.

I, myself, completed a Masters in Theology, plus a Masters in Counseling with a double major in Adult Education. In response to the call to serve God's people, I have ministered as a priest and teacher in the Roman Catholic and The Episcopal Church for over forty years.

As a priest and patriot, I served as a chaplain with the rank of Major in the United States Army National Guard. I have served my local community as a counselor both in clinical settings and during times of natural disaster. I believe that I have been a faithful husband, father, brother and son, offering loving care and support to my family.

This list of achievements by the family is meant to point out how truly rich our family was and became, and what a great influence the family had on me. Our entire family of siblings studied and continues to study actively Theology, Philosophy, and Family Life, and is committed to Christ's values and way of life.

My church family also influenced greatly the persons we became. Personally, I am extremely grateful for the place the church played in the development of my faith life, and I realize, too, how generous the church was in our support in the seminary and in the superb education we received. After I left the Roman Catholic ministry in 1987, what I missed most were my friends, and other good relationships, when they met as a group. I felt a void in my life. I still wanted to be there, however, that whole support system was suddenly gone. Priestly friends were discouraged from validating a priest who had chosen to marry. I believe that what I was looking for was what the people of India called *Namaste*, the honoring or affirming of the person in his or her very being.

I continued to appreciate and love the Roman Catholic Church. There really was no problem with any doctrine. Mostly, I believe that priests should be free to marry, and still be accepted within the church. It was not my intent to offend anyone. I certainly did not believe that I was a traitor to the church. After leaving, I was accepted as a priest in The Episcopal Church. I served several parishes from 1990 to 2005, and retired due to ill health. I continue to serve as I am able.

Finally, I am sorry if I hurt anyone in my relationships. If there were room for me, I might have returned as a priest. I do believe that I remained faithful to my priestly and married vocations. Jesus Christ remains the center of my life, my heart, and my mind. I continue the search for a full life in our loving God whom Jesus called, *ABBA*. Indeed, God is love!

*   *   *   *   *

Many other heartwarming tales could be told of so many supportive and Christ-centered folks who graced my life. I acknowledge them with deep gratitude for the unconditional love they gave.

Thanks especially to my wife Michelle for interpreting and typing my scribbling, and to my sister, Anne who proofread and edited these efforts.

Early Engagement–

Inevitable Separation

Phillip Field

Before I tell my story, a few items should be addressed. First of all, my intentions are threefold: a) to paint a complete picture as to who I was and why I eventually became disillusioned and abandoned my lifelong dream of being "a priest forever;" b) through this clarification, to help create a healthier Church for the days ahead, and c) in no way to take issue with the priesthood itself, only in its administration and in its practice.

A key issue of concern, (and often, pain) is the fact that the Church has operated as though its "realm" is entirely untouchable and its Canon Law is supreme. The thousands of canons (laws) are intended to regulate most every aspect of Catholic life. Too often, the Church ignores the fact that its canons are subject to natural law, individual and natural rights, and, as the Church has come to experience, some secular laws (e.g. sexual abuse of children).

Over a period of fifteen years, beginning in seminary, I had to face my own limitations and those of a warped structure and dictatorial system, ultimately based upon fear.

If ignorance is truly bliss, I blissfully pursued my dream of being a priest without complete knowledge of its parameters within the institutional Church.

As I unfold my story, I draw a parallel between my relationship with the institutional priesthood and what transpires in any and all love relationships. *Mine was such a relationship in all its phases, from introduction all the way through to separation.*

My Story

It was September in Kentucky. My sister, a recent high school graduate, had just entered the Sisters of Charity of Nazareth. For years we had prayed the family rosary every night, with Mother leading each decade praying for "the children to have religious vocations, the conversion of Russia, and for all those we should pray for." This time next September, my two remaining brothers would enter the seminary; one at seventeen, one at thirteen. I can only painfully imagine my Dad, an accountant by profession, picturing his sons growing into manhood and helping make our small farm a success.

His first and second born sons, my brothers, whom I never knew, were already dead. One son had died of leukemia at four and the other son drowned at twelve, when Mother was pregnant with me. I wonder if, having lost her first two children, Mother might have made a pact with God, "If You let my remaining children live, dear Lord, I'll give them all back to You." Three of us became priests and my two sisters, nuns.

In so many other ways, our family was a typical Catholic family in the Owensboro Diocese of Western Kentucky. We attended 8:30 Sunday morning Mass at St. Stephen's Cathedral, ate Mom's delicious fried chicken dinner at noon, and visited cousins, or they us, in the afternoon. We didn't do any work because of the Third Commandment; "Keep holy the Sabbath."

Religion and Church played a cardinal position in our lives, with the pinpoint and ever-present focus being to "save your soul" and "be pleasing to God."

I was an inquisitive boy, who loved the out-of-doors. At Christmas time, I would often go to our hills, gather some evergreen, wild sumac, and ground pine to decorate the homestead. In the seventh and eighth grades I was fond of a pretty and demur classmate, Connie. This fact was my very top secret. Having a girlfriend was not acceptable to my mother, who guarded us brothers from female contact. This reality set me further apart even before I joined. The priest-hood was a dream I had embraced for some years as the highest possible vocation for a boy to have. At fourteen, I entered a minor seminary, St. Mary's College, for high school and college.

Our family was very close-knit and my parents were very loving towards us, but had little show of affection for each another. We children worked and played around the homestead. Our daily routine may have included: feeding the 500 chickens, hoeing the garden, playing marbles, milking the cows, playing basketball, mowing the grass, gathering the eggs for market, etc. I was truly a homebody; so, entering the seminary with twelve years of study until ordination felt like a goal on a distant, foggy horizon; but it was the accepted routine for those who entered after grade school: four years of high school, four years of college, and four years theology.

Even though I had two brothers already in the seminary, being away from my parents and my home during all my teen years predictably arrested a significant part of my normal maturation. This reality was exacerbated by being taught by an all-male, celibate faculty for twelve years, with no female contact three-fourths of the year. Then, it was only with relatives.

In the dorm at night, while others slept, my own nostalgic yearnings called me to the window sill of a tall, open fourth floor window. I sat on the sill with my feet resting outside on a broad ledge, and surveyed the farmland, dotted with homes lit with lights of family warmth. Tangible feelings of loneliness enveloped me. The drone of a single plane, high in the night sky, would often be the only sound. At times I sought solace from the moon, which connected me to home, knowing that my parents would be looking at that same moon.

On several occasions, when returning home from seminary and reaching the top of the driveway, I stepped out of the car and before taking another step, knelt and kissed the home ground. Coming home at the end of May was total joy! Anticipating three months of family life seemed to make it all worthwhile. But, the summer flew by: September closed in and the dread returned. When my brother (three years ahead) had moved on to a seminary in Baltimore, leaving me the only remaining brother at St. Mary's, my loneliness was magnified.

Christmas was our only time off campus for nine months. Going back in early January, with no breaks until the end of May, with mid-term exams facing us within two weeks, was a particularly challenging time for me. And, each year, some friends didn't return after the break.

Yet, the years came and went, and I endured eight years in minor seminary, with endless exams, tests, and scrutinies in pursuit of my dream. *It was a time of discovery and exploration in my relationship with the priesthood of Christ.*

The final four years of studies at St.Maur's Priory, a seminary run by the Benedictines in a former Shaker settlement, became the greatest challenge to my vocation. The buildings were situated on flat non-descript farmland. Our basketball "gym" was in the hayloft of a barn.

Here we were in the prime of our manhood, relegated to a godforsaken place, twelve miles from Bowling Green, Kentucky. For recreation we could walk down a side road, play basketball, or play pool on a broken down table. All presuming you could find others to join you. In total, there were thirty-five, non-Benedictine men scattered through the four theology classes. It was a stark existence both physically, emotionally, and theologically, for these were the days of Vatican Council II (1962-1965). This Council, called by Pope John XXIII, brought in the welcomed winds of change to an out-of-touch institution. Yet, the teachers were still locked into the mindset of Vatican I of the 1870s.

Most of the faculty were not equipped either psychologically or academically to teach or properly administer an institution of theology. This four-year exposure to priests, dedicated to training "other Christs" yet unable to rise to the task, clearly began the long process of my disillusionment between what I sought and what reality was actually in store for me.

Much of what urged me on was the concurrent Second Vatican Council in Rome and classmates who were, like me, reading theologians such as; Teilhard de Chardin, Karl Rahner, and Edward Schillebeeckx, all of whom promoted a Scripturally-based theology, which fearlessly embraced humanity with love and respect. Scholars and theologians such as these gave us hope beyond the desolate classroom. It helped us hold on despite our feelings of despondency.

St. Maur's was a small seminary connected to a Benedictine Priory. Each spring it became a maddening and frightening guessing game as to whom, and under what pretext, the faculty would hold back (clip) those preparing for Minor or Major Orders. The four Minor and two Major Orders were the mandatory steps prior to ordination to the Holy Order of Priesthood. One man was "clipped" from the Minor Orders of Porter & Lector because he had headaches. A third-year theologian was held back from the Major Order of Sub-deaconate because: "You read too many (theology) books." Then, inexplicably, they said: "We don't think you read what you say you read."

I was clipped from Sub-deaconate that same Spring, because they informed me: "You ask too many questions in class." Their other reason was: "The faculty doesn't think you like them." While raising up the inestimable value of the sacred Sacrament of Holy Orders, they used the denial of these sacred Orders as a way to convey some petty misgiving or assert their authority.

We seminarians knew one another far better than they knew us. Our assessment of one another was based on every day contact, in and out of the classroom, chapel, and recreation. At the same time we each had other seminary professors with which to compare this faculty. While my eight previous years at St. Mary's were often underscored with loneliness, the priest faculty at St. Maur's left me totally determined to be different from them. I am aware now, *these four years, ending with the reception of the Deaconate, were a time of engagement in my relationship with the priesthood. A rocky road, but the relationship survived.*

*   *   *   *   *

On the First Day of May, I was ordained a priest of Jesus Christ according to the Order of Melchizedek! My long held dream, now a reality. I designed a beautiful multicolored, cloisonne chalice. My ordination cards were inscribed with: *"Joy is the most infallible sign of the presence of God."* (Leon Bloy) For me, the pursuit of beauty and joy had become dual pathways to God.

The glow of those early months gradually dimmed. The camaraderie, loyalty, and deep friendship bonds of the seminary faded into a treasured memory. I was moved from my first assignment in Owensboro, where there were four resident priests, after a short, three months stint. In any other milieu, this would have been seen as a promotion. Instead, in my new assignment I was spending every meal, every day and evening with a pastor I had never met before, who was over twice my age. He administered sacraments, attended the men's club card parties, did crossword puzzles, and watched television. Few parishioners ventured onto the rectory porch; fewer still made it inside.

There was little to no conversation during meals or counting collections, the two times we were together. The Pastor required little social interaction except with his older sister, who was our housekeeper and lived in the rectory. Apparently, this worked fine for him, but did not come close to my idea of the priest in society. The town had a small Catholic hospital, operated by the Sisters of Mercy and in their chapel I celebrated Mass every morning.

The four sisters and three or four lay women came each morning. Sister Mary Virginia, the hospital administrator, became a dear friend. She provided support, conversation, and safety because she was twenty years older than I. After Mass and breakfast, I would visit the sick and then we might talk in her office for awhile. She played an important role in normalizing my life.

About the same time, a young sister and teacher at St. Vincent's High School came into my life via her Superior, Sister John Lynette, who came to me and asked me to spend time with this sister. She was worried because she had no one her age and was theologically more astute than the other nuns in the convent. This paralleled my situation, so I willingly got to know her. We shared all that was being written and done in the post-Vatican II days. She wrote poetry and taught English literature, two of my favorite topics.

We became lifelong friends. I was twenty-six years old and the experience of having a woman friend opened me to a previously untraveled pathway to the love of God. It was a turning point in my understanding of how God reveals Him/Herself through relationships. I became less wary of women. And, the hovering sense of loneliness was held at bay.

"You don't act like a priest," people would say to me. I always responded (whether the remark was meant as a put down, a compliment, or only an observation) with "Thank you;" hoping to give witness to a new and different type of priest. I was going to be "all things to all men" (sic). I strove to be approachable, empathic, and reverent. I valued celebrating Mass and the Sacraments above all. I always refused to adhere to the norm of the day and "say" a twenty-minute Mass. I gave a homily at each and every Mass.

In administering God's forgiveness in the Sacrament of Reconciliation, I took time with each person. Their penances were designed to counterbalance their grievance. I often gave some action to help them in their harried life, like spending fifteen minutes in solitude walking in the woods. One Saturday evening after hearing confessions, a man approached and said, "They told me to tell you if you preached on race relations again they would kill you." I chuckled. Whereupon, he said, "Oh, I wouldn't laugh, they're deadly serious." I said, "Well, tell them to be sure to come to Mass tomorrow morning." Sunday, having changed my sermon to illustrate the pulpit was not "for sale," the sermon focused on the equality of the races and the sin of racism.

A similar threat, though from a different source, was given to me two years later in Owensboro.

In four years, I taught in three high schools, five grade schools, sponsored several youth Gospel-action groups, and was a member of a team conducting retreats for juniors and seniors, giving me an opportunity to influence young lives. I prize those events and years and hope they benefited as much as did I in working to make "Thy Kingdom come." Today, encounters with former students recounting an impact I had on their lives, brings me comfort and satisfaction. These were the first seasons of consummation; my relationship with the priesthood was rich.

However, my parish assignments were another story - not smooth and rosy. In several parishes of one county where I was stationed, the African American parishioners sat in the last pews, and received Holy Communion last. At the same time, for one parish's summer barbeque-fund raiser (held on parish grounds), the African Americans were quarantined on the opposite side of a farm fence, strewn across the middle of the eating area, which separated the Black from the White parishioners.

At one Forty Hours (a yearly event held to honor Jesus' presence in the Eucharist), I witnessed one of the local pastors, during the clergy dinner, with disgusting fanfare, mock the Black ministers' and morticians' manner of conducting their funerals. This was received with much laughter and no admonitions. The priests and our Bishop sat there unfazed.

Two weeks later when meeting with the bishop, I recalled the state of affairs across the county and brought up this ugly incident. The bishop responded with; "Oh, Father, they were just joking!"

He easily dismissed these institutional sins. I then felt compelled to further illustrate how discriminative and sinful things were in the diocese. So, I told the bishop of a recent incident involving my pastor, where I was the assistant.

One afternoon, the Pastor answered the doorbell, which rang from the side porch. About fifteen seconds later, when I arrived on the scene, I saw Marvin, an African American teen, walking away and already more than sixty yards from the rectory. I presumed Marvin could not have rung the bell since he was too far away, so I asked the Pastor, "Was there someone at the door?"

"Yeah, that nigger."

I was speechless, but finally gulped and found my voice, "What did he want?"

The pastor gave a muffled chuckle and said, "He wanted to become a Catholic."

I sat silently and watched as the Bishop became white, as he angrily grappled with this outrageous event. His response was to stab his index finger down onto the desktop between us and say, "Father Field, that did not happen!"

Without a doubt, the actions of many of the priests were scandalous and the diocese needed to right itself. I had waited too long to act. But, at last I did the right thing. I reached out to the Rome-appointed successor to the Apostles, the Bishop, and came away totally empty. Now, where was I to turn?

The priesthood was still there, but the relationship had taken a serious hit. Technically, the practice of the priesthood does not exist outside of the structure. So, in reality, if one wishes to actively participate in the priesthood, then it must be within the administrative structure of the Church. But, the priest himself remains, for "once a priest, always a priest."

Not long after that, I was transferred to an Owensboro parish, while the previous Pastor, who turned away a young man seeking Baptism, remained in place to continue his discriminating actions without any civil or spiritual accountability.

Soon after my arrival in Owensboro, one of the lay pillars of this parish, Russell, asked me what was wrong with his Pastor. He recounted how shocked he was that his Pastor had hung up on him, when Russell, asked to speak to me. The Pastor never considered this was my hometown, and some of the pillars of "his" church were also friends of mine.

As the days passed, the Pastor's attitude became more personal and hardened. He was rude to youth and others coming for counseling, discounting this as a natural outgrowth of my teaching part-time at Owensboro Catholic High. He told me, "None of 'your people' are welcome here. You'll have to meet with them somewhere else."

I began giving instructions and counseling in nearby restaurants or over at the teachers' lounge in the parish grade school. Soon, he upped the ante and decided to prevent all incoming and outgoing phone calls, by taking the phone off the hook in his room at 10:00 p.m. every night. This, of course, made both of us unavailable, as there was only one parish line. Everyone knew and expected their priests to be available to bring help, support, or the Sacraments in times of crisis, regardless of the hour.

After a short time, I decided to remedy the problem by having a separate phone put in my room. It was to have a distinctive ring, so there would be no confusion when it rang, and would not bother him, thus allowing me to make personal calls and making a priest available to respond to sick calls, accidents, and other emergencies. The following morning when the Pastor discovered the new phone, we had a short give and take as I explained my reasoning and that the parish would not be out a dime. He said he was going to see the Bishop at the Chancery, a hundred yards away. The Bishop called me and said to have the phone removed and then come over to see him.

This I did. In short order, he gave me five options. They were: a) suspension (this is the strictest reprimand short of being defrocked; b) Via Coeli (a monastery in New Mexico for wayward priests); c) a priest psychiatrist at the Trappist Monastery of Gethsemani; d) Our Lady of Peace in Louisville; or e) a psychiatrist of my own choice.

For some long moments, I was speechless. Eventually, I said, "All of this because I had a phone installed?"

He responded, "Oh, the phone has nothing to do with it. It's obvious you are losing your priesthood, and I'm going to save it for you."

Pondering this, I thought; *maybe I'm totally missing something; my Bishop is telling me I'm losing my priesthood, my dream.* So, I asked, "Bishop, I'm unaware I'm losing my priesthood, how do you know I am?"

"Father, there are three signs; a) you are too close to your family; b) you are too close to your classmates; and, c) teenagers like you."

He was right about the teenagers, I let that ride. However, I said, "In the Christian Family Movement (CFM), strong family ties are to be emulated." Then I said, "And, why do you think I am too close to my classmates?"

He said, "Yesterday, you mentioned John Sisk's name and you should have forgotten him a long time ago." (John was from the Albany, New York diocese and I'd had no contact with him since we left the seminary to be ordained over two years ago).

The Bishop concluded, "Go pack and I will let you know what's to happen."

I did just that and lived out of my suitcase in that rectory for the next seven months.

In the meantime, I celebrated Mass, heard confessions, buried parishioners, conducted weddings, counseled people, and gave instructions in the faith. Even though I "was losing my priesthood," I was allowed to fully function in peoples' quest for comfort and salvation. All in the very same parish and rectory.

It was now December. I had been at the parish since late August. Sometime later, though the cold spell between us was still below freezing, I approached the Pastor with what I had finally surmised about his being intolerable, from day one.

I asked, if it was because, he made bravado statements to my previous pastor while playing poker, 'If he were **my** assistant...I'd clip his wings!' Then, the clergy changes came out and there I was in 'your house.'"

I credit the pastor for not ducking or denying my conclusion. He agreed that was exactly what had been behind this whole bloody mess. In retrospect, some of his behavior may have been exacerbated by the fact that he was worried about his heart.

In June, seven months later at the time of clergy reassignments, I was assigned to St. Mary's Parish in Whitesville. But the pastor, who shirked his night time responsibilities to his parishioners, remained untouched.

At Whitesville, Father Charlie Fischer, a great man and beloved pastor, had one house rule; <u>be on time for Mass.</u> My fifteen months there were what I had always presumed a truly functioning rectory would be. I celebrated the early weekday Mass, alternated with Charlie preaching Sundays, taught religion at Trinity High and St. Mary's Grade School, celebrated Mass with the Sisters at the parish convent, made friends with the three Extension Volunteers who lived in a parish house, started the youth "Yes Group," (who helped me visit the parish shut-ins), prayed and worked with a dedicated

Legion of Mary, and attended to all things regular to priestly ministry: baptisms, instructions, anointings, weddings, and funerals.

The relationship had received the healing oil of friendship and common sense.

Then, wishing to have some solidarity with my older brother, who had been forced to take a year's leave of absence, I joined the International Mission Society for a five year stint. I signed up to work in Mexico and traveled to Pusan, Korea for seven weeks, to be trained in the proper way to minister to the poor. But, just prior to leaving for the mission in Mexico City, the lone anchor priest there, John Robinson, OSB, pulled up stakes, the mission folded, and my missionary aspirations ended. However, I was still a priest of the Owensboro Diocese. And, though totally available for a parish assignment, I received no salary from the diocese, despite it being a requirement of Canon Law and having received total permission to join the mission field. Because I had no income, I had to live with my parents.

After a few weeks, I wrote the Bishop and then spoke with him. He said he would assign me, but didn't. Finally, I met with him at his residence on a Sunday. He admitted that his failure to give me an assignment was confessional matter for him. Yet, I received no assignment for another two months. At our meeting, he asked, "Do you need money, Father?" He opened his wallet and offered me ten dollars. Here I was a priest, thirty-one years of age, with my parents supporting me and he offers me a ten.

Since it was more and more obvious this was the way it was and would be, my disillusionment was eroding my life long, deeply rooted trust in church hierarchy. Did my relationship with my dream hang in the balance? My naïveté, with a major slow-to-learn bent, was showing. *In this relationship with the priesthood, I had been cheated on and had been too blind to see it.*

Meanwhile, the war in Vietnam was still very hot with no end in sight. The Catholic bishops of South Vietnam had said to the US government, "For God's sake, stop!"

Before he was assassinated, the Reverend M.L. King had spoken strongly against the war. How could we just let it continue in silence? I felt it my responsibility to actively protest against the war. My non-violent heroes were: Jesus (above all), Mohandas Gandhi, Martin Luther King, Dorothy Day, and Bishop Oscar Romero. So, following their lead, my brother and I, in conjunction with a national anti-war push for Lent, organized The Forty Day Peace Committee, a group of Catholics: religious sisters and lay people.

We passed out flyers, wrote letters, provided draft counseling, motored to Washington several times, often picketed the Federal Building in downtown Owensboro, and held a prayer service on its steps every Sunday evening for three years. These were a remarkable group of Christians (mostly Catholic) who were dedicated to carrying out the peace message of Jesus. At the same time, I was attending to all of my parish work (Blessed Mother in Owensboro).

Though my Pastor never voiced any displeasure with my anti-war involvement, perhaps predictably by now, I was transferred again, this time to St. John's at Sunfish. All transfers come from the Bishop. This parish, because of its remoteness, was considered the Siberia of the diocese. I was given one week to wind up all work, vacate the parish premises, and move to Sunfish. I was thirty-three years old.

The sudden transfer of a priest (for no apparent reason) accomplishes three things: a) it satisfies the chancery/bishop; for there is one less "headache"; b) causes parishioners and the public to question, guess, or gossip about what "Father" had done wrong; and, c) leaves the work started by the priest (e.g. catechetical instructions, marriage preparation, divorce prevention, unwanted pregnancy, personal spirituality, etc.) in a vacuum with little concern for the plight of the bewildered and abandoned flock.

Knowing why I had been transferred, made it difficult for me to go quietly, but I did, with one caveat; the next time I move it will be at a time and place of my own choosing.

I arrived at Sunfish and drove up the half-mile, tree-lined driveway leading to the white frame, steepled church. It was an idyllic setting and perfect for a non-social individual or a recluse, which I, of course, was not. The rectory was about twenty yards from the church. The nights were the darkest I had ever experienced. On clear nights, I found the church by going to where the steeple's outline obstructed the stars. On non-moonlit, cloudy nights, I would walk in the church's direction, arms extended before me, to find the structure. Eventually, I realized I could walk out the rectory's front door, watch to my left, and use the light of the sanctuary lamp showing through the gap between the two front doors, and let the red glow act as a pathfinder.

The people of Sunfish embraced me as one of their own. I was invited to their homes regularly for dinner and family celebrations, which eased my feelings of isolation. After three straight years of my homilies, with no respite, they had heard most every thought of mine more than once.

After three years (as administrator, not pastor) at St. John's in Sunfish, with both Bishops' approval, I took a position with Catholic Charities across the Ohio River, in the Evansville, Indiana Diocese. It was not a permanent arrangement. I wished to work in a social justice ministry and was convinced, if I didn't transfer myself, I could easily have been left out there for the rest of my priestly days. I was thirty-six years old.

Aside: During these years, Bishop Dozier, of the Memphis Diocese, offered me a position. He said I could work anywhere in the United States and he would pay my salary so long as I "was not behind a desk." I probably should have accepted.

Once in Evansville, I worked full time at Catholic Charities, much of it with a Benedictine Sister, who was also committed to social justice ministry. I lived at the Sarto Retreat Center and celebrated Mass and preached in nineteen parishes throughout the diocese, bringing me into contact with many of the clergy. I served on two committees of the Priests Senate. Some of my time involved working with a program at The Little Sisters of the Poor's Home for the Aged, in one of their outreach programs.

This involved live-alone, elderly city residents, for whom I would provide rides to and from Little Sisters for lunch and a program, bingo, or a game. This program was the brain child of the Director of Activities, a beautiful lay woman, who, six years later would become my wife. With our mutual interest in the elderly and other religious and social issues, we became good friends.

Near this same time, my brother, as a priest, entered the spring Democrat primary for the U.S. Congress. It was an intense fifty-eight day run, from March until May. One hundred people volunteered and together we totally pursued this goal. Given the condensed time frame, we needed astute, clear thinkers, who knew the issues, and had great organizational skills. My future wife became a key member of the Steering Committee. Out of six potential candidates for the Democrat Primary, my brother came in second, though he was the last one to "toss his hat in the ring."

Meanwhile, as part of my job while still at Charities, I scheduled workshops on peace and justice issues and attended national conferences. One conference, the First Women's Ordination Conference in 1977 in the city of Detroit, had profound and far reaching effects on me. It was electric and vibrated with the energy and the deep spirituality of these women. I had a surge of hope. Ordained women could save the Church with their Christ-like Spirit, their deep and advanced theology, their compassion, and their willingness to forgive.

Twice, Sandra Boston, a phenomenal trainer from the Philadelphia Life Center, came for several days to engage and train our lay, sister, and clergy leaders in some of the justice issues of the day. During these visits, she voiced to me her total dismay at the Catholic Church's ban of women from the priesthood of Christ. I, of course, gave all the canned answers. All the while I danced around the issue, I could hear the hollowness and illogic of my responses.

Sandra was not a Catholic, but led an extremely committed and Christian lifestyle. Her insights and reasoning ripped away any veiled attempt, which had kept me from facing the Church's discriminatory practice. As days went by, I meditated upon her words and, over time, realized this was tantamount to the Church banning African Americans from the priesthood. This parallel stopped the music and I could no longer continue my dance of denial that the Church's stance of categorically discriminating against women was institutional sin.

My relationship with the institutional priesthood was, no doubt, under serious duress.

After being in the Evansville Diocese for two years, the position at Catholic Charities was discontinued. I could return to the Owensboro Diocese or stay as an independent priest and be available for weekend duty when asked. I opted to stay and got a job with Head Start as Social Services Coordinator. I chose this path because I knew the situation in the Owensboro Diocese and its Bishop had not changed. I chose to protect myself from this toxic environment and stay away.

But, the monumental question lingered; could I remain as an "official" of this Institution? It had been and was a privileged position, in society at large, especially within the Catholic world. I wanted to believe in the possibility Rome would change her mind and welcome sacramentally baptized and confirmed women into the priesthood. Women, with their gifts, abilities, and graces, were sorely needed amidst the all-male clergy.

I had to face reality. Rome, change her spots? Only through the intervention of the Holy Spirit, which I would never count out; but, while I awaited Her interference in the Roman mind set, was I not bearing witness to this evil by remaining a spokesperson of the Church? And, of equal importance, violating my own conscience, thus committing a sin of my own?

The street definition of insanity; "doing the same thing over and over and expecting a different result" was so applicable. At long last, I applied it to my own struggle.

A separation was inevitable.

$$* \quad * \quad * \quad * \quad *$$

Thus, my story ends. After a year's Leave of Absence, I resigned my active priesthood. I had known in the near and real future, my conscience would compel me to resign. In addition, knowing a life of loneliness lay ahead and wishing deeply to have a life's companion, I had, over time, developed a profoundly deep relationship with my future wife. She was a committed beautiful, Catholic woman, with five children, free to marry in the Church. Her wonderful children became mine. I was blessed with an "instant family!"

A new sacred relationship began through the Sacrament of Matrimony and married life.

I was forty-two years old.

My Spiritual Journey
From the Priesthood

Jerry Griffith

"We thought we were gods"

As I write my story, I am able to view my life at a distance. Living day by day is similar to looking at a painting with my nose against the picture. I didn't know why the artist chose this color or that. But now at a distance, I see the whole panoramic view and then I know what the artist had in mind. It becomes a work of art. My life begins on a playground of bullies and continues through the playground of life. Playgrounds can be exciting and frightening.

When I was ten months old during the latter part of the depression, my father lost his job and we moved from Kentucky to New Jersey. When I reached school age, I attended the public schools. The playgrounds were an unsupervised zone. Bullies were everywhere. I was not a fighter so I made excuses of sickness every day in order to avoid school. Before long, we received a visit from the truant officer.

"Mrs. Griffith, the truant officer sternly said, "The law states that you must send your child to school." I remember him as a large, heavyset, stern-looking man. He carried a very large book and a chain for his keys. He further stated, "You can go to prison if you don't comply."

I was thinking, "Who is this guy anyway? We have a right to do what we want. What has school given me, but a playground dominated by bullies?"

My mother seemed to take this seriously.

"I guess the prison was a little scary," I thought to myself. "Oh well, it couldn't be any worse than a playground."

My mother didn't know what to do. She faced my apprehension about continuing in the public school system daily. Her choices were limited. Wanting something close to our home left her with one choice: Saint Margaret.

Even though our family was not Catholic, mother decided to plead her case to the principal of St. Margaret. Mother figured she would stress the immediacy of the situation.

"Sister, I have a son who is scared of going to school. He needs a school where he won't be afraid."

I was going into the second grade.

The principal was silent for a while. Sister stated, "This is highly unusual. He would be required to take Catechism classes, preparation classes for First Communion, and attend daily Mass with the rest of the students. Also we will need to change his name to Gerald since Jerry is not a name of a saint."

My mother, with relief, said, "Oh, yes, that is not a problem."

I think my mother would have said yes even if the principal said that I must take daily Communism lessons. Mother was a Church of Christ member but not a faithful one. She was brought up in a strict Protestant environment that claimed the Catholic Church was straight from Hell.

Well, I thought I had died and gone to heaven. Compared to the public schools, St. Margaret was different as night and day. Due to the discipline, there were no fights or disruptions.

The Mass offered peace and tranquility which I never experienced in previous Protestant worship that I attended with my grandfather. In contrast, I was not impressed with the Protestant service. There was too much noise, shaking of hands, etc. I didn't understand the passing of bread and grape juice.

I asked mother, "Why does the preacher seem so angry when he gives his sermon?"

She laughed since she was not a real fan of the Protestant Church. Her immediate family—especially her brother—were religious fanatics.

I went through the first Communion classes with the rest of my class. So I asked the nun. "Can I receive the body and blood of Jesus?"

"You will need to bring your mother in for permission," she advised me.

I knew my mother would give consent.

I was mesmerized by the receiving of the body and blood of Christ. I understood it as much as any seven year old could comprehend such a doctrine. I always thought like an adult, and thought I knew what was good for me.

I want to divert here to explain my relationship with my mother and why I thought there would be no problem with her permission and why I thought like an adult at such an early age. Usually children at this early age do not join a religion so different from their background. Again, looking at the painting at a distance reveals many things about yourself and others.

I had an unusual fear of death, which a child of my age should never have. So my mother took me to a psychologist.

The psychologist told my mother, "He has an adult mind in a child's body with a child's emotions. He needs to be around children more and not adults."

As I look back I think my mother treated me like an adult also. There may be some reasons for this.

My mother was very close to me. Her first child died immediately after birth. She had waited several years for that child. She had to wait a long time for me. So when I was born in good health, she rejoiced, and I was the favored ever since. She was probably overprotective. She wouldn't even let the doctor circumcise me. No way was anyone touching her baby. This may explain her feelings of an adult relationship but yet not wanting me to grow me up.

And so as I predicted, she granted permission for me to join the Catholic religion with no problem. My mother for good or for bad used to let me do about anything I wanted as long as it was safe. If unsafe, she would respond in the absolute negative. Neither my mother nor my father practiced any religion at the time.

When we visited Paducah the following summer, my uncle, my mother's brother, was upset for allowing a child of seven to make this step. He couldn't believe it.

"You let this child do whatever he wants," he screamed. "Virginia, you mean to tell me you let this child join another faith? Our mother is turning over in her grave right now! He is only seven. He doesn't know what he is doing," he shouted.

I remember thinking to myself, "I know what I am doing."

I was standing by and wondering how this caused a grave turnover of my mama Sanderson. I just dismissed him as a crazy fanatic. It seemed like the argument lasted for hours and finally my grandfather drew them apart before a physical fight would ensue. My mother answered, "He wanted to do it, and he seems to be doing very well."

"Are you crazy? You can't let your child do anything he wants," Uncle James screamed again.

I don't think my mother and her brother talked too much after that encounter. We didn't see him when we returned each summer to Paducah from New Jersey.

And so I was baptized and practiced the religion by myself, as if I were an adult and knew what I was doing. But this is the way my mother raised me, to my uncle's chagrin.

Later my parents and brother joined the Catholic faith after returning to Kentucky. My grandfather remarried a Catholic after Mama Sanderson died.

My uncle James never approved of that marriage. Papa and Mama Sanderson were my mother's and her brother's parents.

We missed New York City, since we did all our shopping there. We always attended the Thanksgiving parade. We visited many times after we moved. You may see anything in New York. I remember when I was about six or seven, while walking in Time Square, right out of the blue, a naked lady ran past us with police in hot pursuit. I couldn't believe what I saw. "Mother, why isn't she wearing any clothes?" I exclaimed.

My mother passed it off with, "Oh, she just has some mental problems," stammering off the cuff.

"Mental problems," I thought, "Wow!"

I loved New York and still do. I am still a Yankee. You can take the boy out of New York, but you can't take New York out of the boy.

My grandparents used to say, "He talks so much like a New Yorker, we can't understand him."

Catholicism is the predominate religion in the East and Protestantism is the religion of the Midwest. So who knows what would have happened if we never moved to the East coast. I would have a different story. When we moved back to Kentucky, my dad took a job in Paducah; I attended St. Mary's grade school.

My spiritual journey to the priesthood began one hot July day when my mother was perusing the Sunday paper. She happened upon a full-page section with pictures and a write -up of St. Meinrad Monastery and Seminary. She read the article to me. After she read it, she pointed out to me, "Look at this full-page write up with pictures of a seminary in Indiana run by Benedictine monks."

I looked at it with some curiosity. It was large and beautiful, with an imposing Abbey Church and Seminary.

She said, "You can begin there after eighth grade. Would you like to go there? You would go for twelve years and then be ordained a priest."

I was rather surprised, since she wouldn't even let me go to summer camp. While mother was very protective and would not put me in the hands of any adult, when it came to priests and religious, she had ultimate trust. Those were the days when the supervision of priests or religious was the safest venture a parent could allow. How well we know it is untrue today. At first, this way of life didn't seem very attractive to me at the tender age of twelve or thirteen. In fact I gave a resounding, "No way!"

So we discussed it more as time went on, and it became more alluring, since she told me there was an active sports program along with prayer, liturgy, and study. I wanted to play football, but my mother wouldn't allow it. I thought this might be a novel way to do what I wanted away from home. In fact, I thought this may be a good way of getting out of parental authority and control. Now I wish I hadn't played football, since now I have a knee replacement due to an injury. I should have listened.

Little did I know I was getting into a much more disciplined life-style. I had it made at home and didn't realize it. I was an altar boy in grade school, and I had a high admiration for the profession of the priesthood. I pondered this idea, and the priesthood seemed more compelling, but an uncertainty seemed to lurk behind my thinking.

So we talked to the pastor, and the long procedure began. My grades in the eighth grade were sufficient to pass the requirement for the seminary. This academic objective served to predict if I could pass the rigorous studies of the seminary. Academics were never a problem for me. I didn't put a lot of effort in school, but it seemed that I didn't need to.

I received good recommendations from my pastor and other supervisors. I also passed my physical. During his examination of me, Dr. Higdon, my internist, pointed out that I would be exposed to some of the most brilliant professors in their field. Yet, training and studying for twelve years seemed like an eternity then.

He said, "You will learn much from these wise Benedictine monks who give their whole life to prayer and study. Take advantage. Not many are exposed to this educational background," he reiterated.

He knew the Benedictine philosophy of "Ora et Labora" (Pray and Work). He and my pastor were friends. My pastor attended St. Meinrad for twelve years.

This made me uncomfortable and anxious since, if that is the case, what will they expect of me? Not being in the habit of knuckling down with homework, I was doubtful about the required intensity in my studies St. Meinrad would require of me. My mother asked the pastor whether I could attend later since I was very young.

His answer to me was, "If you don't go now, you could lose your vocation in High School by dating girls."

Then, that seemed to be the philosophy of the Church in order to nurture vocations. Seminary is a place to protect small seeds. Now it is the opposite. Men enter much older and are mature enough to make a well-informed decision. A child of fourteen cannot make that decision. As a result, many are sheltered from the world and go into a way of life they are not expecting.

So, my mother reluctantly agreed. Bishop Cotton gave his permission to attend St. Meinrad Seminary. This was unusual since most seminarians from my diocese attended St. Mary's in Baltimore. But Bishop Cotton and also my pastor, Father Thompson, were alumni of St. Meinrad. When Owensboro was part of the Louisville diocese, St. Meinrad was the seminary for all candidates.

I will never forget the long journey in the hot, old, stuffy Ford to the "Holy Hill," as we called it. I think, as we traveled along the old black top in the time before interstates, we were having second thoughts about this venture. We were going around endless curves and hills and suddenly the Abbey popped up in all its majesty. I remember that the ride was overwhelming, exciting, but anxiety- ridden. I can still remember to this day the queasy feeling in my stomach and the burning question in my mind: "Do I really want to do this?"

A Benedictine monk showed us around, since I was early on a Sunday—due to my mother and father's work schedule. My parents left me all alone.

Mother asked if I was all right.

I said, "I'm fine."

Mother said, "Are you sure?"

I said, "I'm fine."

Mother said, "Are you sure?"

"Yes," I said, "I feel good; I have no problem." I think I was trying to fool myself here. This was really an unknown, and I was walking right into the mouth of the lion.

I think Mother said this five or six times before she left, because she didn't know whether she was fine. They finally left. All of a sudden I felt like an adult. No one had authority over me. As I look back, I think my mother was regretting her encouragement at such an early age. Afterward, I walked around wondering what I was getting into.

I began to realize that, while I was relieved of parental authority, now I was subject to another authority. I had no idea of what I was getting into. I went into the huge abbey church where the monks were singing the Divine Office. The Gregorian chant seemed to relax me and give me some peace. Although it was in Latin, the chant was beautiful to my untrained ear.

All priests and religious orders are required to pray the Divine Office every day. This is the official prayer of the Church. It is made up of psalms and prayers. At that time, services in Latin were no big deal. The Latin just added mystery. I was used to it. I, like all altar boys, had memorized all the Latin responses even though we had no idea what we were saying. I can remember Father Rhodes going over the "suscipiat" ("may he receive"). I don't know how many times we rehearsed. I don't think I ever got that one right. I mumbled through it.

Father Thompson, my pastor, was very impatient during the prayers at the foot of the altar and would cut in right in the middle of the "Ad Deum qui laetificat"("To God who gives joy to my youth").

Finally, I discovered another classmate who had also arrived early. I learned later from my father that my mother cried all the way home. My father told her to turn around and pick me up, but she drove on through the tears. My dad was really upset. I have never seen my dad this upset. I can still hear him screaming out this story. I don't think my dad was ever in favor of this venture so early in my life, but he always did what mother wanted. No one questioned the Church, then.

So, this is the way I began my long twelve-year journey of work, intensive study, meditation, prayer, comradeship with peers, and physical activity under the guidance of the Benedictine monks. As I review my seminary career, the education was comprehensive in the classical languages of Latin, Greek, Philosophy, and Theology. All the other academics made up a study worthy of an undergraduate degree in Philosophy and Classical languages and a Masters Degree in Theology.

In minor seminary, we studied in a huge study hall. Two assistant principals patrolled the study hall to make sure there was absolute quiet and no one was sleeping. I would get into trouble now and then since I was asking my neighbor about some involved sentences in Cicero or Plato's Republic in Greek. If we disobey a rule we would receive a check which would mean one point off of your conduct grade.

My mother kept strict tabs on our relationship. We exchanged letters every week. One time in the twelve years, I didn't mail a letter. My mother was on the phone asking the rector of the minor seminary if I was all right.

So the rector called me to his office. I don't think she believed him.

Mother said, "Jerry, I didn't get a letter this week. Are you okay?"

"Yes, I'm fine."

"Why didn't I get a letter?"

"I forgot, sorry."

Well, I was a little embarrassed with the rector hearing this conversation. But I never missed a week for the rest of my 12 year stay.

The training in high school was also more rigorous than other high schools. All my classmates used to say that every professor thinks he is the only one and the grade of A is rarely given. There was no grade inflation here. It was more like grade depression. If I earned a C, I was happy.

This was nothing like grade school where A's were easy. I had it made with Sister Stanislaus Kostka who was a rough and tough nun. After I told her I was going to the seminary, I could do no wrong. She appointed me patrol boy and I left school early every day. My grades were great. I was the teacher's pet.

In the seminary, homework was over-whelming . But we were given time to do the work. It was just very strenuous. We had study hall in the morning before classes and study hall after recreation before supper and after supper, seven o'clock to ten o'clock, followed by night prayers. The grand silence, "Magnum Silentium," followed night prayers. So we had time to do our homework. The Magnum Silentium was kept from night prayers until after Mass the next morning for meditative purposes. We even had classes on Saturday. It was strictly kept, or else many checks against the student' conduct would be the penalty.

Our days were full of prayer, classes, study and recreation. If we came to the seminary after high school we would lose a year just catching up with the Latin. In those days we had to know Latin well, since this was the official language of the Church. The Mass was in Latin and most of the Theology and Philosophy books in the major seminary were in Latin. I remember those "special-class" seminarians, as we called them. These were students who came to the seminary after high school. They had nothing but Latin every day for a whole year. Talk about burn out!

The moral training and the military discipline that accompanied my intellectual formation were effective in a sense, but there were negative results also. There were times of scrupulosity, communion with God, discipline of a militaristic style, and rigorous intellectual training that were difficult for a young and impressionable mind. I don't think I will ever rid myself of this background. My conscience is somewhat brainwashed. A victim of scrupulosity sees sin where there is no sin and suffers from anxiety due to this malady. Martin Luther and many other religious have suffered from this. We were taken at an impressionable age and led down an intellectual and disciplinary path with both positive and negative results.

I sometimes wonder how I lasted. It was all I knew, and once I got on the train it was difficult to get off without guilt about leaving. It is almost like trying to get off a train while it's moving. The jump seemed fearful. So, I just stayed, although as my mind matured and the hormones increased, the idea of celibacy seemed more precarious.

When I entered at the tender age of fourteen, celibacy was no big deal. I didn't want to disappoint anyone, especially my parents. But I know that would not have been the case. Some are able to shed this militaristic disciplined life style, but I have not been successful in doing so.

I shared some great camaraderie with many of my peers whom I will never forget. It is always good to renew old acquaintances when I return for class reunions. And so, as in all lives there were good results and bad results from such a venture. I wouldn't trade my classical education for any amount of money. The Benedictine education is superior.

I presently teach Greek and Latin at a community college. I know my background in a classical education has helped me in many ways. The Benedictine monks in all their monastic schools are recognized worldwide for their classical education and their emphasis on Greek and Latin.

As I look back, we were all immature and knew nothing about life as we entered the long twelve-year journey. As a result I have many classmates who realized they made a mistake after ordination.

Today, the Church has changed its philosophy about nurturing vocations. Now those entering are much older and more mature, since they enter the seminary after college. I am sure the number of drop- outs will decline. But back then, in a previous era, vocations were to be nurtured at an early age with strict discipline and militaristic regulations which would bind some student into lasting immaturity and an inability of making decisions. Not all are affected the same way.

Decisions were made for me. Everything was done for me, and all I was asked to do was: "Study, pray, meditate, participate in the liturgy, and keep in physical shape through sports. We were given no practical knowledge not even a shop class. So I have the academic knowledge and the discipline but not much common sense as my wife reminds me. But I'm very thankful for the intellectual training and discipline the Benedictine monks gave me. I still live by much of the philosophy and theology of fathers Adelbert, Bernard, Kyran, and Marion, just to name a few of my mentors. They had a certain practical objective way of viewing reality which I still hold today. Their theology was Thomistic and their philosophy and logic were grounded in Aristotle. Our basic theology text was the "Summa Theologica" by St. Thomas Aquinas, which questioned everything through the logic of Aristotle.

If life was full, as was our schedule, the thinking was that sexual desires would be put to a minimum and you would grow in wisdom and age. But as we know, you can't fight nature. Scrupulosity and emotional turmoil followed for some, due to the guilt caused by the hormones of an adolescent.

The law of celibacy seems to be the issue that causes many priests to leave. This is the cause for a dwindling priesthood as we see today. Unless the Church turns its attention to this problem, the numbers will continue to dwindle. Twelve out of our class of thirty-three have married. That is over forty percent. This is a tremendous loss to the Church. When I think of the waste, I see the need to address this problem. Most of these forty percent entered the seminary when they were only thirteen or fourteen years of age and have similar reasons for leaving.

Years later, one of my classmates aptly reminisced, "We thought we were gods." In the seminary during our last year of theology we were at the top of the heap. We survived twelve years. Everyone looked up to us. We were going to offer Mass, hear confessions, etc. This made us feel godlike. But when we hit the real world, the feeling soon vanished. As the Eagle's song *Welcome to the Hotel California* says, we didn't know whether it was heaven or hell.

I went to a parish where I was active in the Catholic High School. I enjoyed my work. I truly loved all the duties and responsibilities of the priesthood. But once again, the tight reign that is placed upon young priests then was a cause of much unhappiness and lack of freedom.

The presiding bishop had much power over my life and any priest's life. I spent two short years at my first assignment and was doing well with the students and the adults. I taught some classes and started a basketball team. This was a great joy and I was in a place to do much good for the students. But right in the middle of satisfying work, the bishop appointed me by letter to another parish. I was very upset; so, I went to the Bishop. But he still insisted on my transfer. No reason was given.

I accepted the assignment and journeyed to Hopkinsville, Kentucky. I had the misfortune of working with a dominating pastor. The change was like night and day. I suffered from loneliness and didn't enjoy the work as well. I was a chaplain at the state mental institution, and auxiliary chaplain at Fort Campbell, the home of the hundred and first paratroopers. I met some interesting chaplains who also jumped with the men.

After one year—another short stay—I and the Pastor were transferred to Paducah, which I welcomed since my parents lived there. I liked my transfer and enjoyed the work. I was chaplain at the hospital and started a Confraternity of Christian Doctrine group. This is a lay organization devoted to the education of adults. After my sermons on the morality of segregation, the group decided to look more deeply into the morality of segregation. Of course, the conclusion was what society has been doing for years is truly immoral. African Americans deserved the same rights as whites or any other race.

I didn't realize it but rumors were spreading. In those times this was a radical statement. My write up in the paper announcing my move stated that The Confraternity of Christian Doctrine group, headed by Father Griffith, was sponsoring civil-rights meetings. At that time you might as well have said Communist meetings. It doesn't take a genius to know that this was taken to the Bishop by certain concerned laity.

This was the day of separate restrooms, segregated buses, separate entrances to movies, black and white neighborhoods etc. The average white person was not ready to believe this was immoral. People in the parish were not too happy about these "radical statements." The times were very fragile then. Racism was raising its ugly head. The bullies on the playground were now really getting rough and another move resulted.

Then another letter came from the Bishop after only a two year stay. I was told to transfer to the Cathedral parish in Owensboro, Kentucky. The Bishop was in charge of the Cathedral. When I went there, I knew I would be under close scrutiny. I liked the work since it was a large parish. But I always felt like the Bishop and the rector of the Cathedral were looking over my shoulder. I and my fellow associate continued to give sermons on the morality of racism. We also participated in some demonstrations.

The bishop was not too pleased with all of this activity. This was my last assignment before I decided to take a leave of absence. I was completely frustrated with these bullies on the playground. Emotionally I needed a more peaceful life. So as my mother went to St. Margaret School, I went to the Bishop told him about my need to take a leave of absence. He, like the St. Margaret principal, said this was highly unusual.

I met my first wife in the youth club of the Cathedral parish which I supervised. I was a juvenile when it came to women, sex etc. I had one brother and attended an all-male seminary. I really mistook sex for love and I fell deeply in love, or should I say, in love with sex.

She was young. She thought she was in love with me. Celibacy was put to the test. So, I said, "Let's just play it by ear." But I should have said, "Let's end it now before it begins." I was at a lonely point in my life and very vulnerable. The relationship grew deeper and deeper.

The Bishop was very reluctant to grant me the leave. He sent me to counseling, hoping I would come to my senses. All my superiors did not want me to leave. I was successful delivering good sermons, and I was well liked by the people of the parish, though racial sermons were unacceptable at that time. I was also successful with my youth group which was assisting the poor.

The rector of the Cathedral called me in and told me how he would hate to lose me. To my shock and surprise he broke down and cried. I always thought he was a rather cold administrator, who would never succumb to tears. This really shook me up. It's not easy leaving a successful and full life. I still miss the life of the priesthood and would return if the celibacy law changed. But the call of sex was too much and I was overcome.

We married in July, 1969 in St. Louis. I really gave no thought to the speed of this decision or the maturity of my wife. She was only twenty. She was too young to make this decision.

My purpose was to move on with my life. I realize I should have dated many women in order to make a sound decision but my immaturity won out and I lost my reason. My emotions overcame my reason.

The absolute sheltering from the real world in a prayerful, solemn, academic environment under militaristic supervision may cause this. As I view the painting from a distance I probably should have entered the Benedictine order. I thought about it in the minor seminary but ruled it out. If I could have lived with the celibacy, I think I would have been happy in teaching and living in a community. I almost dropped out in first philosophy (third year college).

"Father Adelbert, I don't think I will be happy giving up sex and marriage." I said rather fearfully.

"Think and pray about it for a while and let me know." He replied.

I prayed and thought about it, but it was hard getting off that moving train and so I stayed on.

After I received my leave, I think I was being monitored by the government since, during my very first year in St. Louis my income tax was audited by the Federal government. I made very little money that year. My small priestly salary and a few months teaching in St. Louis was not much. I was very active in civil-rights and was teaching in a black school. I can't believe the government was concerned about such small potatoes. Go figure.

I applied to the Public School system in the city of St. Louis. The first question I was asked, "Will you teach in a black school?" My thought has always been, "Why would they ask this question?" The more years I spent in St. Louis, the more I understood the meaning. This is the racism I fought against in Kentucky years before.

I took a position teaching English Literature. I enrolled in St. Louis University Graduate School to study for a Master's degree in Guidance and Counseling. I graduated two years later. In 1971, I enrolled in the University of Missouri and worked on my principal's certificate. I then became a guidance counselor at Soldan High School.

In 1976 I transferred to Metro High School, an experimental magnet school that specialized in college preparation. I started a Latin program there and served as director of guidance and athletic director. During this time my first wife bore four children who are now functioning well as adults in their various fields. My children have given me much joy and have eased the pain of the many problems in life.

I am presently in my second marriage and very happy since this was a mature decision. I am active in the Church after a dispensation from Rome. So I wonder! Did I do the right thing? Was this God's will? All I can say is that from my perspective now, if I had not made the former marriage decision my four children and seven grandchildren would not exist today. They have taught me about life and brought much happiness to my life.

Even to this day, I feel a lacking in the common sense arena due to my background. As seminarians we had an ideal life. Our meals were prepared. We didn't have a job like most students in school. We didn't have the problems of the world with transportation, tuition, and work. We just answered to bells and gave everything to study without any distractions that people in the world face every day. I can see the reasoning for this disciplined life, but, for me, the practical side of life was not developed.

Today we do not have that situation. Twelve-year seminary programs are a thing of the past. Now, there are only schools of theology. Many men are older and more mature who take the step into the priesthood or diaconate. This should eliminate or lessen the number of defections due to the maturity of the candidates in worldly experience.

Everyone will have a different story in this book, but it will probably be seen that a thread of sameness runs through each story.

You might call us the Vatican II babies. We were ordained during the council and had great hope for the future of the church. Pope John XXIII came in under the radar. The conservative cardinals didn't really know who they were electing. When Pope Pius died they elected an old cardinal who would have a short tenure and keep the status quo. Were they ever wrong! At the beginning, John said that we need to open up the windows and let some fresh air in. The church had been stagnant for a long time.

He called the Second Vatican Council. Then many changes resulted. The Latin Mass and the Friday abstinence from meat were changed. The liturgy underwent great changes. But after John's tenure, the Popes stopped these changes. The hopes of our generation of priests were dashed. All the Popes from John Paul to Benedict have placed a quietus on the fulfillment of Vatican II. As a result, we are observing a mass exodus of priests, and vocations are at a record low. There is no doubt about it. The priesthood is declining in numbers. Older priests are asked not to retire, and many priests are pastoring two or three parishes. The Church needs priests. Deacons, lay ministers, and lay involvement cannot take their place. The laity is wondering what the future of the Church will be. Hans Kung, who was a theological consultant during the Council, states that the Council has been thwarted by the Vatican Curia, the governing body of the Church.

He states, "The tension between a church that embraces reform and an unwilling Curia can only produce a serious crisis."

He is asking for a third council with priestly celibacy as its top issue.

The hierarchy will only allow conservatives to enter their ranks. The church is in a state of little or no change. Change is life and lack of change is death.

The church needs to do something about the dwindling priesthood. The first item to be reviewed should be optional celibacy. In fact, the church has accepted Episcopal and Anglican priests who are married. This is a slap in the face of the married priests longing to serve God. For the first one thousand years of the church, the clergy married. So this law could easily be abolished.

I still feel a need to serve. I applied to serve as a deacon, but at this time Rome is not granting permission. This doesn't make sense in a time of great need. Again I am faced with bullies on the playground of life. The will of God is incomprehensible, but I am sure that He will bring good out of my whole life, no matter what my weaknesses might bring.

e Call

kel

When approached with this project, I will have to admit I was intrigued by the concept of several former Roman Catholic priests each writing a chapter in a book answering the Big Question—"Why I left the priesthood."

How do I articulate something so personal, so intertwined with my being? As that question bounced around in my mind, I realized that the question was one that perhaps I had denied myself the freedom to face objectively, let alone subjectively. I also realized in order to answer the question of why I left is parallel as to why I answered the call in the first place. With the dawn of a new day I had decided to go back to the beginning to search for the ultimate answer.

Having been the first born of seven children, I now realize how that and what it entails, etched its way into my DNA. From my earliest recollections it was, "Richard do this or help with that." As time passed and our family grew, the church was infused into our lives as just part of the way it was supposed to be. Births were followed by baptisms, first confessions and holy communions, confirmations and CCD classes for the Eckels, as there was no Catholic school in our community. It became second nature to help, be it family or anyone else asking or in need.

To further my search I went to my file cabinet, to the bottom drawer in the very back and found a file labeled "High School." I opened it and began to flip my way through its contents. I came to a folder marked "End of Year Summary—Career Counseling 1955." I found a note attached to some printouts labeled "Classes for Fall Semester 1955, Sophomore Year—counselor, Mr. Skibbey." I remembered him and I also remembered the results of that session, namely, I would be pursuing a college prep curriculum for the rest of my high school career, which, by the way, was not exactly to my liking at the time.

It seems like the next two years were probably much the same for me as any other high school teenager at that time, but during Easter time of 1957, after serving Easter Mass, the Pastor and I were talking about graduation and summer plans and he asked me what my plans were after graduation.

"I'm still undecided," I responded.

He then asked, "Are you thinking about college or staying home on the farm with your family?"

I told him I did not want to stay on the farm, that my brothers and sisters could help the family there and that I was just beginning to wonder what there is to life when you are just going to die in the end anyway.

Well, I suppose that was the wrong thing to say because he came back with God's purpose for us here on earth, etcetera, etcetera and finished with, "I think it sounds to me like you need to study and learn about the real answers in life beyond that 'we just die anyway' stuff."

In later conversations with him I decided to begin my studies at a pre-theology college in Kentucky that specialized in church Latin. Four years later I graduated with my B.A. and enrolled in the Major Seminary in Cincinnati.

The summer between college graduation and entry into the Major Seminary I experienced a 'reality check' time. I had the opportunity to enjoy talking with the Mexican migrant workers and their families in my local parish. That was my first real opportunity to relate with people on a 'Faith Encounter' type of experience. These individuals were born in Catholicism, lived in Catholicism, and died in Catholicism. From that time on I began to see my purpose in life was in some way to act as a go-between, a facilitator if you will, between man and his Creator. Was this the calling I had been searching for when I chose to enter the seminary? Was this my challenge, and if so, why me?

Entering the Major Seminary was, in retrospect, like joining the Marines: private dorm-like rooms, a regimented daily schedule, mandatory class schedules, uniform dress code, no leaving the quarters, no visitors, and zero communication with the opposite sex, unless it was family. Why I did not recognize the ultimate goal and resulting effect on me, I do not know. I suppose in short, it was just being caught up in the moment, which was exactly the intent. The end became subject to the means; if you want to be ordained you must conform in every aspect of the program.

I remember in my second year of the Seminary program the professor in scripture class quoted Jesus as saying, "Behold, thou art Peter and upon this rock I will build my church and the gates of Hell shall not prevail against it," as proof of the Papacy and the infallibility of the Pope.

I thought about that for a moment and raised my hand to ask a question.

The professor called on me and I asked, "Professor, isn't that taking an awful lot from one simple sentence?"

"Richard," he said, "see me after class and I'll deal with your problem, there is no need to take the time from the rest of the class for such an ignorant question."

After class I approached the professor and he said, "What the Church teaches on the matter in question, Richard, was, is, and will always remain the same, just remember that." I guess such a response should have been expected. I could only deduce that it is so amazing what a commitment to a calling demands of us.

The Second Vatican Council opened in late 1962 and Pope John XXIII called for a "Renewal of Faith and Liturgy" in the Church. I was thankful for that man and his purpose for bringing the Church into the modern world. As time passed, the spirit of Vatican II began to move toward reform and renewal and the dynamic truly gave hope for me that it would all be worth it in the end. However, with the death of Pope John XXIII and the naming of Pope Paul VI as his successor, that all ended. What the ramifications of that would be remained to be seen, but it had a delayed and profound effect on my calling.

Finally, on May 28, 1965, I was to be ordained. In the preliminary events before the service itself had begun, the Bishop, as procedure dictated, spoke individually with each man to be ordained, asking the question, "Do you Richard wish to be ordained to the priesthood of Jesus Christ in the Diocese of Toledo?"

The expected response was "Yes."

I responded instead with, "Bishop I believe the question should be, "Do you as Bishop wish to ordain me to the priesthood of Jesus Christ in the Diocese of Toledo?"

He appeared somewhat taken aback and glared at me and exclaimed, "I take that as a 'Yes'!"

He then rose to his feet, opened the exit door and said, "Next candidate please."

During the ordination ceremony as I lay prostrate on the cathedral floor, I remember asking my Creator to always be the Way, the Truth, and the Life for me in His service and I wondered how great it would be to fulfill my being as His servant, serving the people He puts into my life.

After the ceremony there was a joyous gathering with family and friends; it was full of memories that are still with me to this day. About a week later I received a letter from the Diocese office informing me that my first assignment was as an Associate Pastor at St. Mary's Parish in Sandusky, Ohio beginning in June 1965.

The following is the first sermon I gave to the parishioners that first Sunday morning at St. Mary's: I found the original copy in the same bottom file drawer that I had found my high school class information.

I would like to take this opportunity to introduce myself to you. I am Father Richard Eckel and my home was in Bowling Green. I'm very happy to be assigned to St. Mary's and I'm looking forward to a full and rewarding stay here.

No doubt, when any parish has a young newly-ordained priest assigned to them, there is the question in the minds of the parishioners, "I wonder what Father is like, what kind of priest is he?" This is a natural question. Of course, we all know that the priest is another Christ, that he is the representative of God, but I believe and I want to be the type of priest we hear described in the ordination ceremony; that type of priest is called "a servant of the servants of God."

Yes, I want to be the servant of God's chosen people here at St. Mary's. But, just what does this mean? I think we can find the answer to that question in the epistle, which was read to you this morning. In this morning's epistle, St. Peter tells you to cast your anxiety on God, because it is He who takes care of you. Yes, St. Peter tells you to go to God, to place your confidence in Him; this you do in your prayers and reception of His life through the sacraments. But God, because of His great love for you, did not leave you alone in this task. No, he called men to take His place here on earth to help His people. He called me to be your servant. So that is what I mean when I say that I am the "servant of the servants of God." I am the messenger of God, the minister of God, the helper of God, in serving His people.

First then, I am the messenger of God—this means that even though I am still a weak human being, I am sent to you with the Word of God, that word which is holy and powerful. Hear my human words, my fumbling, miserable and often repetitious words and try to find in them God's word.

Secondly, I am a minister of God. I have come to bring Him to you and help you to Him by ministering to your needs for Him. Accept me as the one who cares for you.

Finally, I am a helper of God. This means that I, though a mere man, act on God's behalf here on earth. As St. Peter tells you to cast your anxiety on God, I tell you I will try to take your cares upon myself and to help you in times of need and trouble.

Yes, here I stand, a messenger, a minister, a helper. I beg you to accept me as I am, with my faults and limited talents. Help me, pray for me, have patience with me. In return I will give you my all and by this will you know that I am God's priest, that I have love for you. This then is why I have come to you, that I may be a sign to you; a sign that God loves you, that Christ lives with you, that I care about you. God Bless you all!

As a newly-ordained young priest I quickly identified with the younger generation in the community. I was to teach religion in the parish schools, both grade school and high school. I was also a leader in the Catholic Family Movement and in parish adult convert classes. Visiting the hospitals, nursing homes, and others in need of Christ in their lives was a most fulfilling part of my ministry. I would visit families in their homes and bless those homes and share in the Breaking of the Bread, and many other inter-communication experiences so that I could be there for them in their times of need.

I knew that my serving the faithful of St. Mary's had to be more than what my Pastor said, "When the people need you they will come to the church or rectory and then you can deal with them."

To which I answered, "There are four other priests sitting here if they come to the rectory. I'm going out *to* them and serve them in their real life situations."

One of my special ministries took place on Saturday evenings after the priests had heard confessions. I would 'hit the bar and lounge circuit.'

This developed from an encounter with a person I had greeted after Mass one Sunday morning.

I said to him, "So good to see you here this morning after last night."

He looked quizzically at me and asked, "What do you mean Father, 'after last night?'"

I responded, "Well, I stepped out last night for a beer myself and just happened to see you and a couple of your buddies there, but I could only have one as I had a later commitment. I wish I could have had the time to join you guys as it looked like you were out for a fun night."

"Well," he said, "we did have a good time and I even made it to church."

"Yes you did," I responded, "but receiving Christ in communion might have helped to strengthen you for the week ahead."

He replied, "Well, I couldn't go to Holy Communion, Father, because I didn't get to confession yesterday."

I then suggested to him that the next time he was out on a Saturday night and wanted to go to confession that he could just call me and I'd come to him and take care of it.

He said, "No, Father, you don't have to do that."

I replied, "I *want* to do that, deal?"

Somewhat awkwardly, he agreed. That was when I decided to take my confessional to the bars on Saturday night.

I also refused to hear confessions of eight-year-olds before they could take their first communion. Could they really grasp the concept of mortal sin? I'm not even sure *I* do! So the pastor just ordered one of the other priests to do it.

When it came to the Church's position on birth control, the way I dealt with it was to leave that decision to the conscience of the believer where it belongs. There were four confessionals in the church and at confession time the line was longest at mine. Rumor had it that I had a free birth control pill dispenser in my confessional!

The role of women in the Church had always seemed strange to me. It seemed that God's plan somehow was flipped along the way. Women give birth to men and then become the lesser of the two. How could that be? I did not buy into that then or ever, for that matter.

As history often does, a new chapter developed in the mid sixties and with it new challenges. The younger generation was searching for freedom and new frontiers and the older generation was trying to keep the reins tight. Dialogue weakened and widened and became a seedbed for conflict. Where was the Church? Where was direction to come from? Answers seemed to be few!

In 1966 I became active in the Ministerial Association in the local community and spoke out for more dialogue between faiths and active communication by all clergy with their troubled youth. We were able to come together in establishing "Volunteers in Action" in Erie County, which is still in active operation today.

As growth comes with time and from need, we created a 24-Hour Crisis Hot Line. By 1968 we had implemented a program for visitation and dialogue between those incarcerated and the criminal justice system staff.

Due to my involvement with the younger generation and listening to their problems and needs, we concluded that they needed a safe place, away from the establishment to share ideas, beliefs, hopes, fears, and goals in life. The outgrowth of this need was realized with the opening of the Ichtus Coffee House in a downtown empty storefront. The fruits of this labor were absolutely amazing. However, the realization soon became evident that a 24-Hour Crisis Hot Line and the coffee house were not enough.

One evening in 1971 I was sitting in the rectory watching the late evening news with one of the other priests when the doorbell rang. I opened the door to see a couple of young boys running across the lawn and another boy lying on the steps in front of me. I rushed down the steps and asked him if he was OK. He did not respond. I dropped to my knees, took the boy into my arms and discovered he was almost unconscious.

At that moment the pastor appeared behind me and asked what was going on. I told him, "This kid is in bad shape, call 911!"

His response was, "Get the kid off the front steps. We don't need any druggers on our rectory steps," and he walked away.

One of the other younger priests appeared and said he had called 911. I did what I could do, but it was too late.

The young boy died in my arms as I blessed him and said a final prayer and anointed him. This entire incident was treated as if it had never happened, but it had a profound and lasting effect on my future.

Another incident also really rocked my world. Three of the young adults and I found our way to Woodstock, New York for the musical festival of the century. As it was a spur of the moment decision, we threw together a few camping essentials such as sleeping bags, a couple changes of clothes, a box of food items and a cooler with water and soft drinks. As it would turn out, we were fortunate to have taken that much. Somewhere close to the festival area we encountered a huge traffic jam and we were there the day before the official opening. Recorded history verifies that over 400,000 men, women, and children were witness to what turned out to be a once-in-a-lifetime experience.

For me personally, to be a part of that gathering brought the thought of Christ's encounter with the multitude of five thousand as recorded in Matthew 14:17. With a couple of small fish and a few loaves of bread He fed the multitude with the help of His disciples as they distributed the meager bounty until all were fed. So it was at Woodstock, with each one who had something to share, dividing it and sharing with those who had none. And when the pouring rains came, so too came an outpouring of love that reached my heart and soul and gave me a renewed faith in the younger generation. Here were thousands of individuals, but one source of unity, which manifested in care and love for others. There was no running out to the supermarket, to the neighbors, to the fast food shops on the corner. No, we were there and we were staying there. We will never forget it, for we were all better for experiencing it.

This experience brought true meaning to the words on a poster that hung on the wall in my room at the rectory, "Today is the first day of the rest of your life." Yes, a new dawn to my calling—to awake each morning now with a real belief in the meaning behind that. It was, as it were, the coming together of the existential experience and my existing reality. That serving my Creator and serving my fellow man are indeed one and the same reality. That was the moment I decided to resign from the institutional Catholic Church and *live* my calling to be a servant of the servants of God in the real world.

Upon my return from Woodstock I began to lay the foundation for my resignation. Because of all my commitments in the community I made an arrangement with my new pastor at St. Mary's to stay active at the church while giving my extra time to the other projects at hand.

Finally, in the early summer of 1972, I met with the Bishop and informed him of my decision to retire from the institutional church and pursue my calling of service while in residence at the Youth House in Sandusky. The Bishop said I could not just retire because I wanted to, so after a brief exchange of our positions, I said "Good Bye Bishop," and walked out. The pastor later informed me that I had been suspended and told to leave my residency at St. Mary's, which I had previously done, and was living with the residents at the Youth House.

In response to the question as to why I left the priesthood—I didn't. Yes, I informed the Bishop that I was leaving the Parish of St. Mary's in Sandusky, but I never said I was leaving my calling to the priesthood.

That calling was from God, to serve the people of God as I had pledged to do seven years earlier. Interestingly enough it is stated in Scripture and as part of the ordination ceremony that, "Thou art a priest forever according to the Order of Melchizedek."

So you see, I left the Catholic Church, the institution as it were, in order to continue fulfilling my calling as a servant of the servants of God.

The development of the Youth House Program had begun in 1971 as the result of a community meeting with juvenile judges, law enforcement, school counselors, area clergy, and any others who were involved with juveniles who were in need of guidance and understanding. With the help of this gathering of professionals and concerned others, a board of directors was elected and I was asked to be the Director of the program. Its success became a reality for the community and those who were in the program.

I found that the time to move on in a new direction was calling me. I established a resource agency and opened Life Enterprises as a resource for individual and group counseling and guidance. I also fulfilled my need for spiritual growth as well as serving for the spiritual needs of those who sought me out for their own spiritual development. Having my life and its course now somewhat redirected I spent the following year embracing my commitment to these two ends. I decided to marry and have a family during this time. Having a son and daughter brought me another source of responsibility and fullness in living.

The chapter in my life that I am now living took shape in 1993 when I married my soul mate that I had met eight years earlier. We have a full and rewarding life with the added joy of grandchildren. I have the opportunity to officiate at funerals, weddings, and baptisms and offer spiritual counseling and individual guidance to those who seek me out. This in turn enhances my spiritual growth and continued witness to my calling.

While participating in the funeral service for my mother in June of 2011, I had an epiphany about this thing we call Life—Now and The Hereafter. During a prayer I was offering as the casket was being closed the spirit within me spoke and I said, "As all of our Creator's creations are part of the Creator, so Mom are you, and I know that the smile on your beautiful face is a reflection of the Creator. May the life and faith that brought you back to your Creator be yours for eternity."

Now, as was my practice throughout my priesthood, I seldom wrote a sermon or prayer down to read at a specific time. I believed the spirit would speak through me, as was the case at my mother's funeral.

The message to me from my experience at Woodstock more than forty years later and in the prayer for my Mom was continued validation for why I resigned from the Catholic Church's priesthood.

I was called and ordained to serve the servants of God and I will continue to do that until the final breath of earthly life turns into the first breath of eternal life.

It's an Inner Thing

Joe Kirsch

The decision to leave the active ministry was a very complex and difficult decision to make, considering that, at the time, I was happy and content with my disposition in life. The decision came from the depths of my psyche, which I call the "Inner Thing"

By the time I was born the seventh of eight children, my siblings had pretty much established the ways the family approached decisions and problem solving. Thus my own problem solving and decision making was relegated to that "Inner Thing". My decision to enter seminary, my ongoing decision to continue in seminary for twelve years, my decision to be ordained (especially after the death of my father), and all the other significant decisions of my life were a result of processing in that "Inner Thing."

In elementary school, when I started considering the concept of priesthood, I didn't have, nor did I try to find, significant role models who influenced my decision to make the big step. Mine was an inner processing, quiet and personal. I was raised in a loving, Catholic home of the fifties and sixties in the fullest sense of the words. Dad was a strict, hard-working, determined, and simple man who spoke little. Mom was all one could hope for in a mom, full of love, understanding, and encouragement, yet simple in all she did.

Having five brothers and two sisters was a full household; mom and dad also served as foster parents for children from Catholic Charities. I don't remember any time in my early years that I didn't have a foster brother or two around. Mom and dad eventually adopted one of the boys who was a year and nine months younger than me. With such a full home (nine boys and two girls), one was often pushed to process things in an internal way. While we shared spirituality as a family, it was limited to Mass on the weekends, family rosary many times throughout the year (daily during Advent and Lent), and fun celebrations of the Church Feasts. When I shared with my parents that I might want to try seminary, they weren't surprised.

Our home parish was St. Benedict, staffed by monks from St. Meinrad Monastery. I witnessed the community of the rectory and the plentitude of personnel (at one point there were as many as six priests living in the rectory). However, the thinning of the numbers of priests had already begun, as I entered my first year of high school seminary in 1967.

The high school seminary at St. Meinrad Archabbey had closed in the early 60's, and the Bishop of the diocese saw a need to compensate for the loss. The high school seminary opened in 1963, and closed nine years later in 1972. Mine was the fifth class to enter, and we graduated in 1971. We started with a class of twenty five in ninth grade, and by graduation, we had dwindled to eight. Three of us went on to college seminary, graduated, and entered into theology studies.

By Christmas of our first year of theology, we were down to two. My classmate and I were both ordained for the Diocese of Evansville in 1979, the first to be ordained in two years. In a Diocese where it had been customary to have two to four ordinations annually, this was significant. Over the next eight years, there would be only six ordained to the active ministry, yet far more would resign, retire, relocate, or die.

My years in seminary were 1967 thru 1979, which coincide with the main period of time that the initial changes of the Second Vatican Council were being implemented. I always saw myself as one of those on the learning curve, helping to "turn the altars around" (literally and figuratively!). Many of the Liturgical changes were initiated in seminary chapels, and liturgical music became an opportunity for celebrations to express things never before experienced in a liturgical celebration. This, coupled with the stress on "individuality", gave me many experiences in life that always seemed to lead to that "inner thing" about which I speak.

I was often afraid to speak up and voice what I was thinking about current events, as I feared hurting others' feelings. It was easier for me to listen to others, process on the inside, smile, and move on. While growing up in a large family, the younger children were often expected to be seen and not heard. This carried over into my high school and college years.

The seminary was a system afloat with change. Gone were the organized and structured environments I had witnessed when two of my older brothers were in seminary in the late 50's and early 60's; and besides, I had elected to attend college and theology in Cincinnati, Ohio, a break from the tradition of the Diocese of Evansville. Such "inner thinking and decision making" didn't sit well with the Vocations Director, but fortunately Bishop Shea was new enough to the Evansville Diocese that he had yet to be pulled into the established politics of the Diocese.

Thirteen days before my ordination, my father, with whom I was very close, had a massive heart attack. At the time he, mom, and a few others were placing registration papers into the weekly parish bulletin of my home parish, inviting the members of the parish to the celebration. He collapsed, never regained consciousness, and died four days later, just ten days prior to Ordination. The decision to turn off life support was a joint decision between mom and me, as it was clear that recovery would be virtually impossible. I didn't realize until sometime later that this was a seed bed for guilt, as well as extreme anger.

I distinctly remember approaching the Vocations Director during the week between dad's funeral and Ordination, assuring him that I was processing everything to make certain that I was in the right frame of mind for Ordination. Reflecting back, I wonder if that "inner thing" wasn't trying to help someone challenge me as to whether or not I should take some extra time before being ordained, to time reflect and search. It wasn't that I believed I shouldn't be ordained at the time, but, being where I am in life now, were someone to experience something similar, I would be compelled to offer a challenge about them taking time to reflect. Making life altering changes in one's life during a time of flux is risky, to say the least.

Nevertheless, I was ordained, and was blessed with many good life experiences as a parish priest. On the day of Ordination in June, 1979, there were about 114 diocesan and 6 Religious-Order priests serving in the Diocese. This number would steadily dwindle as the days passed, to the point in November, 1993, there were between seventy five and eighty serving the Diocese. The number of Religious had also dwindled to five in active duty in the Diocese. My home parish, which had four to six priests from St. Meinrad in the 70's, shrunk to two in the early 90's. With these sorts of trends, many things weighed heavily on my mind.

I was blessed from the time I was ordained as a deacon in March, 1978, until a few months after I initiated my leave of absence to be affiliated with a fabulous support group of priests. We averaged eight to ten in number, and I can't begin to express how much I relied on them for that "inner processing." It was there that I could be outspoken, honest, and sincere. The life experiences, the openness, and the resourcefulness of the group frequently stimulated the "inner processing" to which I was so accustomed.

From early on, I was disturbed by various situations, church actions (and lack thereof), and individuals I encountered in the active ministry. One of the greatest sources of discord was my uncle, Fr. Mike. My mother was third youngest of thirteen children, and Fr. Mike was two above her in family order.

Being my mother's older brother, he established himself as the "family" priest, especially after his father died at age thirty-nine. Mom was seven years old at the time, and this was in 1923. His going away to seminary left one less mouth to feed, and in the summer months, he worked in a cigar factory. Fr. Mike was a very intelligent man, and prided himself in the role of family priest. Over the years, every one brought problems, difficulties, and conflicts to him, and he was viewed, as many priests were at the time, as the educated one with all the answers. For the time in his early priesthood, that was acceptable, as few were as educated in society as the local priests.

However, with the Second Vatican Council, coupled with the changes happening in society in the 60's and 70's, such wisdom no longer fit the persona of priesthood. Lay people felt empowered, speaking out and becoming educated in theology and church history. The priest was no longer the only source of knowledge in society, and there were times when members of a congregation actually knew more than the pastor who was preaching.

My priest's support group knew well of my struggle with Mike, but seemed often to dismiss it much as they dismissed the importance of Fr. Mike's approach to ministry. During one priests' support group meeting, a really funny "Little Mike" one-liner surfaced with me as the butt of the joke. It was aimed to ease the conflict I was experiencing at the time. While all laughed, I stared at the entire group with a stern face and stated simply, "You know, some things aren't really funny".

It was that day that the group began to realize the conflict I experienced in that "inner thing" over Fr. Mike's persona. He was never "Mike", or "Uncle Mike", or "Uncle Fr. Mike", but "Fr. Mike." I didn't appreciate or agree with much of his approach to ministry, to people, or to priesthood. This was a source of inner conflict for me, because I had a clearly different approach: simple, less removed, and more people oriented.

It drove him nuts when I didn't wear my black shirt and collar to family gatherings, when I didn't dress in alb and stole at the liturgical celebrations on priests' retreats, or when others felt comfortable (as did I) at calling me Joe, rather than Fr. Joe. Others respected me, and called on me as a minister, frequently reminding me that I didn't "act like a priest". Fr. Mike once confronted me with that fact, and I assured him I didn't want to "act like a priest," I just wanted to "be a priest." He couldn't handle it.

He was human, that I could handle. I drove him home one evening after a priests' gathering because his level of intoxication was such that he wasn't safe to drive. He never found out about the parishioners who assisted with that task; I saw to that, because he would have been mortified. His self-righteousness at times like this would make me angry, and then he would pull the superior "Fr. Mike" card on me. Interestingly, I couldn't handle that, and I figured out some years later that this was a real source of conflict for me.

I loved him as my uncle, but grew to despise him as a leader and responsible minister. He seemed to take advantage of his role as priest, at times expecting special treatment because of his collar. This ran contrary to what I understood by humility, service, and ministry. Perhaps the best way for me to reflect on this relationship was to be grateful for what it taught me about being more authentic as a person and minister.

My choice of leaving the active ministry probably stretched over the course of the fourteen and a half years of my ordained ministry as a priest. The pastors with whom I was privileged to serve, save one, were great leaders and mentors, genuinely caring and supportive throughout my ministry.

As a seminarian and deacon, I was likewise blessed with great leaders; what I find interesting is that, in all there were six different "bosses" with whom I ministered in parishes, three as pastors, and four in parish internships prior to ordination. Three of the four preceptors in my internships, and one of the pastors with whom I served left the active ministry over the years for various reasons. I respected them all (and still do!), but I am reminded that the seeds of conflict were always present.

I never struggled with the responsibilities and duties of ministry, and in fact was encouraged and challenged in them. That with which I so frequently struggled wasn't about the issues of ministry, but of others' interpretations of what and whom I should be. The "Inner Thing" was to constantly process others' expectations, and judge the value and realistic nature of the different definitions of "Priesthood".

In February, 1982, at age twenty-nine, I was diagnosed with Rheumatoid arthritis, a major setback in my life. I was healthy, unaccustomed to being sick, one who greeted each day in full stride at daybreak, and didn't slow down until late in the evening. Needless to say, I went through what the Greeks call "metanoia", a total change of person at this point.

Over the course of two to three years, I became perhaps 70% disabled in both arms from the shoulders down due to swelling, aching, exhaustion, fatigue, and depression. There was no warning, no failure of systems, no decline in physical ability. It was a very sudden onset, and very difficult to accept. I suffered to varying degrees with the different stages of the disease for the rest of my years in the active ministry. This disability served to keep me grounded in the important ministry of visitation with the sick in a parish.

The first assignment as an ordained priest was a wonderful experience with a young, vibrant, and growing parish. The people were a challenge, with many needs and an ever-changing congregation. Fortunately, the pastor, the other associate pastor, the parish deacons (of which there were two), the school staff, and the Religious Education directors came together as a team and worked well within the parish.

It was a great time for one with such energy, but after three years I was transferred to an even larger parish with even greater needs, but with quite a different, almost stagnant, congregation. Thankfully, my first impression of this congregation changed in the first year of my assignment. The second assignment was a much more conservative environment than that to which I had become accustomed, and created great struggle for me. It was a congregation that seemed to WANT a priest in the rectory and sanctuary only, taking me back rather quickly to my "Fr. Mike" days.

Within 6 months of my transfer (January, 1983), however, the pastor who had been there for a while announced that he was retiring in June, and a new pastor was appointed about a month later. The fellow associates with whom I served in that assignment were both very genuinely pastoral men, with a commitment to spirituality like I had never before experienced. I learned much from the two of them, and see them as having been a heavenly blessing for me in ministry. They helped me realize that, outside of my support group of priests, there were others deeply committed to simplicity and genuine Christian charity in the priesthood and beyond!

With the new pastor, we faced great challenges in the parish, as many things had come to be accepted as "the way things are done" because no one had ever challenged them. The challenges I faced in this assignment raised my awareness of the changes needing to happen in the church, and the many hurdles to those changes. At this time, the Diocese was also facing a slow decline in the number of men in active ministry; as the clergy aged, new vocations to the priesthood were just not coming forward.

Also at this time, the Church in general was seeing a steady increase in the median age of newly-ordained priests. The issues of married priests and ordaining women to the priesthood were hot topics of discussion, even in the conservative parish in which I was serving, but were not "official" topics for discussion within the "Church". The struggle for me was simple, and yet processed deeply within that "Inner" world that I treasured so much. My Priest Support Group offered a ready venue for discussions, though we were very united in our thinking. All of us had worked in many different situations with females, and all of us knew many women who were most qualified as pastoral leaders. Yet, because they were of the female gender, they were disqualified as potential "Ordained Priestly Ministers." This created great struggle within me, and was frequently the subject of my inner processing. Thus it became part of my "Inner Thing."

During this time, I also experienced the rather sudden death of my mother at age 68. She had not been in ill health, but suddenly suffered a brain bleed one Friday evening. She recovered from the surgery to relieve the pressure on the brain, and was recuperating in the hospital.

Eight days after the surgery, on a Sunday, she suffered a blood clot in the lungs while in the hospital, which killed her almost instantly. I rushed to town from the parish, about an hour's distance, but there was never any hope. That day, I experienced a loss that cannot be measured, and now here I was, age thirty-two, and feeling like an orphan. After mom's funeral, my siblings and I gathered back at the funeral home to take the various plants, planters, etc.

After we claimed the various items, everyone turned to leave, and at that moment, I experienced for the first time a feeling of ultimate abandonment, an emptiness of the "inner" self, and I blurted out, "I really love you guys!" I think it was the first time I had ever shown that sense of loneliness, and my siblings knew little as to how to deal with it. But then, how could they? *I didn't know what to do with it,* something which would come back to haunt me.

During the fourth year of my second assignment, I became aware of the need for increased lay involvement in the parish in the youth program. I had been the designated youth minister of the pastoral team, and it was increasingly apparent to me that, with the steady decline of the number of priests in active ministry, and no reversing of that trend in sight, I approached the pastor with the recommendation that the parish begin an immediate search and hiring of a lay youth minister. I was immediately assigned the task of developing a job description, a list of needs, and then establish a salary recommendation. Little did I realize how my life was about to change.

Over the next several months the task was initiated. The job description was developed, and general estimates of needs, salary, and benefits created. The interviews began, and in the summer of 1986, the new Youth Minister was hired. She faced a challenging task, as I had been the one for four years to whom everyone had brought issues of youth ministry. Despite her hiring, the issues continued to flow to me as the "priest," and again I frequently flashed back to the "Fr. Mike" syndrome. I regretted, and resented, the fact that others couldn't see the wisdom of a lay person in that role.

In the Fall of 1986, after she had been in the position for a few months, I made the decision to put in for transfer the following summer. I saw this as the only way to help the parish realize the importance of her role as youth minister. The inner processing told me that for the Youth Program to continue to flourish, strong lay leadership was essential, and there was no way that could happen as long as I stayed in the picture.

That youth minister and I became good co-workers in the time we served together; not only did we share a common mission in youth ministry, but we grew together spiritually and socially. During Advent and Lent we chose to limit any social contact, and spend that time reading scripture and journaling. During the

Christmas and Easter seasons, we would spend some social time sharing that journaling, growing in that relationship with God through each other. After I transferred the following summer, we maintained contact, often combining youth groups for retreats, mission trips, and other projects.

With my transfer, I became a pastor for the first time at age thirty-four. I had never lived alone, and was not prepared for the experience. In the assignment, I was responsible for two parishes, doing five Masses per weekend between the two parishes. The worshipping communities were quite different in their makeup, not one better than the other, just different. Living alone, I enjoyed being busy. The thought of cutting back on the Mass schedule almost threatened me, though at the time I didn't realize it. In my "Inner Processing", I managed to convince myself that if I reduced the number of Masses per weekend, I would encounter the wrath of the parishioner who had to adjust their routine. I would also have more free time, and this was something I wasn't prepared to handle.

In the first few months of the assignment, I managed to stay very busy between meeting new people, adjusting to new expectations, and learning the layout of the community. However, the loneliness grew on me, like a slow developing cancer. I often hated to see the close of the last Mass on Sunday morning, because, even though I was exhausted physically and emotionally, going into that empty house was like falling into this giant chamber devoid of any humanity.

I would quickly escape the house to some activity, just to keep from being there, alone, empty, and having, seemingly, nothing and no one to share the "let down" of the weekend. I shared this notion of "let down" with my support group, trying through my "Inner Processing" to find a way to face this loneliness. I had lived in a large family, passed through seminary development of twelve years with peers, served in parishes with brothers in ministry, but had never experienced the emptiness of the "letdown". I didn't have smoking, alcohol, gambling, or other habits on which I could fall back. I was limited with my arthritis, which had been in remission, and I suffered a flare up of the disorder, which intensified my depression.

Shortly after I was ordained as a priest in 1979, I had experienced some similar emptiness and aloneness, though not as intense. At that time I approached my "boss", the pastor, who agreed that some psychotherapeutic counseling might not be a bad idea. I met with a psychologist who did evaluative work ups for St. Meinrad Seminary for many years, and we met for therapeutic counseling for about eight to nine months. I processed my feelings of loss, anger, hurt, pain, and struggle over dad's death, and owe a great deal to that man who helped me not only to process these things, but also helping me develop *HOW* to process things of this sort. He is the one who taught me how to go to the "Inner Thing" many times on my own.

Throughout my ministry, I would, on occasion, meet with him for a mental health checkup. Ours was an open and honest relationship, and I genuinely felt I could never shock him. Once I moved into the parish as the sole parish priest responsible for two parishes in two different communities and began to experience the loneliness and emptiness, I knew something was wrong. I remember distinctly calling him one day, a Saturday afternoon, crying and depressed. As an adult in my mid-thirties, I knew something wasn't right about all this, and my depression was worsening.

I struggled to keep this quiet, fearful that someone from the parish might walk in and "catch" me crying, and report me. The counselor spoke with me for a while on the phone, offered an immediate counseling session, even offered to come to the parish to see me. I told him I could hang on until Monday, and so we met on Monday morning. Somehow knowing that I had someone to "go to" gave me the strength to survive. I frequently worried that the parishioners would somehow "find out" about my struggles, and I would be evaluated as unfit for parish life. I feared transfer to a different environment, one that provided the community support, such as a chaplain of a convent or a mental health hospital. In my mindset, this would be failure. No, it needed to remain "an inner thing", and so I struggled. The struggle was not with the responsibilities and duties of ministry, but of the loneliness of that empty chamber devoid of any humanity.

I thoroughly enjoyed the socialization, visitation, and celebrations of ministry. I even volunteered with the Diocesan Tribunal office to help with obtaining testimony in marriage cases in my area. Many times, in the process of an annulment, it is necessary to obtain input from all parties of an annulment. When a non-Catholic was involved, they seldom understood the process, and only saw it as a Catholic divorce that made any children born of the union illegitimate. I welcomed the opportunity to pull a virtual "cold call", as they call it in sales, on the unsuspecting party.

More often than not, I could obtain the information needed to move the case along that had been stagnant for a few years, many times establishing new friendships in the process. Being involved in parish ministry as well as parish business was a welcome event for me, and helped me to grow and develop as a spiritual person. However, after these events, that empty chamber, devoid of any humanity, viciously returned.

My later years in this assignment witnessed an increase in my counseling, as I struggled with the loneliness. I often felt called to more. As the inner struggle grew, it spilled over into the day to day responsibilities of parish life, sometimes leading to conflict with parish business and the many individuals who attempted to assist with the running of the parish. The parish council felt compelled to challenge my position in establishing a process for parish priorities, at times demanding to be the sole determinant of the direction of the parish.

At one point, over half the group decided to go to the Bishop behind my back, reporting my lack of responsible leadership. To his credit, Bishop Gettelfinger summoned a meeting between the council and me that he would chair, in which he reviewed Diocesan policy and the responsibilities of the pastor. Not all were happy with the meeting, and several resignations resulted. None of this sort of pressure ever really bothered me, since, in that "inner thing", I always processed it as part of the responsibility of being a pastor. However, after all was said and done, I returned home to that empty chamber devoid of any humanity.

I put in for transfer once more, and this time was placed at a parish in the town in which I grew up. This was the closest I had ever been to family members, and one brother and his wife and children lived in the parish. The move was a blessing, as it became much easier to be part of family which helped alleviate some of the loneliness, yet being a busy pastor in a large parish whose school was part of a consolidation of three parish schools managed to monopolize my time.

Once again, by the time I was able to organize myself well enough to share time with family, I discovered that their lives were even busier with children and grandchildren. The loneliness grew, intensified by the fact that, even though I was closer to family, I was as distant as I had ever been. I was happy in my pastoral ministry, and truly felt called (as even now I feel called) to be in ministry with/for/to others.

However, I continued to live alone, and this grew more significant in my experience of parish ministry. I struggled with the isolation, being separated with no one to talk to. It just seemed that life had more to offer, and that I was called to more.

Through counseling, I explored the depths of that "seeking more", the experience of which was always influenced by all the supportive and exciting events of the parish in which I served. The school had a wonderful staff, and I was frequently welcomed and affirmed by staff and students alike. Yet, once returning to the rectory, I found the experience of that empty chamber, devoid of humanity.

As many people grow and mature through their twenties, thirties, and into their forties, relationships play a very important part in the development of the personality of an individual. For many priests, family, especially parents, become the central focus of "relationship". Being celibate, priests are limited in how they develop friendships.

For priests, interaction with the laity can be difficult for several reasons: 1) close relationships with members of the parish provide a seed bed for jealousy and suspicion for others in the parish who don't sense that same "closeness" with the pastor; 2) years ago, the numbers of priests were plentiful enough that gathering with other priest friends was an easy thing to accomplish, but those numbers have dwindled enough that priests don't have time for each other and the distance makes gathering difficult; 3) priests are often very public figures, and their activity is often scrutinized by many; and, finally, 4) some priests become accustomed to being alone, and being around others becomes an annoyance and an intrusion into their private space.

To be honest, I never realized just how selfish I was until I married and had children. I have always felt like I missed out on developing healthy relationships since my parents were both deceased by the time I was in my early 30's. Had it not been for a wonderful relationship with my priest support group from early on, I would never have been as happy and successful as I felt I was in the active ministry. Though we gathered only monthly, it was the one time in a month that I could look forward to fellowship and sharing on that "inner level". I realize today how blessed I was with those gentlemen, and how much I miss them even now, after many years of marriage.

So why did I leave the active ministry? There was no one thing, event, person, or situation that I can clearly identify that caused me to leave the active ministry. My decision was a result of a development of my inner processing of many different things going on in my being.

From the time that I was first interested in the possibility of priesthood, I had expectations of the life to which I was entering. I expected to work with others at the task of prayer, leadership, and education; I expected to develop lasting relationships with other priests, nurtured on a regular basis through the camaraderie and friendships of priesthood; I expected to enter an environment of church leaders similar to those I experienced in my home parish; I expected to be an influence in the education and leadership of the local community, a respected individual whose opinion and leadership made a difference. One thing that I did not count on was the influence of the Second Vatican Council on my expectations, and how it would open me to my expectations in ways I never dreamed possible.

The Second Vatican Council's main purpose, as cited by Pope John XXIII, was to open the windows and let the fresh air into the Church. This resulted in greater opportunities for lay participation in governance, leadership, spiritual development, and liturgy. It also called for more dialogue with people of other faiths. In light of these developments from the Council, I was blessed with many opportunities to encourage growth in the life of the Church.

The Benedictine monks who staffed my home parish when I was a child impacted my experience of church and community. The number of priests were dwindling quickly, with some research suggesting that the numbers were anticipated to deteriorate to the point that very early in my active ministry, most parishes would have one resident priest, and some would be served by a non-resident pastor.

My expectations of camaraderie, consultation, friendships, bonding, and mutual support were dashed in these times, as there wasn't time for priests to gather on a regular basis. Clergy who had lived in a home of two or three priests found themselves living alone, or with someone who was vastly different in their thinking. The older priests were struggling with the changes in liturgy, parish leadership, and the direction of the church.

Welcoming lay people into the leadership roles required turning loose of the control the pastor traditionally held, a fact greatly desired by the associate pastor, but often resented by the pastor. Pastors were genuinely concerned that the laity be adequately educated in the theology of the church, and associate pastors envisioned the laity as a breath of new life in the church community. I never experienced any of this as a great struggle, as I was blessed with great pastors both in my five internships prior to ordination, as well as in my roles as an associate pastor.

Just eight years into ordained ministry, I was appointed a pastor of two parishes, providing five Masses per weekend between the two parishes. I had been given no training in being a pastor of a parish, although I don't know that there is a way to train for this sort of an experience. While both parishes were vastly different, they each had a special character of their own, which I truly enjoyed. Bouncing between them was challenging, but helped me to keep a perspective on the wide nature of the theology of the church. My primary struggle during these years was trying to keep a balance between professional expectations of the pastor, and taking care of myself as a person.

I have referred several times previously to my struggle with living alone, and desire for companionship. This led to an increase in the frequency of my counseling with my long-time therapist; and in our discussions, he began to take an interest in the dreams that I was experiencing, helping me to digest the dreams, and to decipher meaning from them. This became a great help in my discernment process, tapping into that "Inner Thing" about which I have spoken often.

Another development for me was the close, supportive, spiritual friendship that I had experienced with the Youth Minister that I had hired in my second assignment. As I stated previously, we maintained contact after I left the parish, and grew together in our understanding of ministry, church, and spirituality. As I also stated previously, at the time of the hiring of that Youth Minister, I had no idea how my life was to change.

She was a very positive, challenging, and supportive force for me from that day forward. She frequently turned to me for explanations and discussions of how things were handled by other priests in the way they were. She was born in 1962, with no previous experience of the pre-Vatican II church; she was the second youngest of 12 children, and her parents were "older". She came from a rather conservative background, and yet found herself very active in an ever changing world of priests, theology, and church practices.

She lacked the fire of a "flaming liberal", but developed great wisdom and passion for the growth of her own spirituality, as well as that of others. Many times her efforts within the pastoral ministry field provided many opportunities for her and me to share ideas and ministry. I personally grew to value her as a person, as well as a spiritual influence. Little did I realize how much all of this influenced my growth and understanding of theology, people, and ministry. Over time, she grew as a very significant influence in my "Inner Processing", helping me to appreciate others who are introverted.

I continued in counseling during those last two years of active ministry, struggling with something I couldn't identify, but feeling in that "Inner Processing" that there was more in my future. In August of 1993, a close friend and member of my support group abruptly left the active ministry. This shook my inner self, and upset me greatly. His departure was announced the Friday before a group of pilgrim youth left to see the Pope in Colorado, and I went along with the group as one of the chaperones. This didn't leave much opportunity for me to process John's departure as part of that "Inner Thing", and returning to the parish after that week and a half in Colorado found me very busy, and again not processing what was going on in my psyche. I finally turned to counseling with my therapist with little success. I felt the call to more in my life, and yet couldn't identify just exactly what that was.

I finally made the decision to meet with Bishop Gettelfinger in the second week of October, 1993, and decided to take a leave of absence from the active ministry. Bishop Gettelfinger and I discussed the situation, and, at his request, I agreed to keep my decision between us so that he could work on my replacement prior to my leave, which was to begin on the First Sunday of Advent. With that decision came an inner peace, yet my inner struggle intensified. I wasn't angry, bitter, or having any negative feelings toward ministry. I loved what I was doing/living, and found fulfillment in ministry. I didn't want to "get out" of ministry, but instead wanted to find more through ministry.

My leave of absence began at noon, officially, on the Saturday after Thanksgiving, once I had completed the second of two funerals after Thanksgiving. The Bishop was gracious enough to have the Masses at my parish that weekend, explaining my absence to the parish, and asking for prayers for me and the Church as a whole. I received a lot of supportive, encouraging notes from many people, letting me know that they cared, and hoped that I was able to do what was best for me. In a way, their understanding and encouragement made my struggle more difficult, because I genuinely felt the love and peace of a loving congregation who cared about me, not just as a priest, but as a person.

In my leave of absence, I set to the task of job hunting, sending out résumés, reading classifieds, and talking to friends. Fortunately, I was contacted by some men who had left the active ministry a few years earlier from my diocese, and they helped me to establish some contacts that eventually led to employment. During the first six months of the leave of absence, finding a job, going to counseling, and processing my future in the "inner self" consumed my energies. I prayed for direction and wisdom, and was challenged to provide for myself. Once I formally resigned, I still searched for something more in my life.

Almost two years after I began my leave of absence, I married Beth, the Youth Minister with whom I had grown personally and spiritually over the years. As I reflect back on the years, it seems to me that we grew in a healthy way as a couple over a nine year period. We were friends who shared a common goal of ministry in a parish, and through that ministry we grew spiritually both as individuals, and as a couple (though at the time, we didn't realize it!) We have been happily married for seventeen plus years, with two teenage boys.

Finally, I am finding just what the "more" was for which I was searching. I continue to grow and discover, and marvel at how much more God has brought into my life. Beth and I married on the principle that a couple doesn't marry to find happiness; rather, you find happiness and marry to share that happiness. Our teenage sons, the product of that sharing, brighten our days, and bring great joy into our lives. The challenge of being a parent in today's world is full of obstacles and opportunities. Growing with our children through the hurdles of life brings new horizons daily, ever enriching that "more" for which I searched. Because of my relationship with my wife, I have come to appreciate a new depth of spirituality in my "Inner Processing."

A Member of Each Family

Jim Koerber

Introduction

Lacordaire begins his definition of a priest – "To live in the midst of the world without wishing its pleasures, to be a member of each family yet belonging to none, to have a heart of fire for charity...."

When I was a newly-ordained Catholic priest in the Archdiocese of Baltimore, Maryland, parishioners often asked me, "When did you first want to be a priest?" Having just completed twelve years of study after grammar school, to achieve the priesthood status, I would often honestly reply, "I really don't know. I guess I always wanted to be one." At least I was honest in my reply, and simple honesty still means a lot to me.

Family

To understand my first inclinations to choosing the priesthood as a way of life you must first know a bit about my early family life. I was born into a German Catholic family in Baltimore County in 1933. I had one brother who was three years older than I. My father was one of six children (two brothers and three sisters) and my mother was one of seven children (three brothers and three sisters). All relatives lived within about a half hour's drive from us, and visiting, or being visited by, family became a major activity every weekend.

No relatives on my father's side of the family were involved in religion beyond going to Mass on Sundays and holydays. My mother's side of the family was a different story. One of her brothers was ordained a priest in the Redemptorist order. Another brother became a lay brother in the Redemptorist order. Two of her sisters became Notre Dame nuns, one of whom died in Puerto Rico just before I was born. Another sister became a Notre Dame nun but left just before her vows became permanent.

On my mother's side of the family religious life became a major focus of attention for everyone. My brother's announcing, at age fourteen, that he wanted to go away to study to become a priest, was no surprise to anyone.

The Roman Rite of the Catholic Church in America embraces about ninety percent of American Catholics. It has two types of clergy – diocesan and religious. Diocesan clergy are ordained to serve a particular geographic area (the diocese of Charleston includes the entire state of South Carolina) and religious clergy (Redemptorists, Jesuits, Franciscans, for example) are ordained to serve a particular religious order whose boundaries may be worldwide. The priestly powers of diocesan and religious clergy are the same, and living conditions are very similar. Diocesan clergy obey their bishop who reports to the Vatican. Religious clergy obey their local superior, who reports to the superior general of the order, who may or may not reside in Rome.

The phrase "enter the seminary" had a special meaning when my brother began his priestly studies. It did not mean jumping on a street car with books and a lunch bag in his hand and coming home each evening. It meant packing up a trunk full of clothes and beginning a fourteen hour train ride to another state. The first time he returned home was ten months later. The minor seminary was just outside of Erie, Pennsylvania. He was given one way to communicate with his family – by letter—and all his outgoing mail was presented unsealed to the priest prefect so it could be read before it was sent. Similarly all incoming mail was given to him – opened – so that it could be read before he got an opportunity to read it. No exceptions. This is just the way things were.

So all through the sixth, seventh, and eighth grades of grammar school at Saint Michael's in Overlea (a suburb of Baltimore) I was for all intents and purposes an only child. Of course there was the constant "oohing" and "aahing" about my brother and about the wonderful stuff he was doing in preparing to be a priest, but I was never too much impressed. I guess it's because for much of my early years at home I remember being unfavorably compared to him with phrases such as "why can't you be more like your brother" and "Charles always did that, and why can't you?" No physical abuse, no neglect, but a sort of constant belittling that implied I should be different than the way I was.

I didn't have a lot friends my own age when I was growing up in Baltimore County. There are many good reasons for this. Very few kids my age lived within walking distance. I can remember only one, Buddy, who lived across the street one or two houses away. But Buddy had a problem he didn't even know about. He was a non-Catholic, and to my hyper-religious family that was tantamount to saying he was at best a leper and at worst a pariah.

Also, I was a Catholic being driven to a Catholic school each day by my mother, and picked up each day at 3:00pm when school was out. In school I could play with classmates during recesses and lunch break. When the school day was over all my classmates walked back to their homes and I got into my mom's waiting car.

When my brother came home after his first year in seminary high school I had not seen him in ten months. For me this absence was not the worst thing in the world, as even when we were in the same location we did very little together. We didn't like each other and we were never taught how to try to do anything different. Two months of summertime with each other brought on a whole new schedule. We had to go to Mass every morning of the week as now my brother was a seminarian. At Sunday Mass, and at visits to all the relatives, my brother was the center of attraction because he was studying to be a priest...and I wasn't. This distinction was never spoken out loud, but the meaning was just as clear as if it had been shouted from the highest hilltop.

I was in the eighth grade of grammar school and not too sure of what I wanted to do. I knew I had to go to high school, I knew I had to get an education, and I knew the very high pedestal my brother had been placed on by becoming a Redemptorist seminarian. Up to the eighth grade, school day contact with classmates was my major way of relating to other people. I may have spent a few hours a week with Buddy who lived across the street, but because he was a non-Catholic this rarely happened.

With my brother away in the seminary ten months out of the year I was isolated as a child even within my own family. Christmas and Easter came and went without him, so I learned to amuse myself by doing homework, listening to the radio, and attending school. On rare occasions there would be a baseball game to play at Glenmore Park or a drum and bugle practice to go to, but this was the exception rather than the general rule.

I wish I could share something dramatic with you about how and when I decided I wanted to be a Redemptorist priest. Nothing dramatic happened. It was expected that since my uncle was a priest and my brother was away in a seminary studying to be a priest, I would go away to do the same. Somehow or other I guess I agreed to follow the great expectations (apology to Charles Dickens) my family had for me.

One thing I can remember as clear as if it were yesterday. My dad was driving me up Ridge Road to the corner grocery store to get some bread for lunch. He looked over at me as I sat next to him on the front seat of the car.

"You know," he said gently, "you don't have to go to North East if you don't want to."

That's all he said. Dad alone picked up on my lack of positive statements about going to North East where no one else had, and I was grateful to him for that.

I answered quietly, "no, I really do want to go." I was too much of a coward to say anything else, but I was really grateful that my Dad had heard the real me. In May just before my brother came home for the two-month summer vacation I took a scholarship examination for the diocesan Seminary in Catonsville, Maryland. To everyone's surprise I won the full six year scholarship, but turned it down because of my previous commitment to the Redemptorist priesthood.

I vividly recall how much my mother and father enjoyed being with us kids and enjoyed having us around them, and enjoyed bragging about our accomplishments to family and friends. Mother really liked to cook, and she gave 100% to every meal she placed on the table. Dad liked to eat with all of us, which meant dinner each evening and all meals on Saturday and Sunday. Church attendance on Sunday was never a chore, but a time to get dressed up and do something important in front of the rest of the world. It was a real time of celebration and it meant a lot to all of us. We always had a vegetable garden, strawberry patch, and fruit trees real close to the house, so a lot of family time was spent planting, cultivating, and harvesting these crops so they could then be prepared to grace the family dinner table.

Nothing much changed, except that in my brother's fourth year in the minor seminary, and my first year there with him, a two week Christmas vacation at home was granted to all for the first time in the history of the institution. As can be seen, family ties and dynamics and relationships meant absolutely nothing to the religious seminary mentality. In fact after the sixth year of minor seminary (second year of college) a seminarian got a one-month vacation and then he never got to visit his home again until ordination six years later. When family is denigrated, and little else of value is put in its place, all sort of chaos follows. The religious seminary system of fifty years ago no longer exists today, and with good reason.

Minor Seminary

This idea, which I had lived for fourteen years, of a closely-knit family life was about to come to a screeching halt. On August 28, 1947, my mother and father took my brother and I to the Pennsylvania train Station in Baltimore, kissed us goodbye, and watched as we climbed aboard a day coach car and waved goodbye through the dirty train windows. Fourteen hours later we arrived in the town of North East, Pennsylvania, and walked about one mile or so to the seminary cluster of buildings.

We were tired and hungry (no dining car or enough money to buy food was available) and scared, and as soon as we got to the main building my brother left me to go see which of his classmates had retuned and which had not. It was a big difference from being one of a family of four people to become one of a group of three hundred fifty strangers. To transition from a dining room where four people ate to one where two hundred fifty people ate was a shock to the system. A room with two beds in it became an area where one hundred twenty-five beds were lined up in perfect order. The immensity of everything was mind numbing, but the changes kept coming and I adapted as best I could.

One of the first things I did upon entering the seminary was to put all my money (change, dollar bills, train ticket) into an envelop and turn it in to the prefect of students who would return it to me in 10 months when I was ready to leave for summer vacation.

I was quickly assigned a place in chapel, the study hall, the sleeping area, and the refectory (dining hall) and the lavatory (60 sinks with running water – cold only). When a bell rang to summon me to each location, I were told that this bell was actually God's voice, and the more quickly I broke out in complete silence and did what God wanted, the better seminarian I was. Difficult, stupid, and intriguing, maybe in a slightly different order, but that's how I remember things.

In my new home away from home one of the first things that happened to me was homesickness. It set in quickly and with devastating effects. No family support, no peer support. I was immediately transformed into being a stranger in a strange land.

Constant interaction with adults I knew and trusted vanished overnight. Parental contact, meeting relatives, visiting adult friends of family- these things didn't happen anymore. Instead I interacted with about one hundred twenty-five peers, strangers within one or two years of my age, and that was that.

Also, the rule of the seminary was, "*Raro uno, nunquam duo, semper tres*: (rarely one, never two, always three)" but not always the same three. Particular friendships were absolutely forbidden and could not only lead to expulsion, but even more importantly, as part of the rule I was expected to observe in its entirety, they were forbidden by God.

The rule I lived by each moment of my life was commanded by God Himself, or so I was told. From age fourteen to age twenty, five days out of every seven, life went something like this. I rose at 5:20 a.m., began to study at 5:45, went to chapel at 6:30, ate breakfast at 7:00, all in complete silence. After breakfast I could talk as I ran upstairs, made my bed, scrubbed my teeth, and got to study hall by 8:00 a.m.

Then more silence, three one hour classes, interrupted by a fifteen minute walk outside unless it was raining. Absolute silence the entire time, except for the walk outside. The afternoon went much the same way, with two one hour classes. A long chapel visit, dinner, and more study time. Student life could have been aptly called "the silence of the lambs".

Academically this was an excellent routine, because if I could not learn what was needed with all this mandatory study time I probably was intellectually substandard. Also, all of our high school professors had their doctoral degrees. One important thing was missing: LOVE/FAMILY.

My family no longer existed. They were hundreds of miles away and I would see them for only two months of the year. My brother was in the seminary with me, and I could talk with him for a few minutes after lunch and dinner each day. That was all that was allowed.

I can still recall that in the second year of high school I had a midterm exam that required that I memorize the four major tenses of two thousand irregular Latin verbs. In the last year of high school I could take the final English exam or write down from memory the one hundred eighty-two line poem "The Hound of Heaven" by Francis Thompson. This was a major part of growing up as a teenager in a religious seminary.

One final comment about high school, the graduation ceremony was a big event. All the fourth year students gathered on stage, dressed in their Sunday best, and received their diplomas amid the applause of the entire seminary student body and faculty. In my first year I sat in the audience and clapped as my brother got his diploma.

My graduation day was not as fortunate. The new director of the seminary decided to eliminate the graduation ceremony starting with my class. My class was told to pick up our diplomas, which would be piled in a laundry basket outside our classroom door, on the way to the train station on June 28. We did just that, stuffing our diplomas into our suitcases with dirty laundry and toothpaste tubes as we ran to catch the train. Thus the seminary celebrated our successful completion of four years of high school.

Lightning Strikes

Freshman year of college started off just like any other year. I was cruising along among the top three in each subject I took. We all took the same subjects; we had no choice. In February we all met in the auditorium where the seminary director read out the grades of every student to all of us assembled there. After he finished reading out my grades, which were mostly in the high nineties, there was a murmur of appreciation and wonder from the student body that one of their group had done so well. The director stopped and cautioned us, "Grades are not everything. There is much more to look at. Mr. Koerber, please see me in my office after this function."

Not only was I stunned, but everyone else also fell into complete silence. After the meeting I left the auditorium and went below to meet with the director. He invited me in and asked me to sit down. He then showed me a yellow wooden pencil that way lying on the desk. He said, "If I told you that the pencil was green, and asked you to say that it was green, would you do it?" I was fully aware of the requirements of blind obedience, and truthfully replied, "Yes, I would." Then what little integrity I had would not be denied, and I added, "But I would know it was yellow."

The director came alive immediately. "I knew it," he exclaimed. "You have no vocation to be a Redemptorist. You can finish the school year here in the seminary, but you will not be allowed to return in the fall. That is all. I have nothing more to say." I left the office slowly. I could hardly fathom how so much had changed so quickly. No recourse was available. That was it.

I went up to see the director of students and he told me he was aware of the seminary director's decision and I was to do the best I could until June 28 when we all left for summer vacation. I said to myself, "Cheer up, Jim, things could be worse." So I cheered up and, sure enough, things got worse.

In early May the director of students called me into his office and told me he just got word that my father had died. I had one half hour to pack my suitcase and then he would drive me to the airport so I could go home to attend the funeral. Similarly to the recent news of having to leave the seminary, I was given no support or counseling to help me deal with this new crisis. I was driven to the airport in silence and flew home for the funeral. At home there was such chaos over my father's unexpected death that I decided not to inform the family then of the fact that when I returned home that summer I would not be allowed to return to the seminary.

When I came home in June I told my mother the news of my dismissal from the Redemptorist seminary. She phoned her brother, Father Schruefer, the Redemptorist priest. He phoned the family's pastor in Overlea, and to make a complicated situation a whole lot less complicated, in less that one week I was accepted as a seminarian in St. Charles College, Catonsville, Maryland. I was able to use the fully paid scholarship I had earned five years ago. Class started in September of 1952, the year my father died. God writes straight with crooked lines.

This was a time of great change, excitement, and adjustment. Simple, but important, differences began to appear. Now I could actually have money in my pocket. I could use the telephone to call home. At Thanksgiving and Easter I could visit home overnight. I could walk through a downtown city with classmates on certain days off. I felt alive again. Since then I have always appreciated my good academic record. Call it the arrogance of competence, but so be it.

I'd like to say the minor seminary in Catonsville was a lot better than the one in North East, but it wasn't. It had a lot more privileges and nuance, but basically it operated under the same premise: "Do what you're told, keep your mouth shut, and things will be okay." I did, and things were okay. Nearness to home meant an awful lot, and seeing the family on a regular basis really gave me a much-needed boost.

Major Seminary

Then came the transition to a new seminary in Baltimore for my last two years of college. It was on Paca Street in downtown Baltimore City and housed in a four-story building which was over one hundred years old. The top story had already been condemned, and no seminarian was allowed to go to that area. Instead of the dreaded dormitories housing hundreds of sleepers, the fist year there you had a semiprivate room, and the second year, a private room.

Each room had running water. You filled a pitcher each night with water from the lavatory at the end of the hall, and in the morning when you tipped the pitcher, the water would run.

Now comes the part that made these two years so special, the faculty. Like all other faculties I experienced, they all had their doctorates. Unlike all the other faculties I was ever associated with, they actually liked what they were doing, they did it well, and they wanted their students to like their subject as much as they did. I still remember the first Philosophy of Education Class I attended. The professor came in, introduced himself, and said, "Those who can, do; those who can't, teach; those who can't teach, teach philosophy of education." Things just got better after that.

Unfortunately the four years of postgraduate work in theology were not as educational and functional for the students. Again the faculty all had their doctorates, but that's about all they had.

The seminary was in the Roland Park section of Baltimore and housed 450 students in four years of study. Today a much-enlarged set of buildings houses less than 100 students in 7 years of study.

Finally I was ordained a priest on May 23, 1959 and celebrated my first Mass the next day in my parish of St.

Michael's Church in Overlea, Maryland. There was a big celebration in a nearby hall after the Mass at which many friends and family members showed up to share their congratulations.

When I went home that night my mother took me aside and walked with me into the kitchen pantry. She gave me a bottle of Canadian Club and told me, "Your father bought this for you the day you were born so you could open it on the day of your first Mass. He did the same thing for your brother." Now do you see where my vocation came from?

St. Peter's Church

Two weeks later a letter came from the Archbishop. As a newly-ordained priest I was assigned to St. Peter's Church, Poppleton Street, in Baltimore. It was the second oldest church in the archdiocese, near the University of Maryland Hospital in West Baltimore. I packed up my things and reported to the parish on the designated day. Would this be everything I had worked twelve years for, and dreamed about for about twice as many years? Yes it was, and more.

I was the only assistant there, the pastor was about twenty-five years older than I, and together we were to minister to about fourteen hundred parishioners and the University Hospital which then had about seven hundred beds.

It was a fabulous six years there. Busy, and worth it. One week I would spend the day visiting parishioners in their homes, walking door to door. The next week I would visit patients in the hospital, going from bed to bed. I also would teach religion to some classes in our grammar school and our two-year business school. Add to this the Sodality, Holy Name Society, Youth Group, and I wound up putting in an eighty-hour work week each week. Also, the week of hospital visitation included bringing Holy Communion to patients who wished to receive on any, or all, of the six weekday mornings. This was priestly work, and I enjoyed it immensely.

One aspect of this hospital was the medical and nursing schools attached to it, so this became an additional ministry called Newman Club work. Challenging, and fascinating at the same time. Finally, in 1965 I wrote and asked the Bishop for two items to enhance my ministry since I could not afford them on my $50.00 a month salary. The first was an air conditioner for the office, the second was an electric typewriter.

The bishop came down, looked around, and informed me that I had delusions of grandeur. I can take "no" for an answer, but it could have been phrased a bit more kindly. So I sent another letter to the bishop asking for a transfer to another parish. This time my request was granted. I was transferred to St. Andrew's Parish that was home to Johns Hopkins Hospital with over one thousand beds.

St. Andrew's Church

In my new parish I resumed my former activities in new neighborhoods, and still enjoyed them just as much. Mornings were spent teaching religion in the eighth grade grammar school and the two-year business school. Afternoons were alternated, one week visiting patients at Johns Hopkins Hospital and next week visiting residents of the parish. Another eighty-hour work week, and it meant everything to me.

I kept alive one of my better intellectual habits. Each week I would buy and read one new book on some aspect of the spiritual life. I realized early on that if I didn't read all the time I couldn't speak intelligently when talking with others. Nemo dat quod non habet. (No one gives what he does not have.) That's just the way it was.

The pastor was about thirty years older than I, and the assistant pastor was about four years my senior. The pastor said Mass each morning and I don't know what else he did with the rest of his day, but he never did the parish and hospital work that we two assistant pastors did.

Then something unusual happened. The pastor was transferred to head up a parish out in the country, so I became assistant pastor and the assistant pastor became pastor. The new pastor announced that he and I were working too hard, and from now on each of us would work one day and have the next day off. I was dumbfounded. I had not studied twelve years to work seven days out of fourteen. So I phoned a priest friend in nearby Delaware (ninety miles away) and asked him if he could use my services on a part time basis to carry on religious education in his diocese in a high school or on an adult ed basis. He was elated. I had found an outlet for my energy and my vocation.

In the spring of 1968, the Archdiocese of Baltimore sponsored for its priests a theology class of three sessions, one each week, put on by a theologian it invited down from the Philadelphia archdiocese. The price was right, it was free, and I attended the sessions.

In the last class, the teacher told us that the current Catholic position on abortion and contraception was intellectually and theologically untenable, and if we would give him out attention for fifteen minutes he would prove it to us. We did. He did. I sat there speechless. My training in theology kicked in and I could recognize the validity of everything he said. I knew my days as a messenger of the episcopacy were numbered.

A messenger's job is to deliver the message exactly as it was delivered to him. But when the messenger knows that the message he must deliver is incorrect physiologically and morally and not part of revealed doctrine, then he has to decide whether a pay check is worth more than the price of personal integrity. The yellow pencil scene from the minor seminary session with the rector flashed through my mind. Later that year I flew out west to visit a priest friend and he was not much help as far as answering my theological questions. I knew what I had to do, I just needed to find out how to do it.

Transition

The next year I asked for a transfer to another parish and the bishop responded affirmatively by sending me to a small suburban church in Maryland. Before I left St. Andrews I phoned a few nun friends of mine and told them I had some spiritual reading books they might like to have as I had too many to move all of them with me. They were delighted to meet me at the rectory and take about five hundred books off my hands. (When you buy one new book a week for ten years they add up quickly.) I arrived at my new duty station and settled in for what I thought would be normal parish life without being chaplain to a major hospital.

I was wrong. The pastor was a nice man. He said Mass every morning, helped with confessions on Saturday, and covered for me on my single day off each week. He also left the parish in his car each morning and said he'd be back that night. He came back each night but seldom in time to eat dinner in the rectory. I don't know what he did all day, and he never told me. He also made a bank deposit each Monday morning and wrote out the paychecks for the parish employees each week.

The parish was in the midst of a building campaign and the fund-raising company wrote a sermon that the archdiocese directed the priests at the parish to preach at all Sunday Masses. I read the sermon and recognized some theological errors and phoned the archdiocese to let them know that in good conscience I could not deliver that sermon as written. I was told that I had to give the sermon.

I didn't.

Monday morning I was called down to the Chancery office and asked if I would like to get some Clinical Pastoral Education at the Medical College of Virginia Hospital in Richmond, Virginia. I knew I had no option, so I told them I would accept if that was what was required of me. It should be noted that no one brought up, or offered to discuss, the statement in the sermon that brought this situation to a head. It was, "If you give

$50.00 to the building campaign, it shows you love Jesus."

My time in Richmond allowed me to finish two quarters of clinical pastoral education and gave me excellent training in group dynamics which has helped me tremendously in dealing with the public in various situations.

The psychiatrist who directed our program helped me to understand that leaving the clerical priesthood would be a necessary first step for me to address some of my problems, but that it would not solve any problems in itself.

He knew what he was talking about. I returned to the Archdiocese and Baltimore and requested a leave of absence. I told the chancery office I was in no hurry, and that I would be happy to go back to my old hospital assignment for as long as it took for the logistics to be worked out.

While I was marking time until a replacement could be found I took over half-time chaplaincy work at Johns Hopkins Hospital. Rather than resume my train trips to Delaware I enrolled at the University of Maryland in the graduate classes of Counseling at their College Park Campus.

One day I got a phone call from the Chancery Office and was asked if I'd like to spend the better part of a week at Princeton in New Jersey taking their battery of vocational aptitude tests. I agreed to do this and the Archdiocese said it would pay for the tests and my living expenses.

I arrived at Princeton one Monday at noon, and left much later in the week and returned to Baltimore. After a week passed I phoned the chancery office and asked if I would get any written report on the tests I took. They told me that since I didn't pay for the tests I would not get a written report. I asked if they could share with me verbally anything that the report said. He said the report indicated the job I was most suited for was that of a prison guard. I thanked them for the information.

Federal Government Job

I remained working at Johns Hopkins Hospital until a replacement was found. This took about six months, and then I moved to an apartment in Rockville, Maryland, and began to look for a government job in August, 1970.

At 37 years of age I had never dated a woman in my life, and I didn't have the foggiest notion of how to go about it. The apartment complex a mile or so down the highway from where I lived advertised a "singles" night so I went down to see what it was all about. Right move, wrong results. About 30 people gathered for two hours or so in an activities room setting, and everyone else either had a job or was trying to impress someone else. Very little meeting of any kind seemed to take place.

The next day I resumed my job hunting in downtown Washington, DC and attended the weekly get together of a group of priests and ministers transitioning to the non-clerical life. We traded job leads, critiqued each others' SF 171 application for employment forms, and tried to reassure each other it was just a matter of time until we got our first (of many, we hoped) paychecks.

While we were consoling each other and renewing our determination to face another week of daily job hunting, Ted, a priest from Baltimore, asked me if I'd like to meet this girl he was dating. Both of them had been classmates at the University of Michigan's School of Public Health Masters Program and were completing internships in Baltimore at the time. I told him that was a great idea and that I'd like both of them to have dinner at my apartment the next night.

The next night at 7:00 pm my doorbell rang. I opened the door. There stood Marilynn. Oh yes, Ted was there too. I invited them in and I was completely blown away. Here was a beautiful young woman; she spoke in complete sentences, and her eyes danced whenever she looked at me. I remember showing her my reclining armchair in the middle of the living room with a poster attached to the ceiling overhead. The poster said,

"Sometimes I sit and think, and sometimes I just sit." She just loved that. The evening went by too quickly, but it soon became obvious we both had a lot in common and wanted to share.

Life took on a whole new meaning for each of us after that first meeting. Her internship was finished at the end of the year and she went back to the University of Kentucky at Lexington. I kept on teaching mental health patients part time at Spring Grove State Hospital in Baltimore while looking for a federal government job.

Logistically it proved a nightmare for both of us. Living in cities over four hundred miles apart, planning a wedding in a third city, and dealing with our families who, to phrase it gently, were less than enthused about our relationship. We managed, and both of our families did also. We have now been happily married for forty-one years, and I flash back to the title of that successful movie, "Guess Who's Coming to Dinner."

Twelve years of training to become, and eleven years of practicing to be, a messenger of the episcopacy did leave an impression on me. It began to dawn on me that the content of the message was more important than the occupation of the messenger. Since the church did not officially want me to represent them, I still knew that my spreading the message was something I could carry out, whether it was officially recognized or not.

In about eight months time I returned to the chancery office and informed the archdiocese that I would be getting married soon. I went through all proper diocesan channels and petitioned the Holy See for laicization. The positive response from the Holy See was given later that same year. The chancery office transmitted this information to me eleven years later. No explanation of or apology for the delay.

The chancery officials asked me why I was leaving and I told them I was unable to believe one thing and preach something else. One chancery official told me he had no problem with that at all. He said he believed one thing and said the exact opposite from the pulpit and in the confessional. I told him I couldn't do that. He also informed me that my salary would be discontinued immediately and I reminded that I was promised this salary for a year, not for 8 months only. He said, "That's the way it is."

For twenty years and three days I worked for the federal government in the field of employment discrimination. This was a fascinating program that actually worked and got measurable results. I bring it up here so that the reader will begin to understand why I felt the message was often more important than the messenger. Sacraments, saying Mass, and saying the breviary each day are good, but getting the message of Jesus Christ to influence the lives of people is even better. This was a meaningful ministry which brought justice in a very concrete way into peoples' lives.

Say a company has a contract with a VA hospital to deliver one hundred million pills of x strength, on day y, for z dollars. Buried in this contract is a piece of paper which says the company agrees not to discriminate in employment decisions based on race, sex, religion, Vietnam era veteran, or handicap status. After receiving notice that Company A fulfilled a government contract, my office would go out to inspect the company's employment practices.

A manufacturing plant that employed five hundred people or so would routinely hire first line supervisors on a continuing basis. It was easy to get compensation records, compare education employment histories, and then note if any discrepancies showed up. I found a Florida company where only Hispanic male supervisors were hired in at the lowest salary. I found a bank in South Carolina where college graduates hired with no banking experience resulted in men being assigned to management training classes and women assigned to teller positions.

I worked in different cities and found the same type problems everywhere. In twenty years of this type of activity my staff and I got back pay of about $15,000,000 and, more importantly, economic justice for people who could not have obtained it in any other way. To me, this was priestly work, not just the world of a messenger from the episcopacy. No Roman collar, no black suit. Just results.

The companies who directly implemented these discriminatory employment practices were just doing their jobs. They were exact replicas of me in my seminary and priestly jobs, doing what I was told and keeping my mouth shut. As my blind obedience adversely impacted me, their silent acquiescence to company policy would not let the equal employment requirements of a government contract be fulfilled.

A compliance review of an industrial plant usually began and ended with a discussion with the plant manager of that particular location. I soon learned a big difference between Catholic institutions (seminaries, parishes, dioceses) and industrial plants. In industrial plants the plant manager was responsible for all the rules and the results they generated. This adult acceptance of responsibility gave me a distinct advantage in ensuring that equal employment opportunity became a reality. I was reviewing a nationwide pharmaceutical sales force at its New York headquarters.

Company policy stated that all approved leaves earned seniority credit for retirement calculations. After checking numerous files of this twelve hundred person sales force I discovered that women on approved maternity leave never received credit for the time spent on leave toward retirement calculations. The sales force was about half male and half female. Immediate changes were made, and calculations for the past two years were also figured in.

As government investigators my staff and I spoke a language that everyone understood – money. Everything that we asked to be done required money to be spent. At the other end of the solution was the money to be lost if the government contract were canceled and/or the case went before a judge with the resultant publicity. It really was a no-brainer, however you looked at it, and in reality I was an agent of change. My job allowed me to get all employees of government contractors to be regarded as human beings, not merely as robots to be slotted into stereotypical roles which said that women cannot be mechanics or that managers must be men. Equality causes some changes, but inequality causes even more problems.

One of my favorite recollections is of a handicapped complaint investigation one of my staff successfully completed at a major U.S. Corporation. We found for the complainant. The company refused to budge. The next day I got a call from my Washington office and was informed that the case was being closed administratively because the company was a major contributor to the political party then in power.

So I had the complainant come to my office the next day and told her what had been decided. I also told her that our agency had a practice whereby the complainant could receive a copy of the complaint investigation free of charge if it were requested. She asked for it, and I gave it to her. She thanked me. I never heard from her again. But months later I did hear that the company had settled a major discrimination case without going to trial.

In 1985 I was the Assistant Regional Administrator of our Boston office, and my minor seminary class reunion was being held in a nearby Connecticut town. My uncle, the Redemptorist lay brother, was also stationed in this town. I was invited to attend the celebration and give a presentation to the former seminarians who were attending with their wives and children. I accepted. After my talk, and during the question and answer session, I was asked if the minor seminary should close as it now had only about forty-seven students compared to the two hundred fifty students back in 1947. I remember asking the alumni and their families if they would want their own children to enter into the kind of student life we endured some thirty years ago. No one responded in the affirmative. The minor seminary in North East closed its doors two years later.

Today that same complex of buildings houses a state technical college which serves eight hundred students.

The chapel alone is unused. "Bare ruined choirs where late the song birds sang."

I finished my federal government service in a blaze of unexpected, and enjoyable, activity. While walking the streets of downtown Dallas I stopped into the office of a local Hispanic organization and asked if they could use the services of a loaned government executive. They said they could. A few weeks later a got a phone call from the Assistant Secretary of Labor who informed me that I would be starting in January, 1988 an Intergovernmental Personnel Assignment with SER, a national Hispanic group, in their Dallas office with all my government pay and benefits being continued by the Department of Labor. This one year of outside experience taught me more than five years of government routing.

This led to my reassignment the next year of another year of loaned executive work, this time with IMAGE, another Hispanic organization. In the midst of these two jobs I was moved, at no expense to myself, to the Washington, DC area where in 1990 I resumed my government job, not in Dallas, but in the National office of the government agency I worked for.

Things went fairly well, but it soon became obvious to everyone that I was not a yes man, and never would be. One day my boss came into my office said, "Jim, we want a black man to do your job." I replied, probably unwisely, "I can do a lot of things, but I cannot do that." He went on. "There is an obscure government personnel practice that if you apply for a promotion outside your commuting area, and win it, and are fifty-five years of age or older with twenty years of government service, you can turn down the promotion and retire." I am slow, but I am not that slow. "Do you know of any such jobs I could apply for?" I asked. He gave me an opening listed for San Francisco in a field in which I did not have one single day of experience. I won the promotion, I turned it down, and I retired from the Federal government with twenty years and three days of service.

State Government Job

After a year or so of loafing I was employed as a mental health professional by the Office of the South Carolina Department of Mental Health. I enjoyed working with the mentally ill and was pleased to help them adjust to medications and therapy in a way that brought them some semblance of order to an otherwise completely disheveled existence.

After seven years of this work I retired once more and volunteered to help one of my former patients lead a better life. He was over seventy years of age, and had been discharged from military service without a pension. I thought this strange and asked to see his papers.

There was an official government document stating he was involuntarily discharged from the locked ward of a psychiatric hospital in New York. I wrote a few letters and asked the VA to reimburse him for 40 years worth of pensions. They did, with a check for over $50,000. I was able to help him, and his mother of 90+ years, to redo the 400 square foot home they lived in. To me, this was priestly work.

Then I worked as chaplain for some local hospices to bring spiritual comfort and the sacraments to hundreds of people as they faced the final days of their lives. The roman collar was seldom worn, but the message of Christ down not need a special garment to be heard.

To end a rather long story I found Rent-a-Priest in about 2004 and have been working with them ever since, performing weddings, funeral Masses, Baptisms, and whatever concrete celebrations of the message of Christ are requested. I am comfortable with myself and my work. I recall the ending of Lacordaire's definition of a priest: "...to go from men to God to offer him their prayers, to return from God to man to bring pardon and hope, to teach and to pardon, to console and bless always, my God, what a life, and it is yours, O priest of Jesus Christ."

"Oh! What a mantra!"

Gerard A. Charbonneau, M.Div., MSW

The Calling

The calling to the priesthood came to fruition with the laying on of hands at my ordination to Holy Orders on May 3, 1969. The ordination ceremony is a very formal liturgy, where the Bishop lays hands on candidates and ordains them priests. From that event, one gets assigned to a ministry. My first assignment to an inner-city parish quickly got me into trouble. I had been assigned to a parish with an older pastor along with a young activist-type priest, my senior by three years.

My ministry rapidly turned into an activist ministry among the inner city poor and disenfranchised. There were protests, there were marches, there were "walks with the people". All of this activity was not the pastor's favorite view of what a representative of Christ (a priest) should be doing. His perception of the duties of a parish priest included: celebrating daily Mass, praying the breviary, visiting the sick as well as elderly, teaching CCD (Confraternity of Christian doctrine) to the young and finally organizing and chaperoning CYO (Catholic Youth Organization) dances and other activities.

The inhumanity of rectory living was getting to me after a while. My "sidekick" priest and I were trying to create a culture of family and community within the rectory. One night we decided that at dinner we would ask the pastor if we could call each other by first name in "our home" (the rectory). The Monsignor objected profusely stating that he expected to be addressed as Monsignor. There was so little warmth in this rectory; it felt quite institutional and nothing like home. I was starting to feel plastic at times.

Within six months of ordination and this assignment, the oil on my forehead barely dry (oil is used as a symbol during the rite of ordination), my sidekick priest and I were called into the Bishop's office. We were clearly told that activism was not an acceptable form of ministry, even though in my mind Jesus had been an activist. We were informed that our assignment in the inner city parish was being terminated. We were not being assigned to another parish, but were instead being challenged to find a pastor in the diocese who could "put up with you and take a chance on you". If we could not find such a pastor in the diocese, then we should consider leaving the priesthood. As unreal as that sounded, those were the marching orders from the Bishop.

As I look back to the fall of 1969, maybe that is when I should have left the priesthood. My idealism of serving as a priest had been betrayed, but not shattered. The inner calling, however, was still too strong and I needed to continue my journey of priestly ministry. With the help of the priests' personnel board, our search became successful. Each of us did find a pastor in a suburban parish, willing to "put up with us and take a chance on us".

My transition to this new ministry proceeded rather well. I began ministering with a wonderful, real down-to-earth pastor. I was able to continue my activist ministry; it was not with the poor and disenfranchised, but with a suburban middle class community dedicated to building a new Church. I obviously did not have to leave the priesthood at this time, as my life in clerical ministry seemed to now be on course.

Transition from Clerical Ministry to Lay Ministry

Though I found my ministry in suburbia challenging, something still gnawed at me. As I interacted with families in the parish, I began sensing the unnatural dimension of celibacy. I wondered at times what it would be like to be married and have a family. The condition of celibacy, to which I had vowed, became more uncertain and more puzzling as the months passed.

My ministry did not bring me the fulfillment I expected. I found it difficult to give party-line church answers to so many questions asked by God's people. I decided to seek some spiritual direction, and I did so from a local retreat center. What became clear to me during this time was my struggle with the Church doctrine position vis-à-vis Humanae Vitae (the encyclical by Pope Paul VI proclaiming artificial birth control a sin). I could not see myself as a priest refusing absolution to people over birth control. I could not see myself telling them how to deal with issues in their sex life. I did not think the Church should be intruding into people's bedrooms.

The movement for married priests was also growing around the world. I began questioning the value of celibacy and this unnatural style of living life on a daily basis. I was looking at some of my clerical colleagues, who were ending up either golfaholics, womenaholics or alcoholics. I knew I did not want to end up like any of them.

My spiritual direction led me to a turning point, where I needed to make a decision about my vocation. At that time, I accepted the challenge of doing the

Ignatian Exercises (a thirty-day scripture-based directed retreat) in Guelph, Ontario. I met with the Bishop, new to the diocese, and received his blessing and support as I moved forward in discerning my vocation. I included him in my exploration, and this led to his kind and gentle handling of me. I left the parish in early November 1972 to go meet God head on in Guelph. God, I believed, had led me to my vocation and God would be the one to lead me out of this vocation.

The Ignatian Exercises

On my drive to Guelph, Ontario, I took control over my anxieties and fears about a thirty-day journey into solitude. Though a gregarious person always ready to bring laughter to a gathering, I was surprised that I felt very much at ease with the prospect of this solitary experience. I found a kind, supportive and gentle man in my spiritual director. He made it quite clear to me that there was no magic in Guelph; God would be there to meet me "tête à tête". I should be able to discern and decide what God wanted from me and what I wanted from me. I received the gift of "peace of mind" as I walked daily through this journey in Guelph.

What I first learned about myself was that I would not be leaving the priesthood. Rather, I would be leaving clerical ministry; BIG DIFFERENCE! Baptism, Eucharist and Confirmation made me a priest, while Holy Orders made me a person of ministry, a servant of God's people. While I suspected that I would be surrounded with guilt from the decision to change my life style, the retreat helped me discard that guilt and feel free to decide what was right for me. In fact, as a result of my meeting with God in Guelph, I left clerical ministry through the front door; I did not need to sneak out the back door, as many already had. In fact, I wrote a letter of announcement to all parishioners and mailed it the day of my departure.

The retreat helped me become honest with myself. My encounter with God allowed me to learn that I could also serve God and God's people in a different profession. The retreat gave me the strength to decide that being retrained as a clinical social worker would be good for me and could offer me new avenues of ministering. I truly believed that the training I received to become a parish priest would only enhance my services in clinical social work and my ongoing interactions with people.

A meeting with my Bishop the day I returned from Guelph, which had been his condition of my receiving permission to leave the diocese for a month, facilitated my departure from ministry in early 1973. Although disappointed, he felt comfortable with my decision to leave priestly ministry. He praised me for being so open with God, with him and myself. I decided to take a one-year's leave of absence in order to help me explore my way as a lay Christian. Because of my openness with the Bishop, changing my canonical status from parish priest to lay priest was quick and easy. I did not have to "fight" with Rome in any way, as many were having to do. My canonical discharge took all of three months.

Transition to Lay Living

My transition to the lay Christian lifestyle became a spectacular gift from God. I took on a personal mantra in my faith life: "Where God has been, God will continue to be". And... Oh! what a mantra! In fact, I continued to stand by this mantra in all of my life's transitions: from the profession of clerical ministry to selling cars for six months, to pursuing an MSW (master's degree in social work), to twenty-five years of service in the field of clinical social work (which included adoption services, mental-health services offering child, individual and family therapy, substance-abuse counseling services, education services in substance abuse and other mental health issues, a nursing home administrator service) and finally serving people in the insurance industry (currently in my sixteenth year of service). My belief and my trust that God leads the walk have accompanied me throughout my life. It has made my life so much easier to live one day at a time.

I received a very unique gift while serving in mental health. I am sure you realize that many folks ask, "Why did you leave the priesthood?" with the hope of getting a glimpse into a person's private story. I rarely but occasionally have shared this story which I am about to reveal to you.

Working in mental health as a clinical social worker provides opportunities to work with and to interact with psychiatrists. This one particular psychiatrist, quite intrigued with my past, wanted to know more about my personal story. He invited me to lunch and even paid for it. He was curious about my past. He wanted to know my family history hoping to better understand the dynamics of a vocation.

When I told him I was the youngest of five siblings and that four of the five had entered religious life, and that three of the four had changed their life status from religious back to lay lifestyle, he began connecting some dots that had never come into my consciousness. Of course, as a clinical social worker I was intrigued to have his take on processing the inner and even unconscious dynamics of my vocation.

The doctor concluded that as children, we had experienced abandonment at the time of our biological mother's death (I was fourteen months at that time). It dynamically and psychologically made a lot of sense that our religious vocation was a response of wanting closeness with her. In fact, we always have and still do refer to our biological mother as "our mother in heaven" ("*Maman au ciel*" in French). The best dynamic to counteract this abandonment syndrome was to embrace a life that would have us be close to God and heaven (where Maman lived).

However, once we grew up and matured in our adulthood and found our own true selves, there was no further need to counteract this abandonment syndrome. Therefore, living out our lives as lay individuals became emotionally acceptable. What an interesting gift and unique insight given to me that day: a veritable psychiatric explanation as to why I may have embraced my initial calling and why I may have journeyed to my new calling.

Faith remained an important dynamic in living my life. In reflecting on my journey through life, there were many junctures which could only be encountered in faith. Without my mantra "where God has been, God will continue to be", I may have not so easily followed the labyrinth of my life.

There have been seven careers to live through from 1969 to this present moment. These careers were not presented to me on a platter; some required additional training and licensing. There was much unknown at every turn, yet I was able to find a peace of mind and personal fulfillment in the choices I made. In fact, my bride of thirty-eight years has described me as a "phoenix", who just keeps rising from the ashes.

I very deeply believe in my heart that my mantra will guide me into my sunset years, my last career known as retirement. This mantra will also help me in my final transition from living this earthly life to breaking through to eternal life, the promise made to us all.

The initial calling to Holy Orders and clerical ordination became a call and challenge to follow God. During my life I have done exactly that. At each new juncture, I responded to what I believed God was calling me. I answered all of the opportunities with an openness to walk life's journey in faith and in trust. I knew in my heart that God would carry me. Who cared what storms lay ahead? My God would calm the rough waters.

Therefore, my life has been filled with serendipities and surprises. God has filled my life with so many of them and I continue to expect them, as I plunge forward each day.

People have asked if I would live my life all over again with all of the choices I made. I absolutely would. Many have also asked if I would go back to clerical ministry, were there to be a married clergy. My answer is absolutely not. The institution of the church would need to change too dramatically for me to recognize that God was calling me once again into clerical ministry. The ministering, which I have experienced in my last forty-three years has been much too fulfilling for me to think I may have been serving in "wrong" ministries.

Certainly God knew what God was doing when I felt the "call". I am just so grateful that I was able to recognize the call in the varied challenges life has offered me. What a great adventure my life has been with a bride, three sons, grandchildren (at the moment two) and varied professions of service to others, which I gladly embraced over the years. It has really been an adventuresome and enjoyable ride!

The call has been wonderful until now and the continued call should be wondrous.

Praised be God for always being there!

Afterword

With the resignation of Pope Benedict XVI, the conclave of Cardinals elected Cardinal Jorge Bergoglio of Buenes Aires as his successor. The new pope chose the name Francis, the first in history.

Pope Francis, since being elected Pope, has made some dramatic claims and statements, challenging the curia and Vatican "business as usual," even calling the Papal court "the leprosy of the papacy."

The stories of bishops and priests, obsessed with power and prestige, show that the stories in this book are not isolated incidents. Pope Francis and his advisers have an enormous task of changing the curia culture in Rome.

But Pope Francis will also have to address the issue of whether celibacy is more important than the celebration of the Holy Eucharist.

With the dramatic shortage of priests worldwide today (120,000 men have chosen to leave the priesthood since 1960), Pope Francis will have to address the issue of whether celibacy is of greater value than have sufficient priests to minister to the faithful.

Many Catholics are aware that married ministers of the Anglican and Lutheran traditions, have for generations been admitted into the Catholic priesthood. Jesus did not require celibacy for his Apostles.

For many priests, celibacy is a gift of the Holy Spirit, and has served them well in their ministry. However, not all of those who have believed themselves called to the priesthood experience celibacy as such a gift. The call to marriage is also a gift of the Holy Spirit.

In the current administration of Pope Francis a married priesthood is actually being discussed. Cardinal Pietro Parolin, the Secretary of State for the Vatican under Pope Francis, stated in an interview in the summer of 2013 that celibacy "is not a church dogma and it can be discussed because it is a church tradition."

The pope himself has said: "Celibacy for priests is a matter of discipline, and as such it can change. Celibacy is not a dogma of faith; it is a rule of life that I appreciate a great deal, and I believe it is a gift for the Church. The door is always open, given that it is not a dogma of faith."

And if the celibacy rule for priesthood were relaxed in a case-by-case situation owing to the need for priests, then what of the many Latin Rite priests who left the active ministry because of celibacy, such as some of the men in this book? Might they – and others like them – be welcomed back to the ministry?

CPSIA information can be obtained
at www.ICGtesting.com
Printed in the USA
FFOW03n1834221014
8245FF